Homelessness and the Law in Britain

by Paul Q. Watchman
and Peter Robson

Published by the Planning Exchange,
186 Bath Street, Glasgow G2 4HG, Tel. 041-332 8541

First edition 1983, ISBN 0 905011 20 1
Second edition (revised) 1989
© 1989, Paul Q. Watchman and Peter Robson

Designed and typeset by Anodyne Publishing Services, Edinburgh.
Printed by Billing & Sons Ltd., Worcester.

ISBN 0 905011 35 X

Contents

Chapter 4. The Circumstances of Homelessness and Priority Need ... 82

Chapter 5. Intentional Homelessness ... 103

Chapter 8. Remedies for the Homeless ... 208

Preface

It is now more then ten years since the Housing (Homeless Persons) Act 1977 was introduced and six years since the first edition of this book was published. In this time there has continued to be a welter of homelessness cases and varying interpretations of the legislation. One of the main reasons for producing this second edition is to examine the changes that have occurred. The authors provide the reader with a fully updated and revised assessment of not only the complex case law but also, to some extent, the multi-dimensional social problem of homelessness itself.

The book will be a useful and accessible aid for the wide range of people concerned with the issue of homelessness. The excessive use of legal terms has been avoided and the preamble on the Legal Framework is a good point of reference for anyone without a legal background. Equally the comprehensive indices of Cases, Statutes and Ombudsman's Reports along with the reading list will allow individuals to pursue specific areas of interest in greater detail.

The authors would like to express their thanks to all those who contributed their experience and expertise to the compiling of the text. A special mention is made of Kenny Miller for updating his original preamble. The law is as stated at 31 March, 1989.

Florence Burke
Production Editor
April, 1989.

The Legal Framework

1. Sources of Law:

There are THREE distinct sources of law:

(a) The statute

The primary source of law on homelessness is the Housing (Homeless Persons) Act 1977. Statutes are the most authoritative source of law in the United Kingdom and a housing authority cannot lawfully ignore the provisions of the Act. It is necessary to stress, however, that the Housing (Homeless Persons) Act 1977 is a statute of a general nature which provides a legal framework within which housing authorities must act rather than a detailed set of rules. It is therefore necessary to refer to other sources of law to discover the way in which a housing authority should act in any given situation.

(b) The Codes of Guidance

Section 12 of the Act provides that in the exercise of their functions housing authorities shall have regard to such guidance as may from time to time be given by the Secretary of State for Scotland or the Secretary of State for the Environment. Both Secretaries of State have issued detailed Codes of Guidance which run to over 30 pages and deal with all aspects of the legislation. The Codes do not have statutory force, i.e. they are not enforceable in a court of law. Housing authorities may depart from the guidance contained in the Code. However, failure to follow the guidance contained in the Code may be grounds for challenging the legality of the housing authority's decision.

(c) Cases

Where uncertainty arises in relation either to the interpretation or administration of legislation that uncertainty may be resolved by litigation. There is no statutory appeal either to an administrative body, such as the Secretary of State or an administrative tribunal, or to the law courts. An aggrieved person, however, may challenge the decision of a housing authority in the courts by way of judicial review or seek damages for breach of statutory duty. Alternatively, if he believes that he has suffered injustice as a result of maladministration on the part of the authority, he can complain to the Commissioner for Local Administration, "the Local Government Ombudsman". Of these two forms of redress by far the most important and the only source of authoritative guidance on the proper meaning of legislation is the law courts.

Any action taken before the courts would involve use of the civil legal system. Such a system is based upon a hierarchy of courts. It is a cardinal principle of both the Scottish and English legal systems that there should be certainty in the law. This is provided for by requiring the courts at the lower levels in the hierarchy to follow and apply the decisions of the superior courts. The operation of the rules of precedent, therefore, is supposed to provide the certainty and consistency in the law which our legal systems demand. Precedent operates in the Scottish and English legal systems as follows.

2. The Civil Court System

(a) The Scottish Civil Court structure

(i) House of Lords
This court is the supreme court for Scottish civil cases. It hears appeals from the Inner House of the Court of Session. It consists of the Lord Chancellor; the Lords of Appeal in Ordinary (the law lords); and peers who hold or have held high judicial office. Two of the law lords are Scottish judges . The quorum for the court is three although five judges normally sit. Its decisions are authoritative and binding on all other Scottish courts. These lower courts, therefore, must follow a decision of the House of Lords unless it is clear that the decision of the House of Lords can be "distinguished". This would involve a judge in the lower court holding that there is some material difference in circumstance between the case before him and the House of Lords case justifying him reaching a different conclusion.

(ii) Court of Session
This court is both a court of first instance and an appellate court, and is

the next most important court in the hierarchy. Its first instance work is carried out by the sixteen (fifteen) junior judges who sit in the Outer House. These judges have exclusive jurisdiction in cases of reduction and status actions and hear the more important damages and personal injury cases. The Inner House exercise the appellate functions of this court where the eight senior judges sit. It is split up into two divisions of four judges each, the First Division and the Second Division. The First Division is chaired by the Lord President, Lord Emslie and the Second Division is presided over by the Lord Justice Clerk, Lord Ross. Both Divisions have equal authority and cases are allocated to either Division at random. The Inner House hears appeals from the decisions of judges of the Outer House and from the Sheriff Court. Clearly a decision of either Division of the Inner House is more authoritative than a decision of a single judge sitting in the Outer House. The Inner House is bound to follow decisions of the House of Lords in Scottish cases and is likely to follow decisions of either Division when in point. An Outer House judge must follow a decision of the House of Lords and decisions of the Inner House. He need not follow decisions of another Outer House judge, although clearly he will treat them with great respect.

(iii) Sheriff Court

This is the only civil court in Scotland which is locally based. Scotland, as a geographical area, is divided into six sheriffdoms each presided over

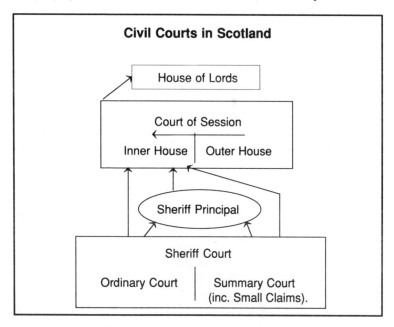

Civil Courts in Scotland

House of Lords

Court of Session

Inner House | Outer House

Sheriff Principal

Sheriff Court

Ordinary Court | Summary Court (inc. Small Claims).

by a Sheriff Principal, who is a full-time salaried judge. He hears appeals from the Sheriff in civil cases and is chief administrator of the court. The local judge is the Sheriff who hears cases for the first time which arise within his sheriffdom. The Sheriff Court has a very wide jurisdiction dealing with everything from debt to damages actions. It could not formerly hear divorce cases. The provisions of the Divorce Jurisdiction, Court Fees and Legal Aid (Scotland) Act, however, give the Sheriff Court concurrent jurisdiction with the Court of Session in divorce actions. It also has exclusive jurisdiction in actions valued at less than £1500. Actions for less that £1500 are raised by summary cause and are dealt with in the Summary Court. The Law Reform (Miscellaneous Provisions) (Scotland) Act 1985 introduces a Small Claims procedure into the Summary Court for certain types of case valued at less than £750. In these types of case the normal rules of evidence and procedure are relaxed and there is a restriction on the amount of expenses which can be claimed from the defeated party.

All other actions are heard in the Ordinary Court. Although the Sheriff Principal acts as an appeal judge for his sheriffdom, there is nothing to prevent a litigant appealing directly to the Inner House of the Court of Session. Both the Sheriff and Sheriff Principal must follow decisions of the House of Lords and Inner House. They are not bound, however, by a decision of an Outer House judge. It is usual practice for a Sheriff to follow a decision of his Sheriff Principal. Sheriffs' decisions do not bind other Sheriffs.

(b) The English Civil Courts

(i) House of Lords

This court is also the final appeal court for England and Wales. Since the 1966 Practice Direction the House is no longer bound by its own previous decisions. It hears appeals, with leave, from the Court of Appeal.

(ii) Court of Appeal

The day to day civil work of this court is carried out by the Master of the Rolls and 21 Lords Justices of Appeal. The Court sits normally in groups of three judges. The jurisdiction of the civil division is entirely appellate. As well as hearing appeals from certain tribunals, the Court of Appeal also hears appeals from the High Court of Justice and the County Court. The Court is bound by decisions of the House of Lords and by its own previous decisions unless it can be shown that these previous decisions were arrived at by a lack of care. Most civil appeals in England go no further than the Court of Appeal.

(iii) High Court of Justice

The High Court consists of three divisions, the Queen's Bench Division, the Chancery Division and the Family Division. It can sit anywhere in England and Wales although the Lord Chancellor has issued directions as to where the court should sit. The Queen's Bench Division consists of the Lord Chief Justice and about 49 other judges. Its jurisdiction over cases being heard for the first time covers commercial matters and most damages cases. It also exercises an appellate jurisdiction from certain decisions of Magistrates. One important function of the Division which is exercised by the Divisional Court is to exercise supervisory jurisdiction over inferior bodies. This jurisdiction allows the Division to ensure that tribunals and other agencies do not exceed their powers. The work of the Chancery Division is carried out by the Vice-Chancellor and about a dozen other judges. The Division deals with the law of trusts and equity and with disputes concerning land transactions. The Family Division, which deals with contested matrimonial cases, adoption and guardianship cases, consists of the President of the Division and about 15 other judges.

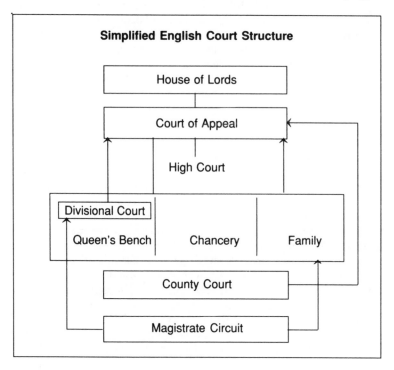

A judge of the High Court is bound by a decision of the House of Lords or Court of Appeal. He is not, however, bound by an earlier decision of a single judge of the High Court. The Divisional Court of Queen's Bench on the other hand as well as being bound by the House of Lords and Court of Appeal is also bound by its own previous decisions.

(iv) County Court

The county court is a local court dealing with minor civil claims. There are over 350 county court districts in England and Wales grouped into circuits each with a circuit judge. The circuit itself is administered by the Registrar. The county court has express statutory jurisdiction and can also hear damages actions up to a maximum value of £5,000. Certain designated county courts can also hear undefended matrimonial causes. Appeals from this court go to the Court of Appeal. A circuit judge is bound by any decision of a superior court including decisions of a single judge of the High Court.

(v) Magistrates' Court

Magistrates' court is the lowest court in the hierarchy although exercising a fairly wide jurisdiction. It is staffed by local Justices of the Peace. Its jurisdiction covers such matters as non-payment of gas or electricity bills, revocation and renewal of licences, and certain types of domestic proceedings. Most appeals go to the Divisional Court of the Queen's Bench Division, although appeals from domestic proceedings go to the Divisional Court of the Family Division. The magistrates' court is bound by a decision of any superior court.

3. Application of Precedent

Since the Housing (Homeless Persons) Act 1977 applies to England and Wales and to Scotland it is administered by two separate systems of courts. The normal rule of law is that a decision of an English court is not binding upon the Scottish courts and vice versa. However, in areas such as the 1977 Act where the same law is applicable to the two systems, it is very likely that a Scottish court would follow its English brethren in construing the Act. Indeed, the higher up the hierarchy from the decision, the more likely it is that it will be followed in Scotland. It should be noted that the Act does not apply to Northern Ireland.

One word of caution should be mentioned in reading judgements of court cases. The judge, in theory, only deals with the particular legal dispute between the parties. He is not concerned with the wider problems of the legislations. However, this does not prevent judges from giving

amorphous and is used in different senses by different bodies. There is insufficiently detailed information on the extent and causes of homelessness. The characteristics of the heterogeneous group which is described by the generic term "homeless" are often portrayed in terms of perjorative stereotyping. Given the complexity of this problem, it is important to examine the ways in which homelessness is defined, measured and explained by governmental and voluntary agencies.

1. Defining Homelessness

Homelessness is a relative concept. Those who may be defined as homeless range from those persons who are roofless through to those in insecure and poor accommodation as well as those whose accommodation does not meet their individual preferences. Where on this continuum of housing need the line of homeless is drawn, is a political issue. However, any distinction tends to be arbitrary and reflects a subjective perception of competing priorities.[4]

In 1971 the authors of the Greve Report, *Homelessness in London*[5], noted that there was no universally accepted definition of homelessness. There are, however, a number of recognised definitions:

(a) **Rooflessness**
(b) **Houselessness**

    (i)   long-term institutions
    (ii) bed and breakfast

(c) **Insecure accommodation**
(d) **Intolerable housing conditions**

(a) Rooflessness

Perhaps the narrowest definition of homelessness is the one which equates "homelessness" with rooflessness. Jeremy Sandford, for example, defines homelessness in his study of the lifestyle of vagrants in terms of "the thousands of people who ... are sleeping rough in derelict buildings, barns, hedgerows, under the sky, wrapped in newspapers, old sacks, old clothes."[6] Until the early 1970's this, very broadly, was the definition

---

4. Helen Austerberry, Kerry Schott and Sophie Watson, *Homeless in London 1971-1981*, International Centre for Economic and Related Disciplines 1984.
5. J. Greve, D. Page and S. Greve, *Homelessness in London, op. cit.*, pp. 279-282.
6. J. Sandford, *Down and Out in Britain* (1971), p.130.

accepted by government. There was, however, an additional requirement which the government placed on persons without shelter before they could be regarded as homeless. That requirement was that they had applied to the welfare department of a local authority for assistance and had been admitted to temporary accommodation. Otherwise, in the government's view, those persons were not "truly" homeless.[7]

(b) Houselessness

A second, and in many ways more realistic, definition of homelessness is "houselessness". This definition includes not only those who sleep rough but also persons who occupy emergency accommodation, accommodation which may not strictly be of an emergency nature but which in essence offers little more than a bed, accommodation which for a limited period of time provides special supportive resources and facilities and other forms of short-stay or temporary accommodation. Accommodation which traditionally has been regarded as falling within this definition includes night shelters, local authority reception centres, model lodging-houses, working men's hostels, and alcoholic recovery units.[8] This definition lays stress on the adage that "a house is not a home" and gives recognition to the fact that there is quite a considerable overlap between persons who sleep rough and persons who occupy night shelters, reception centres and lodging-houses.[9]

In recent years there has been a concerted effort to stretch this definition of homelessness in two directions:

(i) Long-term institutions

The first direction has been the attempt by pressure groups such as MIND to extend the definition of "homelessness" to cover persons who are admitted to mental hospitals and other long-term institutions simple because they have nowhere else to go.[10] If the definition of "homelessness" as "houselessness" includes persons who stay in short-term accommodation, it is argued that the definition should clearly also include physically and mentally handicapped persons who reside in long-term institutions not because they have special medical needs or are

---

7. *Press Statement* by Mr. David Ennals, the Minister of State for Health and Social Security, dated 29 April, 1969, quoted by Des Wilson in *I Know It Was The Place's Fault* (1970) p.19.
8. See "Emergency Accommodation" below; *R. v. Ealing London Borough Council, ex p. Sidhu* (1982) HLR 45; *R. v. Waveney Borough Council, ex p. Bowers* [1983] QB 238.
9. J. Leach and J. Wing, *Helping Destitute Men* (1980) pp. 33-40; National Assistance Board, *Homeless Single Men*, (HMSO, 1966).
10. *Better Services for the Mentally Ill* (HMSO, Cmnd. 6233, 1975); MIND, *Even Better Services for the Mentally Handicapped* (1972); R. Bailey, *The Homeless and the Empty Houses* (1977) pp. 37-48.

a danger to society but because there is no suitable accommodation available for them in the community at large. The logic of this argument cannot be faulted. The "circuit of homelessness"[11] extends to hospitals and prisons as well as sleeping rough and night shelters. Admission to a long-term institution therefore may be viewed as being only one point on that circuit.

The government White Paper, *Better Services for the Mentally Ill,*[12] acknowledged that institutionalisation could be harmful and that the lack of accommodation available in the community results in a large number of persons being kept in mental hospitals who do not need to be there. However, successive governments have been extremely reluctant to extend the definition of "homelessness" to cover persons in hospitals or custodial institutions.[13]

(ii) Bed and breakfast

The second direction in which this definition has been attempted to be stretched is to cover families living in bed and breakfast accommodation which do not supply a sufficient degree of privacy or adequate facilities to enable families to carry on a normal family life.[14] The extension of the definition of "homelessness" to cover bed and breakfast and other forms of similarly unsuitable accommodation is implicitly recognised by the legislation[15] and explicitly accepted by the Code of Guidance.[16]

(c) Insecure accommodation

A third definition of homelessness includes not only persons who are without a roof but persons who occupy accommodation of an insecure nature. Although this substantially covers the same ground as the second definition of homelessness it is much wider than that definition.[17]

Insecurity may arise from the legal status of occupancy, personal circumstances or extraneous factors. Under the first heading of insecure accommodation are persons without any security of tenure or with limited security of tenure.[18] Thus, persons occupying unauthorised

---

11. Department of the Environment, *Single and Homeless* (HMSO, 1981) p.49.
12. See above at fn. 10, *supra.*
13. See R. Crossman, *The Diaries of a Cabinet Minister,* Volume 3, Secretary of State for Social Services 1968-70, (1977) Monday, 29 September, 1969, p.662.
14. *R. v. Hillingdon London Borough Council, ex p. Puhlhofer* [1986] AC 484; J. Conway and P. Kemp, *Bed and Breakfast: Slum Housing of the Eighties* (1985) p.5; P.Q. Watchman, 'Heartbreak Hotel' [1988] JSWL 147.
15. Section 58 of the Housing Act 1985 (as amended); section 24 of the Housing (Scotland) Act 1987.
16. ECA 2.14; SC 4.15.
17. B. Glastonbury, *Homeless Near A Thousand Homes* (1971) p.18.
18. Both public and private sector tenants are protected against arbitrary eviction by the Rent (Scotland) Act 1984 and the Housing (Scotland) Act 1987 in Scotland, and by the Rent Act 1977 and the

squats, "holiday" or out-of-season lets, tied accommodation, sharing with their landlord, residing in lodgings or under what are known in England as licences or non-exclusive occupancy agreements might be regarded as occupying insecure accommodation, particularly where their "landlord" has set in motion court proceedings to enforce a clear right to re-possession.[19] The second form of insecurity arises in circumstances such as demolition or rehabilitation where it is clear that the occupier will be displaced from his home within a short period of time.[20]

The final form of "homelessness" arises in circumstances where a person is residing with relatives or where occupation of available accommodation may expose him or her to an unacceptable risk. Examples of persons who may fall under this heading are young couples living with their parents or relatives, and battered women who may be assaulted if they return to a violent partner.[21] Although not as sweeping as the definition of homelessness indicated here, the statutory definition of homelessness recognises that persons occupying insecure accommodation must in certain circumstances be treated as if they were homeless or threatened with homelessness.[22]

(d) Intolerable housing conditions

Voluntary housing bodies have suggested that homelessness should be defined in relative terms. In their 1969 report *Face the Facts* and in subsequent publications, Shelter for example, have argued that "those people who live in conditions so bad that a civilised family life is impossible are homeless in the true sense of the word." Although this definition of homelessness has not been firmly accepted by government, the challenge to government orthodoxy which it represents has had a major impact on policy-making. To some degree this view has recently found favour with the government as the definition of homelessness now includes provision for those occupying overcrowded or unsatisfactory accommodation. Taking the estimates of the number of houses unfit for

Housing Act 1985 in England and Wales. The position of tenants entering into contracts after the introduction of the Housing (Scotland) Act 1988 and the Housing Act 1988 is weaker as regards security of tenure. However, they may not be evicted arbitrarily.

19. These mechanisms erected to defeat the Rent Acts are not likely to be a feature of the post-1988 private rented sector since the 1988 Housing Acts effectively remove protection for tenants as regards rent levels and security of tenure beyond the terms of the lease.

20. Section 39(1) of the Land Compensation Act 1973 (as amended) places a duty on local authorities to rehouse displaced occupiers. That duty, however, is not an absolute one but a duty to act reasonably and practically, see *R. v. Bristol Corporation, ex p. Hendy* [1974] 1 All ER 1047 and *Glasgow District Council v. Douglas* unreported, discussed by E. Young, "Rehousing Displaced Occupiers", 1979 SCOLAG 76.

21. See "The Causes of Homelessness" below at pp. 19-24. .

22. See "Homelessness and Priority Need", pp. 82-102.

habitation, lack of basic amenities like exclusive use of a hot water supply, or a fixed bath or an inside water closet or unacceptably damp houses recent studies[23] have indicated that on these very basic standards over 2.5 million households in England, Wales and Scotland would fall into a category of homeless persons.

2. Measuring Homelessness

It is difficult, if not impossible, to obtain a reliable estimate of the size and scope of the homelessness problem. The official statistics on homelessness are unreliable because they only record the articulated demand for accommodation and ignore the many thousands of homeless persons who do not approach local authorities for assistance, families living with their parents or in overcrowded or insanitary housing, and the patients admitted to medical institutions simply because they have no fixed abode.[24] It is important, however, that some attempt is made to gauge the size and scope of the problem. For without a reasonably clear picture of the overall number and characteristics of the homeless, government policy may be an ill-conceived and consequently an ineffective or inappropriate response.

There are FOUR methods of measuring homelessness:

(a) Surveys of the "visibly" homeless.

(b) Admissions to local authority homeless accommodation.

(c) Applications to local authority homelessness units.

(d) Aggregation of "visible" and "hidden" homelessness.

(a) Surveys of the "visibly" homeless

The first method is to conduct a survey of the number of persons sleeping rough in one area on one particular evening or of the number of persons admitted to emergency accommodation, such as model lodging-houses, night shelters, hostels, or reception centres. Although this crude head-counting provides no more than a "freeze-frame" of one point on the homelessness circuit it has been extensively used by the medical profession and government departments to obtain details of the main

---

23. *Scottish Housing: A Consultative Document* (HMSO, Cmnd. 6852, 1977) para. 2.10 and *Housing Policy: A Consultative Document* (HMSO Cmnd. 6851, 1977) para. 2.04-2.05. The House Conditions Survey of 1981 estimated that over 1.1 million houses in England and Wales – 6% of stock – were unfit for human habitation and 1 in 10 houses were unfit, lacked basic amenities or were in need of major repairs. The Scottish Affairs Committee Report on *Dampness in Housing Session* 1983-84 (HC 206 - I) para. 16 et seq. revealed that there were some 500,000 houses in Scotland which were affected by dampness.
24. See "Defining Homelessness" above at pp. 9-13.

characteristics and circumstances of the single homeless.[25] There can be no mistake that if this was the only method employed it would result in a serious under-estimate of the size and a distortion of the scope of the homelessness problem. However, it is a useful supplement to other methods of measurement and a barometer of extreme housing stress.

(b) Admissions to local authority homeless accommodation

The second method, on which goverment statistics were based prior to 1968, is to equate the number of homeless persons with the number of persons *admitted* to local authority accommodation on the ground of homelessness. This method was criticised by both the Morris Committee and by Greve, Page and Greve in their study of homelessness in London. The main thrust of the criticisms levelled at this method of measuring homelessness by the Morris Committee was that it ignored persons living with relatives and friends and other forms of "hidden homelessness".[26]

The authors of *The Greve Report* were, if anything, more scathing and wide-ranging in their condemnation of the number of admissions to local authority temporary accommodation as a measure of homelessness. The official statistics, they argued, gave "a distorted and incomplete measure of homelessness" and were descriptive of "not so much the trend in homelessness but rather the trend in the provision of temporary accommodation."[27] In particular it was noted that this measure failed to record two main groups of homeless persons: those who did not approach a local authority for assistance, and those who did approach a local authority for assistance but who were not admitted to temporary accommodation. In the first group were included families without a home of their own who live with relatives or friends and families living in accommodation of an insecure nature. In the second group were the single homeless, childless couples, families with teenage children and the "foreseeably" homeless. In addition to the inherent defects in this measure, *The Greve Report* noted that its potential as a reliable indicator of the number of homeless persons was undermined by the local authority practice of requiring applicants to prove their homelessness. This remains a matter of some difficulty where an applicant alleges that

25. M. Sargaison, *Growing Old in Common Lodgings* (1954); S.I. Laidlaw, *Glasgow's Common Lodging Houses and the People Who Live in Them* (1956); National Assistance Board, *Homeless Single Persons* (1966); Scottish Development Department, *Single and Homeless in Scotland – Some Facts* (1974); P. Wingfield-Digby, *Hostels and Lodgings for Single People* (HMSO, 1976); S.M. Wood, "Camberwell Reception Centre: A Consideration of the Need for Health and Social Services of Homeless Single Men", 5 *Journal of Social Policy* (1976) 389.
26. Scottish Development Department, *Housing and Social Work – A Joint Approach* (HMSO, 1975) paras. 8.8 - 8.10.
27. J. Greve, D. Page and S. Greve, *Homelessness in London* (1971) pp. 59-61.

relatives or friends are no longer able or willing to continue to provide him with accommodation.

(c) Applications to local authority homelessness units

A third method of measuring homelessness, the one on which the current homelessness statistics are based, is the number of persons who apply to local authorities for accommodation. While this is a more reliable indicator of the number of homeless persons, it suffers from the same deficiencies as a measure of homelessness as do housing waiting lists for measuring housing needs.[28] In short, it becomes rapidly outdated, and it fails to register "hidden homelessness". Additionally, as the authors of the *Greve Report* noted, it is an underestimate of the number of homeless persons because some local authorities deflate the number of applications for assistance by making a rather tenuous distinction between *applications* which are recorded, and *enquiries* about homelessness, which are not recorded.[29]

(d) Aggregation of "visible" and "hidden" homlessness

Finally, attempts are made to measure the size of the homelessness problem by estimating the number of "hidden" homeless persons. This is achieved by adding together figures from many sources. For example, housing statistics provide estimates of the number of overcrowded and sub-tolerable houses or houses lacking one or more standard amenities, censuses provide details of the number of households comprising two or more families, and medical and prison statistics give an indication of the number of persons in such institutions because they have no place to go. This measure is unreliable because the statistics have not been gathered in any systematic sense as a measure of homelessness. It is important, however, that some estimate of "hidden homelessness" is made if persons who occupy unsatisfactory accommodation are not to be ignored.

A reliable measure of the number of homeless persons can only be made by combining these methods of measurement.

3. Who are the Homeless?[30]

The public image of the homeless is of two homogeneous groups of

---

28. Central Housing Advisory Committee, *Council Housing Purposes, Procedures and Priorities (HMSO, 1969) paras. 37-40.*
29. This tenuous distinction, however, has been accepted by the courts: see *R. v. Cherwell District Council, ex p. Howkins* (QBD) 14 May, 1984.
30. See R. De Friend, "The Housing (Homeless Persons) Act 1977" 41 *Modern Law Review* (1978) 173.

social misfits: problem families and vagrants. Around these stock caricatures self-serving myths have been woven to justify antipathy and neglect. A cursory examination on the Parliamentary debates on the Housing (Homeless Persons) Bill[31] or media reports of the attitudes of some local authorities towards the homeless[32] reveals concern for discouraging fecklessness through social discipline. The homeless, in short, are said to form part of the undeserving poor — the residuum, the submerged tenth, the dangerous classes to borrow terms of Victorian disapproval — for whom the workhouse rather than welfare is the appropriate response.

In spite of *Cathy Come Home*,[33] *Edna, the Inebriate Woman*,[34] *Johnny Go Home*,[35] and the challenge represented by the diligent campaigning of Shelter and the Campaign for the Homeless and Rootless (CHAR) this view remains a particularly tenacious one. However, it is a view which is directly contradicted by the findings of a number of research studies.[36]

(a) The single homeless

The archetypal single homeless person is perceived to be a "punk" with spiky hair, or a middle-aged disease-ridden alcoholic who has chosen an austere lifestyle of sleeping rough and living in hostels or lodging-houses. It is an image which unfortunately, and no doubt intentionally, has been reinforced by Orwell and those who have subsequently followed his footsteps[37] in joining the single homeless in their endless tramp between "derries, dosshouses and spikes."[38]

That view however, has been refuted by the *Single and Homeless* report.[39] In their study of the circumstances and needs of 7,360 single homeless people Drake, O'Brien and Biebuyck identified four broad

---

31. See "The Housing (Homeless Persons) Bill", below at pp. 33-36.
32. For example, N. Finnis, "The Heartless and the Homeless", *Roof* (1978) 138; "Homes Galore for Single Mums", *Sunday Mail*, 6 January, 1980; "Why Single Mums Want Babies", *Sunday Mail*, 18 November, 1979 and *Roof* (1980) 85.
33. J. Sandford, *Cathy Come Home* (1976).
34. J. Sandford, *Edna, the Inebriate Woman* (1971).
35. *Johnny Go Home* Television Documentary (1976).
36. J. Greve, D. Page and S. Greve, *Homelessness in London* (1971); *Single and Homeless* (DOE, 1981).
37. G. Orwell, *Down and Out in Paris and London* (1933); and J. Sandford, *Down and Out in Britain* (1971).
38. A "derry" is a derelict house, a "dosshouse" or "kiphouse" is a common lodging house and a "spike" is a state or local authority reception centre where the destitute can obtain free accommodation: J.Sandford, *Down and Out in Britain*, op. cit., p.9.
39. M. Drake, M. O'Brien and T. Biebuyck, *Single and Homeless* (DOE, 1981). This report is controversial, not in the sense that its findings are disputed but because it was delayed and gutted by a government hostile to some of its recommendations. In particular recommendations for better health care, a house building programme, and changes in the way social security payments were made to the single homeless were deleted from the report. See *The Guardian*, 8 and 9 March, 1982.

categories of persons who fall within the category of the single homeless:[40]

    (i)   Young single people.
    (ii) Victims of technological change.
    (iii) Middle-aged "dossers".
    (iv) Elderly people.

(i) Young single people

This sub-group comprised persons under twenty-five years of age, some of whom had a history of institutional care, but who were unlikely to have any evident disabilities and who were more often than not employed rather than unemployed. The young single homeless had drifted away from homes to major cities, in particular to London, in search of work or following a family dispute or the breakdown of a teenage marriage.

(ii) Victims of technological change

The second sub-group could reasonably be described as the victims of technological change; middle-aged workers with obsolete skills, predominantly male workers who had not received any further education and who were now employed in manual labour. This group, like the young single homeless, had no evident social or medical disabilities and again family or marital breakdown would appear to be a factor in their homlessness. It is conceivable, given the increase in divorces and the impact of new technology, that this group will form an increasingly large part of the single homeless.

(iii) Middle-aged "dossers"

The third sub-group identified by the study were middle-aged "dossers"; men and women who had severe multiple disabilities, and who had become locked into the homeless circuit of medical, penal and rehabilitative institutions, refuges and the streets. Many had recently been employed in casual low paid jobs in the building or service industries.

(iv) Elderly people

The final sub-group was the aged; elderly people without a family to care for them or with a family who did not wish to care for them and who were forced to spend the last years of their lives as long-term hostel dwellers.

(b) Homeless families

Prior to the National Assistance Act 1948 the problem of homelessness was very largely perceived in terms of vagrancy. The homeless quite simply were vagrants and casual labourers who migrated from rural areas to the major cities to spend the winter on the streets, in the House of Correction, or labouring in the casual wards of the poorhouses.[41] The 1948 Act, however, led to a redefinition of homelessness and consequently to a shift in perception. Although the Act specifically referred to homeless *persons,* in practice local authorities were loathe to provide temporary accommodation to anyone other than homeless *families,* or more exactly mothers and dependent children.[42] Homeless families, like the single homeless, have been caricatured as anti-social, feckless and undeserving; a crude over-simplification which serves to justify a failure to examine what kinds of families become homeless.

The problem of homeless families was a focus of debate on housing during the 1960s.[43] The number of persons applying to London County Council for temporary accommodation has steadily increased since 1958 and following a particularly large increase in 1961-62 the Council commissioned an investigation to study the underlying causes of homelessness.[44] That investigation found that London's homeless were primarily young families attempting to live on low pay and that their greatest need was for decent housing at a reasonable rent. Yet it was not until 1966 that episcopal campaigning, media reporting and careful research were converted into public indignation.[45] In November of that year Jeremy Sandford's *Cathy Come Home*[46] was televised. Based on interviews with homeless families and media reports *Cathy Come Home* traced the disintegration of a young family as it fell through the safety net of the welfare state. Described by *The Sunday Times* as "[t]he most important piece of dramatised documentary ever screened", the impact of *Cathy Come Home* was immediate. Many local authorities discontinued the practice of splitting families. However, if the impact of *Cathy Come Home* was immediate it was also short-lived. Des Wilson, the then Director of Shelter, was to write less than four years afterwards: "For all the hullabaloo, Cathy is still homeless."[47]

The number of homeless persons in temporary accommodation continued to rise during the 1960s[48] and in the spring of 1969 the

40. *Ibid.,* pp. 15-17.
41. G. Stedman Jones, *Outcast London* (1971) pp.88-91; N. Longmate, *The Workhouse* (1974) pp. 232-250.
42. J. Greve, D. Page and S. Greve, *Homelessness in London* (1971) p.59.
43. On the housing debate in the 1960s see K.G. Banting, *Poverty, Politics and Policy* (1979) pp. 14-65, especially at pp. 22-21.
44. J. Greve, *London's Homeless* (1964).
45. *The Guardian,* 18 December, 1961, 2 July and 29 December, 1962 and *The Times,* 30 July, 1962 and 21 August, 1963.
46. J. Sandford, *Cathy Come Home* (1976).
47. D. Wilson, *I Know It Was The Place's Fault* (1970) p.10.
48. See "The Growth of Homelessness" below at pp. 24-25.

Department of Health and Social Security appointed two research teams under the leadership of John Greve and Bryan Glastonbury to study the problem of homeless families in Greater London and South Wales and the West of England. The findings of these studies[49] broadly confirmed those of Greve's earlier study of London's homeless. Homeless families were largely young families with an above average number of infant children. The head of the household frequently was unskilled or semi-skilled and therefore low paid, or had a history of unemployment or irregular employment. Additionally, one parent families and chronic illness or disability were not uncommon characteristics of this group. These disadvantages combined with an inadequate supply of decent, secure low-cost housing to produce a social and economic vulnerability to homelessness. The one major exception to the findings of the 1962 study was the increasing number of homeless immigrant families in Inner London. These families differed substantially from other homeless families in terms of age, family size and economic status. Immigrant families on the whole were older, larger and more skilled than non-immigrant families.[50]

4. The Causes of Homelessness

As with other social problems the reasons why some people become homeless whereas others in similar circumstances do not are complex, multi-dimensional and obscure. Cause and effect tend to be confused and the immediate cause often disguises the real reason why someone becomes homeless. For example, eviction may be the reason given by a homeless family for approaching a housing authority for assistance, yet their homelessness more correctly may be attributable to some other underlying cause such as marital breakdown, poverty or illness. This point is well made by Drake, O'Brien and Biebuyck in their study of the single homeless:

> "Homelessness is caused by processes occuring at many different levels: the individual level, the family level, the social group level and the societal level. Housing and labour market factors, migration, demographic and socio-cultural factors interact to create the preconditions of ... homelessness in the mismatch of housing and job supply and demand."[51]

This definition of the causes of homelessness underlines the fact that homelessness cannot be explained adequately in terms of a

49. J. Greve, D. Page and S. Greve, *Homelessness in London* (1971) pp. 90-120, and B. Glastonbury, *Homeless Near A Thousand Homes* (1971) pp. 46-53.
50. J. Greve, D. Page and S. Greve, *Homelessness in London* (1971) pp. 91-93.
51. M. Drake, M. O'Brien and A. Biebuyck, *Single and Homeless* (DOE, 1981) p.12.

straightforward linear equation which links cause and effect. It is possible, however, to examine the social and economic factors which combine to produce homelessness and to attempt to illustrate the ways in which these factors interact.

(a) Economic factors

Of the economic factors relating to homelessness listed by Drake, O'Brien and Biebuyck the one most frequently mentioned by commentators is the unavailability of decent low cost accommodation.[52] Martin Partington, for example, states that "homelessness still exists because there are insufficient units of accommodation of decent standard, located in the places which people want or have got to live, and available at prices that even the poorest families can afford."[53]

For those unable to buy their own homes the problem is primarily one of access. Access to the private rented sector is particularly difficult for families. Not only has there been a rapid decline in the number of houses available for rent, but landlords have adopted allocation policies which effectively exclude families.[54] However, if the private sector does not cater for the housing needs of families the public sector has been equally reluctant to provide accommodation for single people and childless couples. Local authority allocation policies generally are weighted against single people and, with the closing of lodging houses and an overall reduction in the number of beds available, this group faces substantial difficulties in securing public sector accommodation of any kind.[55]

Related to the problem of access to the housing market is the uneven geographical distribution of available housing. The problem has two aspects. Firstly, although there is now a crude surplus of dwelling houses, many houses are unoccupied.[56] Some empty houses are dilapidated or in a serious state of disrepair. Others remain unoccupied while renovation work takes place or because of the time lag between a house becoming available for occupation and tenants moving in. Secondly, a number of houses are empty simply because they are located in the wrong place. This mismatch between the demand for labour and the

52. *Ibid.*
53. M. Partington, *The Housing (Homeless Persons) Act 1977 and Code of Guidance* (1978).
54. M. Wicks, *Rented Housing and Social Ownership,* Fabian Tract 421 (1973); L. Reynolds, *Some Effects of the 1974 Rent Act in London,* Middlesex Polytechnic (1978); D. Maclennan, 'The 1974 Rent Act – Some Short Run Supply Effects', *The Economic Journal* (1978) 331; D. MacLennan, 'An Economic approach to rent control: tenants and the 1974 Rent Act', *Social Policy and Administration (1981) 181.*
55. M. Thomson and L Naumann, *Lochgelly – The Closing of a Lodging House* (1978); D. Brandon, "Lodgings", *New Society* (1972) 597.
56. R. Bailey, *The Homeless and the Empty Houses* (1977).

supply of housing has created a situation where houses stand empty in declining areas where there is little employment whereas in areas such as London where the demand for labour is greatest few houses are available for occupation.[57]

Other economic factors which are related to housing, and which may be cited as important causes of homelessness, are insecurity of tenure and the poor condition of housing. Private sector and public sector tenants generally are protected against eviction except in a number of specified circumstances. However, many occupiers of rented accommodation who are neither protected tenants nor secure tenants have little more protection against eviction than their contractural rights and the prohibitions against harassment and illegal eviction. Thus, for those persons living with friends or relatives or sharing with their landlord, squatters, service occupiers and hostel dwellers the threat of eviction is very real. Greve, Page and Greve, for example, noted in their 1971 study of homelessness in London that "the actions of private Landlords ... are the immediate cause of admission for nearly two-fifths of all homeless families taken into temporary accommodation and for almost three quarters (71%) of those directly rehoused."[58]

In addition to eviction by private landlords action taken by public authorities to close or demolish unfit property or to prevent overcrowding may result in homelessness. Other economic factors which are major causes of homelessness, but the effects of which are most difficult to gauge, are poverty, low wages, and unemployment. As we have already noted, the surveys of homeless families in Greater London and South Wales and the West of England, revealed that low pay, irregular employment and deprivation were the main characteristics of families admitted to temporary accommodation.[59]

Writing in the 1980s on housing has stressed the particular problems experienced by women. Housing is particularly significant to women as they are most likely to spend time in the home. For a woman the home is not a place of relaxation to which she can return after work. With domestic labour still falling primarily on women, home and the workplace are one and the same.[60] Moreover, women's inferior economic status and their primary domestic role restricts their independent access to housing in the British allocation system, in the sense that the private housing sector is not concerned with housing need, but economic purchasing power. Hence, for example, the owner-occupied sector limits access because of women's inferior economic status. Although public allocation systems are based on meeting housing needs traditionally

---

57. J.H. Johnston, J. Salt and P.A. Wood, *Housing and the Migration of Labour in England and Wales* (1974).
58. J. Greve, D. Page and S. Greve, *Homelessness in London* (1971) at p.76.
59. See "Who are the Homeless?" above at pp. 15-19.
60. M. Brailey, *Women's Access to Housing* (Planning Exchange, Glasgow, 1985).

the public sector allocation has been geared towards the nuclear family. Female headed single-parent households accordingly experience double discrimination.[61]

(b) Social factors

Whilst economic factors create a vulnerability to homelessness, they do not provide an adequate explanation of why people become homeless. Economic factors are general in their application, and therefore cannot fully account for why one family becomes homeless whereas another family in exactly similar circumstances does not. Clearly social factors do have some bearing on why people become homeless and must be taken into consideration together with economic factors.

Any assessment of the personal circumstances of homeless persons, however, is fraught with difficulties. To give an example, domestic disputes are regarded as a major cause of homelessness.[62] Yet, Madeline Drake has argued that domestic disputes themselves may arise because of inadequate housing.[63] The close interrelationship between economic and social factors therefore must be kept in mind when looking at government statistics on the causes of homelessness.

According to the Scottish Development Department and the Department of the Environment, the most common cause of homelessness recently has been domestic disputes.[64] These commonly take two forms: family breakdown and the unwillingness or inability of relatives and friends to continue to provide accommodation. An analysis of the Scottish Development Department statistics for 1986[65] reveals that 72.2% of homeless persons, accepted as being homeless, gave a domestic dispute of some kind as the main reason for losing their accommodation. Similar figures emerge south of the border. The Scottish figures can be further sub-divided: 42.2% of such applicants became homeless because their parents, relatives or friends were reluctant or unable to continue to supply accommodation; 13.8% had become homeless because of a violent dispute with a partner; and 16% because of a non-violent dispute. Equally disturbing is the fact that in Scotland — excluding Strathclyde where over half the population lives — the number of children in care solely because their parents have no accommodation where they can live as a family has ranged between 71 and 46 in the years 1984 and 1986.[66]

61. S. Watson, "Women and Housing or Feminist Housing Analysis" *Housing Studies* (1986) 9.
62. S. Watson with H. Austerbery, *Housing and Homelessness* (RKP, London, 1986).
63. M. Drake, *New Society* (1977) 464.
64. Scottish Development Department, *Scottish Housing: A Consultative Document* (HMSO, Cmnd.6852, 1977) para. 7.9; Department of the Environment, *Housing Policy: A Consultative Document* (HMSO, Cmnd.6851, 1977) para. 12.12.
65. Scottish Development Department *Scottish Housing Statistics* (1986); at p.43.
66. HC Debates, Vol. 130 (25 March, 1988) col. 254, p.19.

Closely related to the problem of domestic disputes is the increasing trend of single people to set up home on their own rather than to share accommodation with parents, relatives and friends. This may be a matter of personal preference but it has led to increased pressure on both the private and public housing stocks.[67]

Unemployment and poverty have been listed as economic factors which lead to homelessness. However, they are commonly part of a sequence of events such as illness, family crisis and debt. It is important to note therefore that many of the families who get into rent arrears and who are subsequently evicted from their homes experience personal difficulties of these kinds. Many of the single homeless suffer from physical or mental disabilities and families who have difficulties in eking out a living on low wages or income support are drawn into a downward spiral which results in homelessness.[68]

These factors have been recognised as causes of homelessness. However, the Parliamentary debates on the Housing (Homeless Persons) Bill firmly focused on the nebulous concept of self-induced homelessness and to a lesser extent local connection. research findings indicated that the number of persons who intentionally bring about their own homelessness is minimal and government statistics have long demonstrated that persons rehoused in local authority temporary accommodation are rarely "outsiders".[69] Yet without any hard evidence, some Members of Parliament attributed the causes of homelessness to the voluntary acts of the homeless. The homeless were quite simply said to be queue-jumpers, feckless or nomadic Scots and Irish. Fears, such as these, that the homeless manipulate the system to their own advantage may be sincere but it would appear from the evidence that they are unfounded.[70]

(c) Summary

Attempting to find the effective cause of homelessness in any particular case is rather like unravelling the *Gordian knot*. Social and economic factors interact in a complex and unpredictable manner. Illness and family problems may lead to unemployment or irregular employment which in turn may result in or exacerbate poverty. Indeed, the experience of homelessness itself may be an important factor in limiting a family's housing opportunities. A family evicted from their home because of rent

67. M. Drake and A. Biebuyck, *Policy and Provision for the Single Homeless: A Position Paper* (1977) quoted by R. De Friend, 'Housing (Homeless Persons) Act 1977', 41 MLR (1978) 173; *Beyond the Hostel*, National Association of Youth Clubs, Leicester, 1982.
68. J. Greve, D. Page and S. Greve, *Homelessness in London* (1971) pp. 75-88; B. Glastonbury, *Homeless Near A Thousand Homes* (1971) pp. 54-96.
69. *Scottish Housing Statistics* and *Housing and Construction Statistics* 1978-1986 passim.
70. See "Governmental Policy and Homelessness" below at pp. 25-45.

arrears, for example, may find it difficult to obtain accommodation from either public or private landlords. To label the homeless as feckless or problem families may be convenient. However, given the diversity of circumstances in which homelessness may occur, it is hardly helpful. If, as the Scottish Development Department observed, "[t]he solutions are not necessarily simple"[71] it would be surprising if the diagnosis of the causes of homelessness was any less so.

5. The Growth in Homelessness

Whatever definition of homelessness is adopted or standard of measurement applied, it is clear that the scale of the problem of homelessness has dramatically increased in post-war Britain. Admittedly the increase has not been uniform. In the immediate post-war period an overall shortage of habitable homes combined with a rapid population growth to produce a homelessness crisis. The Ministry of Reconstruction estimated that at the very minimum some 1.25 million houses were required to meet housing needs and to complete the slum clearance and overcrowding abatement programme.[72]

Yet, despite the housing drive launched by the Housing (Financial Provisions) Act 1946, it was estimated in 1951, when the post-war Labour administration was replaced by a Conservative government, that at least one million families remained without a home of their own.[73] During the period from 1951-64 a housing boom and relaxation of rent controls increased the supply of housing with the result that the homelessness problem became obscured by an apparent fall in the number of persons admitted to local authority temporary accommodation.[74] That fall in the number of persons admitted to temporary accommodation, however, disguised the fact that the housing needs of the single and the childless remained unmet.

By the end of the 1950s the number of homeless persons admitted to local authority temporary accommodation, the official barometer of homelessness, began to rise again. By the early 1960s concern for homelessness in London had been translated into action. The London County Council set up a special Committee of Inquiry into Homelessness in 1961, commissioned John Greve to conduct a study of the underlying causes of the increase in homelessness in the same year,[75] and in 1963

71. Scottish Development Department, *Scottish Housing: A Consultative Document* (HMSO, Cmnd.6852, 1977) para. 7.9.
72. S. Merrett, *State Housing in Britain* (1979) p.237.
73. M. Partington, *The Housing (Homeless Persons) Act 1977 and Code of Guidance* 1978; J. Greve, D. Page and S. Greve, *Homelessness in London* (1971) pp.57-58.
74. D. Donnison and C. Ungerson, *Housing Policy* (1982) p.264.
75. J. Greve, *London's Homeless* (1964).

reinstated the practice of a "midnight count" of people sleeping rough.[76] However, little was done to halt the increase in homelessness. According to official statistics homelessness in England and Wales increased by 190% in the period from 1960-68.

This trend was to continue in the period 1968-1977. In his study of the use of bed and breakfast accommodation by local authorities in England and Wales, Ron Bailey estimated that the number of families applying to local authorities for temporary accommodation increased by about 11,000 in the four years from 1969 to 1973, from 22,454 in 1969 to 33,225 in 1973.[77] In the year immediately prior to the introduction of the 1977 Act the number of persons applying to local authorities rose to 52,570, of whom 31,070 were found permanent accommodation and 6,450 were found temporary accommodation.[78]

In Great Britain the trend over the ten years of legislation has been a marked increase in applications. In 1978, 53,110 persons were accepted as homeless by housing authorities in England and Wales. This rose to 70,010 by 1981. Thereafter a slightly different basis for the collection of figures was used but the underlying trend has been the same rising, from 73,600 in 1982 to 102,980 in 1986 according to the DOE statistics.[79]

In Scotland the rise has been even more dramatic. Although in the first five years the figures fluctuated around 15,000 per annum, since 1984 there has been an explosion in the number of homeless applications. In 1985 there were 19,791 applications, in 1986 23,315 and in 1987 the number of applications topped 30,000.[80]

6. Governmental Policy and Homelessness

Prior to 1948 homelessness was not regarded as an independent social problem requiring governmental intervention but rather as being symptomatic of other social ills. The failure to perceive homelessness as a problem in its own right had and has important consequences. Indeed, it is arguable that contemporary attitudes towards the homeless and the objectives of government policy on homelessness cannot be fully or even adequately comprehended without examining the historical development of homelessness as a social problem. For, as Paul Rock observes in the foreword to Paulus's examination of the emergence of anti-adulteration legislation:

"[L]aws do not arise full-grown children of the dragon's teeth. They do not

---

76. J. Greve, D. Page and S. Greve, *Homelessness in London* (1971) p.xiv.
77. R. Bailey, *Bed and Breakfast,* Shelter (1974) p.3.
78. *Hansard,* HL Debates, Vol 385 (15 July, 1977) col.1133.
79. *Housing and Construction Statistics* 1986 and 1987, parts 78-81.
80. Scottish Development Department, *Scottish Housing Statistics,* 1986 Table 1, p.43.

enjoy an uncomplicated and unproblematic relationship with the settings and intentions of their original drafting. Rather, they undergo natural histories whose unwindings shape them in ways never anticipated by their first authors."[81]

(a) Punishing the homeless

Historically, the response of local and central government towards homeless persons was derived from the Poor Law. The function of the Old Poor Law, broadly was twofold — to license begging and discourage vagabondage.[82] The latter function was achieved by cruelly punishing homeless vagrants. A grim Tudor statute of 1530, for example, sought to repress vagabondage by empowering parish officials to have vagrants tied to the tail of a cart and whipped "until the blood streams from their bodies." Subsequent statutes provided for the scourging, branding, mutilation and execution of incorrigible vagabonds and rogues. The Heritors and Kirk Sessions of Scotland, it has to be said, were no less diligent or enthusiastic in discouraging idleness amongst the able-bodied poor.[83]

Hostility towards the homeless, and in particular, homeless vagrants, did not end with the introduction of the New Poor Law. Those authorities which were unable to remove able-bodied paupers legally under the law of settlement[84] and baulked at illegal removal,[85] provided the homeless with the very minimum of assistance. This meagre assistance commonly took the form of the provision of bare boards and a sparse diet of bread and gruel. However, such assistance was not provided free, but had to be earned. Separated from the other workhouse inmates in separate deterrent casual wards or in night asylums and mendicity offices, vagrants were

---

81. I. Paulus, *The Search for Pure Food: A Sociology of Legislation in Britain* (1974) p.10.
82. See, for example, R.A. Cage, *The Scottish Poor Law* 1745-1845 (1981); R. Mitchison, 'The Making of the Old Poor Law', *Past and Present* No. 63 (1974) 58; R. Mitchison, 'The Creation of the Disablement Rule in the Scottish Poor Law', in T.C. Smout (ed.) *The Search for Wealth and Stability (1979).*
83. Studies of the law regulating vagrancy include C.J. Ribton-Turner, *A History of Vagrants and Vagrancy and Beggars and Begging* (1887); K. Marx, 'Bloody Legislation Against the Expropriated, Since the End of the 15th Century. Forcing Down Wages by Acts of Parliament', *Capital*, Vol.1 (1977) Ch.XXVIII, 896; J. Pound, *Poverty and Vagrancy in Tudor England* (1971); W.J. Chambliss, 'A Sociological Analysis of the Law of Vagrancy', in W.G. Carson and P. Wiles (eds.) *Crime and Delinquency in Britain* (1971) p. 206.
84. F.C. Montague, 'Settlement and Removal' (1888) 4 *Law Quarterly Review* 40; M.E. Rose, 'Settlement Removal and New Poor Law' in D. Fraser (ed.), *The New Poor Law in the Nineteenth Century (1976)* p.25.
85. The City of Glasgow did not baulk at illegal removal. In the nineteenth century that city deported thousands of destitute Irishmen irrespective of their rights and needs. See J.C. Woodham-Smith, *The Great Hunger: Ireland 1845-9* (1962) p.279.

set to work breaking stones, grinding corn or picking oakum.[86] Only when they completed their appointed task were they to be released to search for work. While breaking stones was undoubtedly less draconian than the forms of punishment provided for by the Old Poor Law, it was no less a form of punishment.

Thus the persistence and continuity of the view that homelessness primarily was a criminal matter to be discouraged by harsh penal sanctions can be seen to be a major influence in shaping policy prior to 1948. As if to underline this point legislation passed during the nineteenth century created a series of criminal offences specifically related to vagrancy and unauthorised begging. The best known example of this was section 4 of the Vagrancy Act 1824[87] which created the offence of loitering with intent and provided the police with broad discretionary powers to arrest persons on suspicion.[88]

(b) A war-time legacy

Described by Bevan as "the coping stone of the social services of Great Britain",[89] the National Assistance Act 1948 not only brought an end to the Poor Law but heralded the dawn of a more humane approach to the problems of vagrancy and homelessness. Firmly rooted in the experiences of war-time Britain and shaped by post-war optimism, the Act required the National Assistance Board and local authorities to accept responsibility for the resettlement of vagrants and for the temporary rehousing of homeless persons. In particular, section 21(1)(b) of the 1948 Act obliged local authority welfare departments to provide:

"[T]emporary accommodation for persons who are in urgent need thereof, being need arising in circumstances which could not reasonably have been foreseen or in such other circumstances as the authority may in any case determine."

This provision, although well intentioned, was to falter partly

---

86. S. & B. Webb, *English Poor Law Policy* (1910) pp. 96-99 and 172-174; N. Longmate, *The Workhouse* (1974) pp.232-256.

87. The Vagrancy Act 1824 (applied to Scotland by section 15 of the Prevention of Crimes Act 1871); the Vagrancy Act 1838; the Trespass (Scotland) Act 1865, which made trespass a criminal offence in Scotland, and the later Vagrancy Act 1935 are examples of criminal statutes specifically intended to limit the civil rights of vagrants and to create a second class of citizen.

88. The archaic and arbitrary power to arrest a person loitering with intent was abolished in England and Wales by section 8 of the Criminal Attempts Act 1981 after years of serious criticism: see the Home Affairs Committee, "Race Relations and the 'SUS' Law". *Parliamentary Papers,* HC 559, 21 April, 1980. Loitering with intent, however, remained a criminal offence in Scotland (see *Cole v. Cardle* 1981 SCCR 132) until it was abolished under section 137 of and schedule 4 to the Civic Government (Scotland) Act 1982.

89. *Hansard,* HC Debates, Vol.444, (24 November, 1947), col.1603.

because it was an inadequate response to the problem of homelessness and partly because of the misplaced belief that the solution to the housing problem was simply a question of building sufficient houses to meet general housing needs.[90]

The central flaw in the policy illustrates the influence of the Poor Law tradition on the policy-makers. By placing responsibility for the provision of temporary accommodation for the emergency homeless upon local authority welfare departments, rather than housing departments, the problem of homelessness was by implication defined to be a welfare problem rather than a housing problem. This had the consequence not only of emphasising a traditional pathological social work approach to homelessness, that is to say, the use of counselling, the case-work method and other social work skills, but also placed an intolerable strain on the little accommodation which welfare departments were able to offer. Faced with a problem which they were ill-equipped to deal with, some welfare departments devised policies of splitting families and providing inadequate hostel and bed and breakfast accommodation.

The effects of these policies were strongly criticised as inhumane, inefficient, expensive and of doubtful legality.[91] In Scotland, for example, the Morris Committee discovered that no fewer that 14 out of the 18 Part III hostels used by local authorities to provide homeless persons with temporary accommodation were former poorhouses and that in many cases admission to the hostel was restricted to women and children, while men were directed to model lodging houses or hostels for single men.[92] Families placed in bed and breakfast accommodation[93] scarcely fared better than those admitted to hostels. Denied the privacy necessary for normal family life and, in some cases, forced to spend long periods of each day out-of-doors, the plight of families placed in such accommodation tended to be exacerbated rather than ameliorated. Central government and some local authorities, to be fair, were not unaware of this deficiency and almost 60% of local authorities in England and Wales voluntarily implemented the recommendation of DOE Circular 18/74 to transfer responsibility for the temporary housing of homeless persons from their welfare departments to their housing departments. However, over 40% of local authorities refused to do so and, with the reorganisation of local government into a two-tier structure in the early 1970s, local government conflict over responsibility for the homeless was intensified.

90. On the development of UK housing policy see S. Merrett, State *Housing in Britain* (1979) and D. Donnison and C. Ungerson, *Housing Policy* (1982). A Holmans, *Housing Policy in Britain* (1987); and A. Power, *Property Before People* (1987).

91. Shelter, *No Place to Call Home* (1972); R. Bailey and J. Ruddock, *The Grief Report* (1972); R. Bailey, *Bed and Breakfast* (1974); R. Bailey, *Blunt Powers Sharp Practices* (1976).

92. Scottish Development Department, *Housing and Social Work – A Joint Approach* (HMSO, 1975) para. 8.25.

93. See "Preventing Homelessness" below at pp. 50-55.

If the failure to perceive homelessness as a housing problem and to allocate primary responsibility for the homeless to local authority housing departments rather than welfare departments was the central flaw in the policy, it was not the Act's only flaw. Nor was it the only factor which limited the effectiveness of the policy. For example, the duty to provide temporary accommodation to homeless persons was directly limited in THREE important respects by the wording of the statutory provision:

    (i)   Urgent need.
    (ii) Unforeseeable homelessness.
    (iii) Temporary accommodation.

(i) Urgent need

This duty was not owed to all homeless persons but only to persons who had an urgent need for temporary accommodation. Yet in spite of the central importance of the distinction between urgent and non-urgent need, the Act failed to give local authorities guidance on this matter. This failure resulted in a lack of uniformity in local authority practices as to persons who were recognised as having an urgent need for accommodation and in 1974 it was found necessary to issue a joint circular identifying priority groups who were to be regarded as having an urgent need for accommodation.[94]

(ii) Unforeseeable homelessness

The duty to provide temporary accommodation only applied if the need for such accommodation arose in circumstances which could not reasonably have been foreseen, or in other circumstances in which the local authority were willing to accept as giving rise to this duty. During the passage of the National Assistance Bill, Members of Parliament forcibly argued that the effect of the foreseeability test would be to call upon local authorities to exercise an unacceptable degree of moral censorship in determining applications for assistance under the Act and, therefore, should be omitted. The Ministry of Health, however, successfully resisted this attempt arguing that the foreseeability test would cause little practical difficulty.[95] That view was not borne out.

    In practice local authorities ignored Ministerial circulars which reminded them that the distinction between foreseeable and unforeseeable homelessness was artificial,[96] and that temporary accommodation should

94. Circular 18/74, paras. 8-12.
95. *Hansard*, HC Debates Vol. 444, (24 November, 1947) col.1642 and Vol.448, (5 March, 1948), cols. 689-692.
96. Ministry of Health, Circular 20/66.

be provided to persons who had been made homeless as a result of fire, flood and personal tragedies such as eviction.[97] A consequence of a narrow interpretation of the foreseeability test and an extreme reluctance to make use of the discretionary power, which the section gave to local authorities to help foreseeably homeless persons, was the exclusion from temporary accommodation of persons who had been evicted because of rent arrears or anti-social behaviour. Criticisms of local authority practice, however, became muted following the decision of the Court of Appeal in *Southwark London Borough Council v. Williams*.[98] In that case both Lord Denning, the then Master of the Rolls, and Lord Justice Edmund Davies gave their support to the view that the duty of local authorities under section 21(1)(b) was narrowly circumscribed.

Lord Justice Edmund Davies opined that:

> "[T]he whole structure and wording of the sub-section seems to me to deal with an emergency [such as] cases of dispossession or deprivation of accommodation by sudden events such as a fire, flood, or something of that kind".

Lord Denning warned homeless families who were evicted from lodging in one area and went to another area without arranging accommodation for themselves or who voluntarily terminated the tenancy of accommodation (no matter how poor the condition of their accommodation might be) that local authorities were entitled to regard their homelessness as foreseeable and, therefore, outwith the ambit of their duty to provide temporary accommodation.

(iii) Temporary accommodation

The final direct limitation arising from the wording of section 21(1)(b) was that the duty was to provide temporary accommodation only. Again, in spite of the importance of the meaning of the word "temporary", the Act did not provide local authorities with guidance as to the way in which they should interpret the word in the discharge of their statutory obligation. Some guidance was given to local authorities some years later when the meaning of this word was litigated in the High Court. In the first of two cases on this problem, *Roberts v. Dorset County Council*,[99] Mr Justice Griffiths held that the obligation imposed upon local authorities under section 21(1)(b) was not to provide accommodation for as long as an urgent need for accommodation persisted, but merely to provide accommodation on a temporary basis and that it was not unlawful for a local authority to formulate guidelines to determine when

---

97. Ministry of Health, Circular 87/48.
98. [1971] Ch. 734. See also *McPhail v. Persons Unknown; Bristol Corporation v. Ross* [1973] Ch. 447.
99. (1977) 75 LGR 462; *The Times*, 2 August 1976.

the provision of temporary accommodation should cease. The second part of this decision was later discussed by the High Court in the unreported case of *Bristol Corporation v. Stockford*.[100] In this case Bristol Corporation adopted a blanket policy whereby homeless families would be provided with accommodation for a fixed period of 28 days. The High Court held this policy to be unlawful because local authorities must not fetter their discretion[101] and must take into account the actual or potential needs of homeless families for accommodation when determining the length of time for which temporary accommodation would be provided.

In addition to the limitations arising from the wording of section 21(1)(b) two further factors which limited the effectiveness of the 1948 Act are worthy of note. In framing the National Assistance Act 1948 the post-war Ministry of Health provided a default power. A person aggrieved by the failure of a local authority to discharge any of their duties under the Act could apply to the Minister of Health who was empowered by section 36(1) of the Act to compel local authorities to discharge their function. The provision of extra-judicial remedies, can and often does have the effect of excluding recourse to the courts.[102] This Ministerial default power was no exception to that general rule. *In Southwark London Borough Council v. Williams* [103] the Court of Appeal held that the provision of an extra-judicial remedy excluded recourse to the courts, thus effectively ending a campaign by squatting organisations to establish a right to decent housing through the courts.[104]

Another factor which did much to undermine the policy of the 1948 Act was local authority practice. Many local authorities interpreted the obligation under section 21(1)(b) to apply exclusively to homeless families, or more exactly to mother and children of homeless families, rather than to homeless persons.[105] This had the adverse effects of excluding the single homeless and homeless fathers from temporary accommodation. Other examples of what has been aptly described by Ron Bailey as local authority "sharp practices",[106] such as the artificial distinction between "applications" for assistance and "inquiries", the

---

100. This case is not officially reported but appears in R. Carnwarth, *A Guide to the Housing (Homeless Persons) Act 1977* (1978), p.129.

101. See "Remedies for the Homeless", below at pp. 208-242.

102. C.T. Reid, 'Failure to Exhaust Statutory Remedies' [1984] JR 185; J.G. Logie, 'Enforcing Statutory Duties: The Courts and Default Powers' [1988] JSWL 185.

103. [1971] Ch. 734.

104. On this campaign see D.C. James, 'Homelessness: Can the Courts Contribute?' (1974) 1 *British Journal of Law and Society* 195; M. Weaver, 'Common-sense and the Homeless: A Study of the Limits of Judicial Discretion' (1978) 8 *Kingston Law Review* 169.

105. In his study of homeless families in South Wales and the West of England, Bryan Glastonbury points to the institutionalisation of the practice of splitting up "foreseeably" homeless families: *Homeless Near a Thousand Homes* (1971) p.44.

106. R. Bailey, *Blunt Powers – Sharp Practices* (1976).

issuing of rail warrants, and the use of bed and breakfast and other substandard or inadequate forms of temporary accommodation can be
mentioned.[107]

It is fair to say that by the early 1970s local government obduracy
and central government apathy had combined to create a "national
disaster".[108]

(c) Towards a corporate approach to homelessness

At the same time as the homelessness problem began to take on the
proportions of a national disaster the sources of criticism of government
policy shifted. While it was always possible for government to discount
the findings of research by academics and voluntary housing organisations
on the grounds of selectivity and partiality, it was more difficult to do so
when demands for a radical re-appraisal of policy came from committees
set up by government itself.

In the late 1960s and early 1970s a number of important and
influential committees made such a demand. One by one the Seebohm
Committee on local authority and allied services,[109] the Cullingworth
Committee on council house allocation policies,[110] the Greve Report on
homelessness in London,[111] the Finer Committee of one-parent families[112]
and the Morris Committee on the links between housing and social
work[113] recommended that primary responsibility for the homeless
should be transferred from local authority social work or social services
departments to their housing departments. The reason put forward by
these Committees to justify this transfer was that the latter had resources
and expertise not possessed by the former. In addition to recommending
the re-allocation of responsibility, the Morris Committee noted that
whereas it was evident that homelessness was a matter of mutual concern
to both social work and housing departments and presented an overwhelming
case for effective co-operation, in many parts of Scotland co-operation
between those local government departments was either minimal or non-
existent.[114]

---

107. J. Greve, D. Page and S. Greve, *Homelessness in London* (1971) p.62; D. Hiro, 'Homeless Duties
   Must be Enforced', *Roof* (1976) p.7; R. Bailey, *Bed and Breakfast* (1974); R. Bailey & J. Ruddock,
   The Grief Report (1972); Shelter *No Place to Call Home* (1972).
108. R. Bailey, *The Homeless and the Empty Houses* (1977) at p.58.
109. *Committee on Local Authority and Allied Personal Services*, (HMSO, Cmnd. 3203, 1968) paras.
   396-398.
110. Department of the Environment, *Council Housing: Purposes, Procedures and Priorites* (HMSO,
   1969) para. 51.
111. J. Greve, D. Page and S. Greve, *Homelessness in London* (1971) p.270.
112. *Report on the Committee of One Parent Families*, (HMSO, Cmnd. 5629, 1974) para. 6.60.
113. Scottish Development Department, *Housing and Social Work – A Joint Approach*, (HMSO, 1975)
   paras. 8.18-2.22 and recommendations 54 and 55.
114. *Ibid.* at para. 8.2.

32

Progress towards a corporate approach to homelessness was not interrupted. In England and Wales the Local Government Act 1972 temporarily reduced the duty of social services departments under the 1948 Act to a power. That duty was re-established by Ministerial directive in February 1974.[115] In the same year the issue of DOE Circular 18/74 calling on local authorities to transfer responsibility for the homeless voluntarily to their housing departments, and the institution of a major departmental review of the working of the 1948 Act, appeared to herald a first step towards a new approach to homelessness and to implement the recommendations of the circular[116] indicated that progress based on consensus would be slow.

By November 1975 Anthony Crosland, then Secretary of State for the Environment, had conceded the need for legislation. Yet recognition of the deficiencies of the 1948 Act and the need to compel local authority housing departments to accept responsibility for the homeless was not translated into a commitment to introduce legislation. The omission of proposals on homelessness in the Queen's Speech in November 1976 was greeted with a sense of disbelief and betrayal by the voluntary housing organisations which had campaigned for so long for a humane homelessness policy. In an attempt to pacify their outrage Reg Freeson, the Minister of Housing, undertook to lend the Department of Environment's support to any Private Member who wished to introduce a Bill on that subject.

(d) The Housing (Homeless Persons) Bill

The Housing (Homeless Persons) Bill was introduced to the House of Commons by Stephen Ross, the Liberal Member of Parliament for the Isle of Wight, on February 18, 1977. The Bill was a Private Member's Bill only in the sense that it was not directly sponsored by government. For the Bill which was presented to Parliament, as Ross acknowledged during its Second Reading, was one which had originated in the Department of the Environment following the 1974 review of homelessness policy.[117] The main purposes of the Bill were to compel local authorities in England and Wales[118] to implement DOE Circular 18/74 by transferring

---

115. Department of Health and Social Security, Directive D/N 120/8 dated 11 February, 1974 quoted in M. Partington, *The Housing (Homeless Persons) Act 1977 and Code of Guidance* (1978) in A. Arden, 'Homelessness: A New Criminal Offence', *New Law Journal* (1977) 1140.
116. *Hansard*, HC Debates, Vol. 296, (18 February, 1977) col. 899.
117. *Hansard*, HC Debates, Vol. 926, (18 February, 1977) col. 896.
118. Initially the Bill did not apply to Scotland. The Campaign by the Scottish Homeless Group to have the Bill extended to include Scotland is discussed by Peter Gibson in "How Scotland Got The Housing (Homeless Persons) Act" in N. Drucker and H.M. Drucker (eds.) *The Scottish Government Yearbook 1979, (1979) 36.*

responsibility for housing homeless persons from their social services departments to their housing departments and to replace the limited duty to provide homeless persons with temporary accommodation with a range of more extensive and comprehensive duties. However, in spite of government assistance in the drafting and presentation of the Bill and all-party support for the policy underlying it, the Bill's passage through both Houses of Parliament was made difficult by local authority opposition.

Ignoring research findings the local authority lobby attacked the Bill as a "Scroungers' Charter". Members of Parliament argued that the Bill would in effect provide the undeserving poor with a right to council housing. Hordes of displaced miscreants from the hinterlands of Britain and abroad, it was said, would descend on seaside resorts and areas which had major seaports, airport and rail termini clamouring to be housed. Despite the transparency of these arguments and government support for the Bill, Labour's fragile majority at Westminster made an accommodation to local authority interests necessary. The price of their appeasement, however, was the acceptance of a number of amendments which were effectively to transform the nature of the Bill. Rather than a measure which provided the homeless with an enforceable right to housing, the Bill became a series of obstacles to be negotiated before that right can be claimed.[119]

The debate on the Housing (Homeless Persons) Bill focused on whether the proposed legislation should impose on local authorities a clear duty to house homeless persons in priority need or should provide local authorities with discretion to determine the nature and extent of their obligation. At the end of the day it was the view of the Association of District Councils which prevailed. The duties of local authorities under the Bill, and subsequently the Act, were based on a series of discretionary decisions.[120]

The transformation of the Bill from a rights-based measure to a discretionary one was not without difficulties. In particular it was foreseen that those local authorities which had failed voluntarily to transfer responsibility for the homeless to their housing departments might exercise their discretion in a cheese-paring and moralistic manner. To avoid this occurring it was provided that an enforceable Code of Guidance should spell out in clear terms exactly how local authorities would be expected to exercise their discretion.[121] In addition to the provision of a Code of Guidance Lord Gifford put forward an amendment, at the suggestion of John Smythe of Shelter, during the Second Reading

---

119. P. Robson and P.Q. Watchman, 'The Homeless Persons Obstacle Race', [1981] JSWL 1 and 65.
120. See chapters 4, 5, and 6.
121. Hugh Rossi, *Hansard,* HC Debates, Vol. 934/35 (8 July, 1977) col. 1619. In *De Falco v. Crawley District Council* [1980] QB 460, however, the Court of Appeal held that the Code of Guidance was directory and not mandatory. This decision has been followed in Scotland: *Mazzaccherini v. Argyll and Bute District Council* 1987 SCLR 475.

of the Bill in the House of Lords whereby applicants aggrieved by housing authority determinations could appeal to the courts.[122] Unfortunately, this amendment was withdrawn.[123]

Two amendments which were not withdrawn and which continue to exercise housing advisers and the courts, concerned local connection and intentionality. These amendments were introduced at the insistence of the Association of District Councils and are intended to limit the scope for abuse by queue-jumpers and the itinerant poor. The origins of the local connection amendment can be traced back to the Old Poor Law of settlement and, like that concept, was made as a concession to a few rich parishes, particularly in London and the South West of England, which feared an invasion of displaced paupers seeking more congenial surroundings and support from the rates. "Scroungers and scrimshankers, rent dodgers, beach scroungers and queue-jumpers",[124] it was argued, would be attracted to the areas of certain "magnet authorities"[125] making those authorities responsible for a disproportionate number of homeless persons. The Act therefore provides housing authorities with a discretionary power to inquire whether homeless applicants have a local connection with the areas of any other housing authority in Scotland, England and Wales and, in certain circumstances, to transfer responsibility for the permanent housing of priority need applicants to such authorities.[126]

The second amendment formed "the nub of the debate of the Bill since Second Reading"[127] and has the effect of reducing the nature of the obligation of a housing authority to a priority need applicant who is homeless or threatened with homelessness where the housing authority can demonstrate that the present circumstances of that applicant were brought about by a previous culpable act or omission on the part of the applicant.[128] The concept of "intentional homelessness", described by Lady Soper as "gobbledygook",[129] was the major concession made to the local authority lobby and effectively reinstitutes the discredited notions of the deserving and undeserving poor and foreseeable homelessness. It is the prize loophole in the Act and has given rise to extensive litigation.[130]

---

122. *Hansard*, HL Debates, 15 July, 1977, col.1170 and P. Gibson, "How Scotland Got The Housing (Homeless Persons) Act" in N. Drucker and H.M. Drucker (eds.) *The Scottish Government Yearbook 1979*, at p.46.
123. See, "Remedies for the Homeless" below at pp. 208-242.
124. W.R. Rees-Davies, *Hansard*, HC Debates, Vol. 926 (18 February, 1977) cols. 905-921 and 972 and Vol. 934/5 (8 July, 1977) col. 1658.
125. Hugh Rossi, *Hansard*, HC Debates, Vol. 926 (18 February, 1977) col. 956.
126. See below at pp. 164-181.
127. Robin Cook, *Hansard*, HC Debates, Standing Committee A, Vol. 936 (27 July, 1977) col. 879.
128. See below at pp. 123-161.
129. *Hansard*, HL Debates, (15 July, 1977) col. 1157.
130. See below at pp. 103-163.

The Bill which emerged bruised and bloodied from the Houses of Parliament then was in many ways unsatisfactory. Some of those opposed to the Bill, such as Mr George Cunningham, did so on the ground that it was "the worst drafted, worst constructed, worst conceived and worst prepared Bill [he] had ever seen;"[131] others because the Bill was viewed to be an inappropriate, if well-intentioned, response to the problem of homelessness.[132] Many more who had originally supported the Bill, however, were driven into opposition because of the concessions made to the local authority lobby. For example, Lord Gifford, who had assiduously and ably argued Shelter's case in the House of Lords, thought the Bill in its final form to be a "little bit of window-dressing",[133] whereas Lord Soper regarded it as "contaminated ... to an intolerable extent."[134] In short, the Bill pleased no-one and arguably had achieved little more than shifting the terrain of debate.[135]

It was against this background of compromise, hypocrisy and dissent that the Housing (Homeless Persons) Act 1977 received the Royal Assent on July 28, 1977 and was brought into force in England and Wales on December 1, 1977 and in Scotland four months later on April 1, 1988.

(e) The Housing (Homeless Persons) Act 1977

Whatever its many defects, the 1977 Act undoubtedly represents a major shift in governmental policy towards homelessness. By placing the Act within the general framework of the housing statutes, and by transferring responsibility for housing the homeless from local authority social work or social services departments to local authority housing departments, recognition is given to the fact that homelessness is primarily a housing problem In saying that, however, the role of other governmental agencies as providers of accommodation for homeless persons should not be overlooked. Regional social work or social services departments, for example, retain residual responsibility for housing persons in special need.[136]

The Act is a general statute supported by a Code of Guidance.[137] The Act provides a framework of duties owed by housing authorities to

---

131. *Hansard*, HC Debates, Vol. 936, (27 July, 1977) col. 864 quoted by N. Finnis, "The Heartless and the Homeless" *Roof* (1978) 138.

132. *Hansard*, Baroness Young, HL Debates, Vol. 385, (15 July, 1977) col. 1134.

133. *Hansard*, HL Debates, Vol. 386, (22 July, 1977) col. 684.

134. *Hansard*, HL Debates, Vol. 385, (15 July, 1977) col. 1157.

135. R. Widdowson, "The Night Before the Battle", *Roof* (1978) 131.

136. Section 12 of the Social Work (Scotland) Act 1968; Section 1 of the Child Care Act 1980; Section 21(1)(a) of and para. 8(3)(b) of Schedule 6 to the National Assistance Act 1948 (as amended).

137. As the Acts and the Codes are the subjects of this book we have provided the briefest of sketches of their provisions here.

homeless persons and the Code informs those authorities how their duties should be discharged in the particular circumstances of each case. Briefly, housing authorities must, in addition to giving a reasonable preference to homeless persons in allocating council houses,[138] do one of FOUR things if a person who is homeless or threatened with homelessness applies to them for assistance:

    (i)   provide advice and appropriate assistance;

    (ii) take reasonable steps to avert homelessness;

    (iii) provide advice and assistance and temporary accommodation;

(or) (iv) provide permanent accommodation.[139]

Which of these forms of assistance a housing authority are obliged to provide depends on the results of their inquiries into the personal and housing circumstances of the applicant and the circumstances leading up to the applicant becoming homeless or threatened with homelessness.[140]

The policy which underpins the Act is quite straightforward. No homeless person should be unable to turn to their local authority for help and those in greatest need, in other words priority need applicants, should not be left on the streets. The simplicity of the policy, however, belies the difficulties which have arisen in implementing the legislation.

(f) The implementation of the 1977 Act

"The Act is a nonsense, conceived by fools and implemented by idiots for the benefit of scroungers."[141]

The reaction of Mr Terry Dicks, former chairman of the housing committee of Hillingdon London Borough Council, to the 1977 Act may be extreme but it accurately reflects the attitude of a substantial minority of local authorities to the legislation.[142] In the years since the Act was introduced some local authorities have gone to quite extraordinary lengths to avoid or limit their statutory obligations to homeless persons.

---

138. Section 20 of the Housing (Scotland) Act 1987 and section 22 of the Housing Act 1985. In Scotland, but not in England and Wales, residential qualifications for admission to council waiting lists and the allocation of council houses have been prohibited by sections 19-20 of the Housing (Scotland) Act. For criticism of residential qualifications as exacerbating the problem of homelessness see the Cullingworth Report, *Council Houses, Purposes, Priorites, Procedures* (HMSO, 1969) at para. 169 and Scottish Housing Advisory Committee Report, *Allocation and Transfer of Council Houses* (SDD, 1980) para. 4.2.

139. See Ch.7, below at pp. 186-192.

140. See Chs. 4-6.

141. *The Times*, 11 July, 1980. See also 'The Lobby Against The Homeless Persons Act', Roof (1980) 85.

142. We wish to stress that the vast majority of local authorities have adopted a responsible and humane

Thus far six cases: *Din; Islam; Hillingdon London Council, ex p. Commission for Racial Equality; Cocks; Brown,* and *Puhlhofer,*[143] have been debated as far as the House of Lords. To those six cases must be added the hundreds of cases which have been heard in other courts. It may be objected that litigation, while illustrating the determination and tenacity of litigants, is hardly a reliable barometer of antipathy towards legislation and that litigation alone is a misleading guide to local authority practice. However, careful monitoring by Shelter and other charity groups reveals a pattern of local authority practice which is consistent with the issues coming before the courts.

Essentially, THREE major complaints have been levelled against housing authority practice:

    (i) Ignoring the law.
    (ii) Misinterpretation of the law.
    (iii) Accommodation.

(i) Ignoring the law

It is claimed that housing authorities intentionally ignore their clear obligations under the Act. Two specific examples of wilful disregard of the law can be put forward. The policy of the 1977 Act included,in the words of Lord Lowry in *Islam,*[144] "the object of keeping and bringing families together." The Act specifically provides that a person is homeless if he has no accommodation which he and any other member of the family is entitled to occupy. However, in spite of the clear wording of this section and judicial recognition that families are to be brought and kept together, Shelter report almost callous indifference.[145]

Another example of housing authorities openly flouting the law is the failure of some authorities to fulfil there statutory duty to provide temporary accommodation. The Act aims to ensure that any homeless person who has a priority need for accommodation is not left on the streets, irrespective of the reason for his homelessness. Yet in *Galbraith v. Midlothian District Council* [146] the housing authority refused to provide temporary accommodation for Mrs Galbraith and her children and in *R. v. CRE, ex p. Hillingdon London Borough Council* [147] an African family was dumped on the pavement outside the Foreign Office

---

attitude towards the Act.

143. *Din v. Wandsworth LBC* [1983] 1 AC 657; *R. v. Hillingdon LBC, ex p. Islam* [1983] 1 AC 688; and *R. v. Commission for Racial Equality, ex p. Hillingdon LBC* [1983] AC 799; *Cocks v. Thanet District Council,* [1982] AC 286; *Brown v. Hamilton District Council,* 1983 SLT 397; *R. v. Hillingdon LBC, ex p. Puhlhofer* [1986] AC 484.
144. *R. v. Hillingdon LBC ex p. Islam,* [1983] 1 AC 688 at p. 716.
145. R. Franey, "Apart From the Law", *Roof* (1980) 172.
146. (1979) SCOLAG 122.
147. [1983] AC 779.

as a protest against the hidden burden which the legislation places on authorities to house homeless immigrants.

(ii) Misinterpretation of the law

Considerable concern has been expressed about the way some housing authorities have interpreted the Act. In particular, some authorities have attempted to argue that persons occupying emergency accommodation, such as night shelters and battered women's refuges, are not homeless in terms of the Act[148] and the homeless statistics throw up significant variations in the number of applicants considered to be intentionally homeless by different authorities.

(iii) Accommodation

Housing groups have been critical of the nature and standard of temporary and permanent accommodation offered to homeless applicants. The practice of housing homeless persons in inadequate temporary accommodation was one of the major criticisms made of local authority practice prior to the introduction of the 1977 Act. However, while the Code of Guidance[149] points to the unacceptability of temporary accommodation which splits a husband from his wife and children and to the need to secure permanent accommodation for homeless persons as soon as possible, it is clear that some housing authorities are forcing homeless people to live in interim accommodation for a fixed period of time. The practice of "dumping" the homeless in hostels, former poorhouses, hotels, guest houses, bed and breakfast accommodation and disused army camps also persisted.[150] Indeed, one unfortunate family were "rehoused" in a 6ft. by 4ft. tent.[151]

Permanent accommodation, if anything, is a more intractable problem than temporary accommodation. The Act places a duty on housing authorities to secure that accommodation is made available to homeless applicants who have a priority need for accommodation and who did not become homeless intentionally.

---

148. See Ch. 4.
149. See Ch. 7.
150. Shelter, *Where Homelessness Means Hopelessness* (1978); S.Billcliffe, 'Dumped in the Interim', *Roof* (1979) 118; *R. v. Beverley Borough Council, ex p. McPhee, The Times*, 27 October, 1978, where a woman and four children aged between 7 and 13 were forced to spend one year in a 17ft by 14ft room in a hostel; *Galbraith v. Midlothian District Council* 1979 SCOLAG 122, where a woman and children were provided with damp, fire-damaged and vandalised property; *Delahaye v. Oswestry Borough Council, The Times*, 29 July, 1980, when a mobile home was provided only after the applicant had spent three weeks under canvas; Commissioner for Local Administration *Investigation* 641/H/78 – 25 March, 1980 (West Dorset), where the Council housed people in a converted army camp.
151. *The Guardian*, 15 September, 1980 and more generally R. Franey, 'Apart from the Law', *Roof* (1980) 172.

Subject to the limitations imposed by the courts in relation to the physical condition and geographical location of accommodation,[152] housing authorities have a very wide discretion in their allocation of houses to homeless persons.[153] Some authorities, however, are in a better position than others to adopt sensitive allocation policies which do not result in homeless persons being concentrated in difficult-to-let houses in "sink" estates without family support, transport or shopping and recreational facilities. The problems faced by authorities in attempting to balance the interests of the homeless against those of persons on the housing waiting list and existing tenants seeking transfers to better council estates, no doubt are difficult. However, consigning the homeless to poor housing in peripheral estates will only serve to reinforce their demoralisation, stigmatisation and isolation.[154]

Although these three areas are not the only sources of complaint, it was hoped by the homeless lobby that they would be tackled together with the question of the legal status of the Code of Guidance and the extension of the priority groups to include the single homeless when the Department of the Environment completed their review of the Housing (Homeless Persons) Act 1977.

(g) Review of the Housing (Homeless Persons) Act 1977

On May 13, 1982 Mr Michael Heseltine, the then Secretary of State for the Environment, reported to the Commons in a written answer, the conclusions of the Department of the Environment's review of the operation of the 1977 Act in England and Wales.[155] The Minister's statement was surprisingly brief, little more than a column in Hansard or 560 words in length,[156] and primarily reflects local authority interests.

Briefly, the Government did not propose any changes to the Act at present but hinted at indirect measures to assuage the fears of those local authorities which remained convinced that the Act was a "Scroungers' Charter".

---

152. *Galbraith v. Midlothian District Council* (1979) SCOLAG 122 and *Glasgow Herald*, 20 December, 1978; *Brown v. Hamilton District Council*, 1983 SLT 397; and *R. v. Wyre Borough Council, ex p. Parr*, (1982) 2 HLR 71.
153. *R. v. Bristol City Council, ex p. Browne* (1979) 1 WLR 1437; *R. v. Hillingdon LBC, ex p. Streeting* [1980] 3 All ER 417.
154. On the creation of housing ghettos see: O. Gill, *Luke Street, Housing Policy, Conflict and the Creation of the Delinquent Areas* (1977) and S. Damer, 'Wine Alley – the sociology of a dreadful enclosure', 22 *Sociological Review* (1974) 221.
155. *Hansard*, Issue no. 1244, 14 May-20 May, 1982, House of Commons Debates, 13 May, 1982, cols. 317-318.
156. We acknowledge the numeracy of Les Burrows, 'No Respite for the Single Homeless', *Roof* (1982) 29; see also M.Skinner, 'Why the Review of Homeless Persons Law is Taking so Long', *Local Government Chronicle* (1980) 1329; M. Drake, 'Review Sketch', *New Society* (1982) 301; and H. Wilkinson 'Review of the Homeless Persons Act', *New Law Journal* (1982) 708.

These measures included:

— a tightening of the Code of Guidance "[t]o ensure that authorities are clear about the extent of their duties, the ways in which they may fulfil them, and the very wide discretion they have to deal with abuse";

— a substantial diminution of local authority rent arrears consequent upon the introduction of the new housing benefits scheme in November 1982;

— a revision of leaflets issued by overseas embassies to prospective immigrants;

— an amendment of the immigration rules to bring immigration practice into line with the safeguards against abuse outlined by the courts,[157] and

— to ease the financial burden which the legislation places on the "magnet" authorities, the Government revised the homelessness indicator for the 1982-83 housing investment programme (HIP) allocations.

It would be pleasing to report that Government concessions were not all one way. However, the Government resisted considerable pressure to extend the priority need groups to include the single homeless[158] indicating that, in their view, shorthold,[159] homesteading and increased expenditure on hostel accommodation would, by increasing the availability of accommodation, substantially reduce the hardship suffered due to the exclusion of non-priority need groups from the protection of the Act.

(i) The Puhlhofer amendments

In the first eight years of the 1977 Act various tests were successfully put forward in the court to the effect that anyone occupying unacceptable housing conditions should also be considered as being homeless as it would not be reasonable to expect a person to occupy such accommodation.

---

157. *Din v. Wandsworth LBC* [1983] 1 AC 657; *R. v. Hillingdon LBC, ex p. Islam* [1983] 1 AC 688; *Lambert v. Ealing LBC* [1982] 2 All ER 394; *De Falco v. Crawley Borough Council* [1980] QB 460; *R. v. Tower Hamlets LBC, ex p. Monaf and Ali, The Independent*, 28 April, 1988.

158. On the need to include the single homeless under the priority need categorisation of homeless persons see N. McIntosh, 'Homelessness: four big gaps in the new Act', *New Society* (1978) 516 and L. Burrows, "No Respite for the Single Homeless", *op. cit.*

159. It is interesting that the Government should cite short tenancies as one of the measures which would increase the supply of accommodation available to non-priority need applicants, for Mr. John Stanley, the Minister of Housing, in relaxing the safeguards of tenants of such occupancies indicated the Government's disappointment at the failure of that policy to encourage landlords to let their homes: see "Administrative Legislation", (1981) SCOLAG 339. Variants on this type of letting arrangement now form the centrepiece of the 1988 housing legislation which is aimed at revitalising the private rented sector.

41

These tests were variously accepted as covering housing "unfit for human habitation where they cannot be rendered habitable within a short period of time",[160] "uninhabitable accommodation".[161] "unsuitable for human habitation"[162] and "inappropriate accommodation".[163]

However, the question of the minimum level of accommodation was taken on appeal to the Court of Appeal and subsequently to the House of Lords in the *Puhlhofer* case. Their Lordships took the view that there were no standards of accommodation which would require a person to be classified as homeless. Beyond the suggestion that the property in question would have to be capable of being described as accommodation there were in their Lordships' opinion as expressed in Lord Brightman's judgment "no rules".

The campaign spearheaded by Shelter (Scotland) and later taken up south of the border by Shelter was instituted to secure a change to the formal legal definition of homelessness. Initially the suggestion was that applicants should be regarded as homeless if they did not have their own satisfactory self-contained accommodation. Eventually, as a result of the views of those prepared to sponsor the amendments in the House of Lords, two quite different tests emerged to "neutralise" *Puhlhofer*. The test for England and Wales is a relative one centring on what is regarded as reasonable relative to the housing conditions in the area. In Scotland there is a twofold objective test which requires accommodation to be both overcrowded and a threat to health. Thus far these tests have yielded limited case law[164] although the effect of the English amendment is to change the way in which the intentional homelessness test operates.[165]

There can be no doubt that in general the position of homeless persons has been substantially improved by the 1977 Act. The worst fears of the local authority lobby have not been realised and there is a discernible change in attitude within housing management and the elected members of local authorities. Homelessness, like rent arrears, has come to be regarded as an administrative problem. Indeed, a substantial number of housing authorities recognise the concept of intentional homelessness to be an unworkable irrelevancy and have consigned it to the lumber room. It is to those officials and councillors that the success of the legislation is largely owed. However, there are a number of administrative and substantive reforms which the experience of operating the legislation indicates are urgently required and on which the continuing success of the legislation largely hinges.

---

160. *R. v. Dinefwr Borough Council, ex p. Marshall* (QBD) 13 November, 1984.
161. *Brown v. Hamilton District Council*, 1983 SLT 397.
162. *R. v. South Herefordshire District Council, ex p. Miles* [1983] 17 HLR 82.
163. *R. v. Preseli District Council, ex p. Fisher* [1984] 17 HLR 147.
164. *R. v. Westminster City Council, ex p. Tansey* (QBD) 6 March, 1987, and in re Tansey CA 5 October, 1988.
165. David Hoath, 'Homelessness Law After the Housing and Planning Act 1986: The "Puhlhofer" Amendments' [1988] JSWL 39.

In 1975 the Morris Report called for a joint approach to housing.[166] At that time the bulk of the Committee's criticisms were directed towards the intransigence and inflexibility of local authority housing departments in dealing with homelessness. Today, however, criticism would be more correctly addressed to those social work or social services departments which, relieved of *primary* responsibility for the homeless, regard themselves as being under no obligation to provide housing departments with much needed assistance and expertise. The establishment of formal structures of communication and liaison committees may not be enough. What is needed is a commitment to the spirit of the Morris Report.[167] Yet, important though this reform undoubtedly would be, it is also essential for the Department of Social Security to accept that Income Support and the Social Fund provide an inadequate "safety net" for the homeless and those faced with the loss of accommodation due to rent arrears. All too often eviction and homelessness are the consequence of the insensitive handling of conflicting rules by different government agencies.[168] A second administrative reform which has been consistently urged by the homelessness lobby is the provision of a quick, cheap accessible and independent method of challenging housing authority decisions. Unlike its predecessor, the National Assistance Act 1948, the 1977 Act did not provide an extra-judicial remedy. Homeless persons aggrieved by the decisions of housing authorities may challenge the validity of housing authority decision-making only in the superior courts.[169] However, if the legislation has proved anything it is that the procedures and remedies of these courts do not constitute an adequate mechanism for dealing with the urgent problems which arise when a housing authority fail to fulfil their statutory duties to homeless persons. As Lord Gifford pointed out during the Second Reading of the Bill in the House of Lords:

"If the local authority gets it wrong where does the applicant go? If a local authority says, 'We don't believe you are genuine; you are intentionally homeless' or we don't believe that you are vulnerable', or if they make some error, whether through prejudice or out of sheer incompetence, there is no remedy at all in this Bill. There is no tribunal to which a rejected individual can turn. There is no place where justice can be obtained."[170]

While Lord Gifford may be justly accused of a degree of exaggeration

166. Scottish Development Department, *Housing and Social Work – A Joint Approach* (HMSO, 1975).
167. It is, in our view, unfortunate that the Stodard Report, *Committee of Inquiry into Local Government in Scotland* (HMSO, Cmnd. 8115, 1981) paras. 84-88 and 98-104, rejected the need to make housing and social work a joint District/Regional authority responsibility.
168. D. Wilkinson, *Rent Arrears in Public Authority Housing in Scotland* (HMSO, 1980) paras. 7.42-7.48 and para. 8.21.
169. See Ch. 8 below at pp. 208-242.
170. *Hansard*, HL Debates, Vol. 385 (15 July, 1977) col. 1170.

there can be no doubt that he accurately sums up the dilemma faced by homeless persons wrongly turned away by a housing authority. If battered women and their children are not to be left to walk the street or to return to violent partners, it is essential that speedy and independent arbitration be made available.[171]

One can speculate that if the decision of the Court of Session in *Brown v. Hamilton District Council* [172] had prevailed to allow disputes to be dealt with in local sheriff courts that this would have overcome some of the problems of homeless persons in Scotland unlawfully refused assistance. However, it would not have been a panacea because the existing forms of judicial remedies are singularly inappropriate and it is undesirable to subject the decision of elected representatives to review by an appointed official or an appointed tribunal. These fears, while understandable, are misplaced. The establishment of an appeal procedure, whether by way of an administrative tribunal, such as a housing court, or statutory appeal to the sheriff court, will not displace the discretion of housing authorities to determine the nature and level of assistance to be provided to homeless persons, but will ensure that housing authorities have acted lawfully. It seems perverse, for example, that a publican refused a late-night licence in Scotland can appeal to the sheriff court whereas a homeless person must seek judicial review in the Court of Session.

Of the substantive reforms the three most pressing concern the enforceability of the Code of Guidance; the tightening up of the definition of intentional homelessness, and the extension of the priority need groups to include the single homeless.[173]

The Code of Guidance is the lynch-pin upon which the uniformity of treatment of homeless persons depends. Hugh Rossi, the architect of the amendments which effectively transformed the Housing (Homeless Persons) Bill, recognised that if the legislation was to be effective it was necessary that the Code of Guidance should be mandatory.[174] *In De Falco v. Crawley Borough Council* [175] however, the Court of Appeal held

---

171. 122 *Solicitors' Journal* (1979) 345.
172. 1983 SLT 397.
173. Scottish Homeless Group, *No Recourse for the Homeless* (1979) pp. 19-20.
174. "The code of guidance to be produced by the Government for local authorities will spell out to local authorities the way in which the Governement and Parliament expect local authorities to act when exercising their discretion under the Bill. *That is the fail safe system.* It is impossible to spell out in taut legal language wording to cover every possible permutation and combination of human activity. All we can do is use words that cover as best we can the generality of cases. But within that and especially where discretion is being allowed, as it is being allowed here, the local authority could determine rehousing in certain circumstances and guidance and help can be given to those authorities by the Secretary of State in more protracted and extended language in the code of guidance. That code is something that will have a statutory backing." *Hansard,* HC Debates, Vol. 936 (27 July, 1977) col. 885 (our emphasis).
175. [1980] QB 460.

that the Code of Guidance was advisory only. Thus, while housing authorities must take the code into account in processing applications for assistance, they are free to deviate from its guidance where they think it is appropriate to do so. This decision has had the effect of seriously undermining the effectiveness of the legislation and it is hoped that legislative intent will prevail over judicial interpretation.

One area in which the impact of the *De Falco* decision has been particularly felt is in determining whether an applicant has become homeless intentionally. Whereas the Code of Guidance lays down a straightforward test of causality,[176] the courts have adopted more complex tests from criminal and civil law. The law in relation to causality is now so obscure that it is difficult to state with confidence when an authority will not be justified in denying permanent accommodation to a person who has transgressed at some time in the past.[177]

The third substantive issue relates to the progressive extension of the priority need groups to include the single homeless.[178] While it is clear that central and local government are reluctant to accept the case for extension, it is equally clear that unless housing authorities are willing to take a more liberal view of their housing obligations to this vulnerable group, many single persons will be forced to continue to be shunted between institutional care and emergency accommodation.

7. Homelessness: A Decade of Distress and Disappointment

It is now more than a decade since the Housing (Homeless Persons) Act 1977 created a floor of rights for homeless persons and, by locating responsibility for housing homeless people with housing departments, gave explicit recognition to the fact that homelessness is primarily a housing problem rather than being attributable to the personal inadequacies of the homeless. It would be churlish and misleading therefore to fail to recognise the major improvements which have followed as a consequence of this legislation. Many homeless persons who in the past would have received only short-stay accommodation in a local authority hostel or bed and breakfast accommodation have been rehoused in mainstream accommodation. During the 1980s approximately 15% of mainstream allocations in the public sector were made to homeless persons,[179]

---

176. SC 2.19; EC 2.18.
177. See Ch. 5 below at pp. 103-163.
178. In their report, *Single and Homeless* DOE (1981), Drake, O'Brien and Biebuyck state that the vast majority of single homeless persons expressed a preference for mainstream housing. It was hoped that local authorities aided by central government, would take note of this finding and make special provision for this much neglected group. However, it is clear that this hope has not been realised.
179. See generally, L. Thompson, *An Act of Compromise* (Shelter, 1988).

although in some areas with limited housing stocks the proportion of allocations of mainstream housing to the homeless has been considerably higher.[180]

There has also been an important change in attitude towards the homeless. Local authorities and voluntary organisations have combined to seek new and imaginative ways of providing help for homeless persons. Public stereotypes of the homeless have been substantially challenged and the media have highlighted the plight of the single homeless who are forced to sleep rough in increasing numbers.

These improvements, however, have been offset by a series of factors which together have created a homelessness disaster on a scale quite beyond anything experienced in recent times. During the last decade homelessness in Great Britain has grown rapidly in size until now almost 150,000 people are *officially* recognised as being homeless.[181] At the same time, government expenditure on housing has been reduced in real terms. As the Social Security Advisory Committee stated in their Sixth Report:

"The reduction from £4.4 billion in 1980/81 to £2.4 must be seen in the light of the increase in housing inflation: over this period the retail price index for housing increased by over 75%. In real terms the fall in value on housing amounts to over £5 billion at 1987/8 prices."[182]

There has not, however, been a reduction across the board; the area of expenditure which has been most savagely cut is capital expenditure. This has resulted in a dramatic fall in the number of houses being built in the public sector[183] the traditional supplier of low cost housing on a needs basis. Combined with the impact of the 'right to buy',[184] this has resulted in an overall loss of public housing and consequently has reduced the ability of local government to respond to the problem of homelessness.

At the same time as capital expenditure has been reduced, there has been a rapid increase in the amount of money spent on bed and breakfast accommodation and board and lodging. By March 1987 it was estimated that 7,792 homeless families were occupying bed and breakfast accommodation in London, twice as many as 15 months before.[185] The

---

180. City of Glasgow District Council, *Housing Plan 9* (1986).
181. In *R. v. Peterborough District Council, ex p. McKernan* (QBD) 17 July, 1987 it was stated that approximately 75% of mainstream housing was allocated to homeless persons.
182. *Scottish Housing Statistics* (1986); *Housing and Construction Statistics* (1986); and C. Wolmar, 'Revealed: Rising Tide of Homeless', *The Observer*, 6 November, 1988.
183. Social Security Advisory Committee, Sixth Report (HMSO, Cm. 1988).
184. The number of new dwellings started by local authorities in Scotland fell by almost two-thirds, from 4858 to 1693, between 1979 and 1985: SDD, *Statistical Bulletin*, June 1987.
185. Since 1979 over one million public sector houses in Great Britain have been sold. Of this number approximately three-quarters have been sold to tenants exercising their right to buy: M. Kerr, *The*

cost of providing bed and breakfast accommodation to the London Boroughs alone has increased from £8.5 million to £63 million between 1983 and 1986.[186] Significantly, the number of claimants claiming benefit as boarders has also increased from 69,000 in 1981 to 139,000 in 1984 and the cost to the Exchequer has increased in line, from £166 million in 1982 to £500 million in 1984.[187] In the last decade therefore, we have come to a position where there are more homeless persons and more money being spent on bed and breakfast accommodation than ever before, but less provision of mainstream housing which means that the chances of a homeless person obtaining mainstream accommodation have been substantially reduced and that, as has been pointed out, much of the mainstream housing which remains in public ownership is rapidly deteriorating.[188]

If the last decade has been one of distress for homeless persons it has also in many respects been one of disappointment about the operation of the legislation. The vast majority of housing authorities it should be said have faced up to their responsibilities in implementing the law but a significant minority are still resistant to change. Adjacent housing authorities of similar size and housing stocks differ markedly in the proportion of cases which they find intentionally homeless[189] and the voluminous case law which has developed as a consequence of litigation bears testimony to the tenacity of a small group of authorities in seeking to limit assistance to homeless persons.[190] A conservative estimate of the cost of litigation to authorities would be in the order of £1 million.

The courts too have not played a distinguished role. The 'fail-safe' Code of Guidance was quickly discounted as directory rather than

Right to Buy: a National survey of Tenants and Buyers of Council Houses (HMSO, 1988) p.1; see also M. Foulis, *Council House Sales in Scotland* (Scottish Office, Central Research Unit, 1985); Institute of Housing Scottish Branch, *House Sales: The Management Implications* (Institute of Housing, London, 1986).

186. London Research Centre/Shelter, *Survey of Bed and Breakfast and Homelessness in London, Roof* (July/August) 1987 pp. 12-13. See also J. Greve et al, *Homelessness in London* (GLC, London, 1986) pp. 23-26 and L. Bonnerjea and J. Lawton, *Homelessness in Brent* (PSI, Research Report No.667, April 1987).

187. London Research Centre/Shelter, *Survey of Bed and Breakfast and Homelessness in London,,supra*; see also *Home Not Dole: The Economics of Ending Homelessness in Brent* (London Borough of Brent, 1986). The latest official estimate of expenditure by local authorities on bed and breakfast for the homeless for 1986-87 is £45m. for England (£31m. for London, alone), *Hansard*, HC Debates, Vol. 125 (21 January, 1988) col. 826.

188. R. Middleton, "The end of the line: boarders and single homeless people" in S. Ward (ed.), *DHSS in Crisis* (CPAG London 1985) pp. 67-80; see also J. Conway and P. Kemp, *Bed and Breakfast: Slum Housing of the Eighties* (SHAC, London, 1985) and P.Q. Watchman, 'Heartbreak Hotel' JSWL [1988] 147.

189. Scottish Affairs Committee, *Dampness in Housing* (HC 106-I) 1984; *English Housing Conditions Survey 1981* (HMSO, 1982); *The Inquiry into British Housing*, National Federation of Housing Associations (1985); D. Hughes, 'Housing Repairs: A Suitable Case For Reform' [1984] JSWL 137.

190. *Scottish Housing Statistics 1984-85*, Table 4 and *Hansard*, HC Debates (24 February, 1987); DOE, *A Duty to Act* (1988); "Council in 'Apartheid' Accusations", *Scotland on Sunday*, 30 October, 1988.

mandatory;[191] the test of causation became convoluted to an extreme degree;[192] and more importantly, the courts have begun to express grave doubts as to whether judicial review is a suitable remedy for homeless persons dissatisfied with housing decision-making.[193] This doubt can be appreciated, given the limitations of judicial review, but in the absence of a right of appeal to the county court or sheriff court to deny homeless persons this remedy would leave them without any means of recourse to the courts. Even though Northern Ireland has had to wait over a decade for similar legislation to be introduced, that legislation still fails to provide a right of appeal.[194]

However, if there is one area which has been consistently ignored in the debate about the homeless and one which requires fuller consideration after a decade it is to address the problem of those who are substantially excluded from the benefits of the legislation. Much has been written about the needs of the single homeless but an equally pressing consideration is the needs of the intentionally homeless. After a period in temporary accommodation the housing authority's duty towards this group is ended. They are, of course, free to apply for housing through the general allocation scheme and must be given a reasonable preference. Moreover, housing authorities are instructed that it is wrong to regard a person as intentionally homeless forever, and that they must review their circumstances periodically. However, we know little of how many of this group are allocated mainstream housing and, if they are not, what their final destinations may be. The lesson of the first decade therefore is that while some groups of homeless persons have gained through the legislation others have become marginalised and forgotten.

8. Homelessness in the 1990s

The signs for the future are far from encouraging. The Government are at the moment conducting a review of the homeless persons legislation and already there are some indications that radical change may be on the agenda. It is difficult to be precise on the Government's thinking on this matter as contradictory noises are being made by spokesmen in the DOE and the Scottish Office. It has been reported that a market oriented approach to homelessness is being seriously considered by the Secretary of State for the Environment.[195] Two suggestions that are being aired

191. Any roll call would include Hillingdon, Camden, Ealing, Swansea, Cardiff, Hammersmith and Fulham, Eastleigh, Wandsworth, Westminster, Wyre, Monklands and Midlothian.
192. *De Falco v. Crawley Borough Council* [1980] QB 460.
193. The case law is discussed below.
194. *R. v. Hillingdon LBC ex p. Puhlhofer* [1986] AC 484; see also *Mazzaccherini v. Argyll and Bute District Council* [1987] SCLR 475.
195. *The Guardian*, 23 November, 1988; J. Stearn 'Home Truths' *Housing* (November, 1988)13; A Crisp, 'Who Will House the Homeless?' *Housing* (November, 1988) 9.

currently are the possibility of defining homelessness as rooflessness, thus excluding those who are living in insecure or unsatisfactory accommodation, those at risk of domestic violence, and travelling people, from the ambit of the legislation and the reduction of the duties of housing authorities to a single duty to provide temporary accommodation – in other words no home for Cathy.

These suggestions certainly appear to be in line with the limitation of the role of local authorities in housing outlined in the Government's 1987 White Papers on housing.[196] On the other hand voluntary bodies, such as Shelter, have been reassured by Government spokesmen who point to the fact that it would be contrary to their decision to extend rights to the homeless in Northern Ireland to seek to undermine the legislation in Great Britain and that the Government's intention actually is to strengthen the legislation by, for example, including non-domestic violence as a circumstance which makes it reasonable for a person to give up accommodation.[197]

Our guess is that these contradictory views represent two parts of a current debate within government as to the development of housing policy. However, of the two views it is likely that the first will prevail as it seems to be impossible for local government adequately to meet the needs of the homeless if their role as providers of mass housing is to be further eroded. In America today thousands of homeless families live in welfare hotels in much the same way as homeless families live in bed and breakfast establishments.[198] Yet, so far, we do not have emergency warehouse shelters which have been America's primary response to the needs of the homeless.[199] This, we think, could be the homelessness scene in Great Britain in the 1990s; a fitting monument to the United Nations' International Year of Shelter for the Homeless?

---

196. *Housing: The Government's Proposals* (HMSO, Cm.214, 1987); *Housing: The Government's Proposals for Scotland* (HMSO, Cm.242, 1987).
197. *Inside Housing*, 11 November, 1988.
198. P. Marcuse, 'Isolating the Homeless' (Mimeo). Paper delivered at the International Housing Conference, Glasgow, 6-10 July, 1987; *Homlessness: Critical Issues for Policy and Practice* (the Boston Foundation, Boston, 1987).
199. R.K. Schutt, 'Shelters as Organisations: Fully Fledged Programs or Just a Place to Stay, in *Homelessness Critical Issues for Policy and Practice supra* p.43; Institute of Housing, *Who Will House the Homeless?* (1988).

Chapter 2
Preventing Homelessness

In addition to the reactive duties imposed upon housing authorities by the legislation, the Code of Guidance encourages housing authorities to adopt a positive role in the prevention of homelessness. The Code stresses the importance of identifying the symptoms of potential homelessness and urges housing authorities to take preventive action at an early stage.[1] The prevention of homelessness is to be achieved in THREE ways:

1. co-operation with other housing authorities and social services and social work departments and liaison with other bodies such as local social security officers and the courts;
2. training staff to deal with various aspects of housing and social security law which relate to homelessness; and
3. the development of housing aid centres.

1. Co-operation With Other Bodies[2]

The duty of housing authorities,[3] social services or social work departments to co-operate in the administration of the legislation is a general responsibility.[4] However, arguably the most important aspect of this duty concerns the prevention of homelessness. In particular the Secretary

1. EC 3.1 - 3.3 and A1.1-A1.17 and SC 3.1.-3.17.
2. Section 72 of the Housing Act 1985; section 38 of the Housing (Scotland) Act 1987; EC 7.1-7.6 and A 4.1-4.3; SC 7.1-7.8.
3. In this context "housing authority" also includes development corporations, registered housing associations and the Scottish Special Housing Association (Scottish Homes).
4. Section 72 of the Housing Act 1985 and section 38 of the Housing (Scotland) Act 1987 empowers housing authorities to make three types of request for assistance: (a) they may request assistance in discharge of their general duties (e.g. in respect of inquiries, the provision of accommodation, and the transfer of responsibility to provide permanent housing) from other local authorities in England, Scotland and Wales, new town and development corporations, registered housing associations, and the Scottish Special Housing Association (Scottish Homes); (b) request social services departments in England and Wales or social work departments in Scotland to exercise any of their functions in

50

of State for Scotland recommends most strongly effective and speedy co-operation and the development of formal administrative structures between housing authorities and social services or social work departments, as recommended by the report of the Morris Committee.[5] The importance of establishing links between housing authorities and social services or social work departments in identifying potential causes of homelessness (e.g. financial or budgeting difficulties, domestic violence or marital breakdown), in providing a 24-hour service for dealing with homeless persons who are particularly vulnerable because of illness, physical or mental handicap or difficult family circumstances should be self-evident.

Yet, the need for such links to be developed had to be restated by Lord Ross in *Kelly v. Monklands District Council* [6] where the failure by the housing department to liaise properly with the social work department contributed to their failure to appreciate the vulnerability of the sixteen year old girl. Although the view of the social work department that the applicant was considered to be vulnerable was communicated to the housing officer concerned, this information was not considered by him. The decision taken was therefore held to be unlawful as there had been a failure to have regard to a relevant consideration, namely the view of the social work department. However, the fact that an authority require to take account of such views does not mean that they have to agree with the assessment of the social worker or social services authorities.[7]

In addition the Secretary of State stresses the importance of co-operation and liaison with bodies such as New Town Corporations and the Scottish Special Housing Association (SSHA) (and by inference its successor under the Housing (Scotland) Act 1988, Scottish Homes) which may be able to offer homeless persons a fresh start in a different environment. Registered housing associations may also be able to make accommodation available either on a temporary or permanent basis. Liaison with the sheriff court or county court likewise is vital because virtually "all possession orders leading to eviction originate there."[8] The importance of such liaison in providing an early warning of potential cases of homelessness can not be over-estimated.[9] Additionally, co-

---

respect of a case which the housing authority are dealing with as a homeless person or a person threatened with homelessness; or (c) request help from another local authority in England, Scotland or Wales in respect of their functions relating to the protection of property. If such a request is made it is the duty of the authority, when the request is made to co-operate with the housing authority and to render such assistance in the discharge of their functions to which the request relates *"as is reasonable in the circumstances."* On the meaning of reasonable assistance in this context see R. Carnwarth, *A Guide to the Housing (Homeless Persons) Act 1977* (Knight, London, 1978) p.69.

5. Scottish Development Department, *Housing and Social Work: A Joint Approach* (HMSO, 1975).
6. 1986 SLT 169.
7. *Steventon v. Monklands District Council* 1987 GWD 15-576.
8. EC A1.5; SC 3.6.
9. On the problem of rent arrears in the public sector see Diana Wilkinson, *Rent Arrears in Public Authority Housing in Scotland* (HMSO, 1980).

operation is suggested between housing authorities in relation to cases which do not fall within the ambit of the provisions relating to transfer of responsibility between housing authorities. For example, a housing authority may be able to provide assistance in cases involving domestic violence where it may be of paramount importance that the victim should feel safe from a repetition of violent conduct or pursuit. In such cases the Code recommends collaboration between housing authorities to enable movement across local authority boundaries.

2. Staff Training

An important and necessary part of housing authority action to prevent homelessness is the training of their officers in those aspects of social security, welfare, housing, and property law which are relevant to the problems of homelessness.

(a) Housing and property law

The Code stresses that staff dealing with homelessness should have a working knowledge of the relevant provisions of the Rent Acts. These relate broadly to the status of occupancy, the level of rent, security of tenure and harassment and illegal eviction. It is important, albeit difficult, for a housing adviser to be able to explain the rights of occupants of private rented sector dwellings. For example, increasingly problems will arise as to whether or not tenants are occupying accommodation under the Rent Acts or whether they are covered by the Housing Act 1988 or the Housing (Scotland) Act 1988. In situations where the Rent Acts apply it will be important to know whether an occupier is a protected tenant or has a short or shorthold tenancy or occupies property under a restricted (Part VII) contract or a service occupancy or is merely a guest or lodger, as this has important implications for both the level of rent which a landlord is entitled to charge and security of tenure.[10]

Additionally, it is of considerable importance to housing authorities in the discharge of their duties under the legislation, to ascertain in cases of threatened eviction whether a landlord seeks to recover possession under one of the mandatory or discretionary grounds laid down in Schedule 15 of the Rent Act 1977 or Schedule 2 of the Rent (Scotland) Act 1984. Where repossession is sought under one of the mandatory grounds, the Code of Guidance[11] provides that where it is clear from the

---

10. See, for example, A. Arden and M. Partington, *Housing Law* (Sweet & Maxwell, London, 1983) and Second (Cumulative) Supplement (Sweet and Maxwell, London, 1986).
11. EC A1.3; SC 3.5.

facts that tenants have no defence or counter-claim to an application for possession, housing authorities should not insist on tenants remaining in possession until a possession order is obtained and a date of eviction fixed before agreeing to assist an applicant.[12]

In due course the 1988 Acts will require local authorities to reconsider the guidelines they have applied in the past to identify the level of security enjoyed by tenants. Basically private sector tenants in Scotland and England in future will be able to obtain an assured tenancy or a short assured tenancy. There is to be no security of tenure in the case of the short assured tenancy beyond the agreed term.[13] The landlord of the assured tenant will also be able to regain possession in a number of instances where in the past the court had discretion to refuse an order. It will therefore not be possible for authorities to make the same distinction between secure and insecure accommodation as they have in the past.

The Code[14] reminds authorities that where a tenant has no defence to an action for possession it is counter-productive to treat an applicant as having become homeless intentionally because he leaves accommodation before a possession order is obtained or, where a possession order has been granted, to insist that a warrant for possession is also obtained.[15]

The advice given to housing authorities on how to deal with cases of harassment has been significantly altered. In the original Code[16] authorities were informed that action could be taken against landlords where there was evidence to substantiate the offence. The revised Code[17] envisages a two stage approach: firstly, the authority are to attempt to dissuade landlords from harassing their tenants; and secondly, if such an approach fails, the authority are to consider instituting legal proceedings without delay.[18]

Given the derisory fines imposed by the courts[19] it would appear to be reasonable for authorities to attempt to achieve conciliation between landlords and tenants where the conduct complained of is of an anodyne nature. In Scotland local authorities do not have similar powers

12. *Krishnan v. London Borough of Hillingdon* (1981) LAG 137; *Din v. Wandsworth London Borough Council* [1981]; *R. v. Mole Valley District Council, ex. p. Minnett* (1983) 12 HLR 49; *R. v. Portsmouth City Council, ex p. Knight* (1983) 10 HLR 115; *R. v. Exeter City Council, ex p. Gliddon* (1984) 14 HLR 103; *R. v. Surrey Heath Borough Council, ex p. Li* (1984) 16 HLR 79.
13. Sections of the Housing Act 1988; section 33 of the Housing (Scotland) Act 1988. On assured and short assured tenancies see M. Partington 'The Housing Bill – Impact on the Private Rental Sector' 138 NLJ (1988) 75 and 111.
14. EC Al.3
15. See *Din v. Wandsworth London Borough Council* [1983] 1 A.C. 657; *R. v. Portsmouth City Council, ex p. Knight* (1983) 14 HLR 115; *R. v. Exeter City Council, ex p. Gliddon* (1984) 14 HLR 103 in which Mr Justice Woolf stated that it may be harmful to force a landlord to bring possession proceedings; and *R. v. Surrey Heath Borough Council*, ex p. Li (1984) 16 HLR 79.
16. EC A1.4 [1st edition, 1977].
17. EC A1.4 [2nd edition, 1983].
18. See D. Nelken, *The Limits of the Legal Process* (Academic Press, London, 1983).
19. See, for example, First Report of the Government Committee, *The Private Rented Housing Sector*, Volume III, session 1981-82 (HC 40 - IV, 40 i-v) p.12.

of investigation and prosecution to those possessed by local authorities in England and Wales, the responsible bodies being the police and the Procurator Fiscal, but changes introduced by the 1988 Housing Acts should improve the protection available to residential occupiers against harassment.[20]

It is also of importance where owner-occupiers are threatened with foreclosure[21] by building societies or other lending institutions that housing advisers are able to explain their rights and what assistance may be available from the Department of Social Security or by way of loan from housing authorities. In times of recession this may prove to be an increasingly important aspect of the work of housing advisers, particularly as many owner occupiers appear to be paying the ultimate price of the expansion of the property-owning democracy by forfeiting their homes.

(b) Social security law

The Code of Guidance states that "housing authorities are right to use every endeavour to prevent arrears."[22] In addition to adopting the administrative measures recommended by the Wilkinson Report[23] in relation to the payment by and collection of rent from their own tenants, the Code suggests that housing advisers should "check that the tenant is getting the benefit of any rent or rate (community charge) rebate *or other relevant benefit to which he is entitled.*"[24] This recommendation in our view, is wide enough to provide for housing authorities undertaking take-up campaigns and certainly includes checking entitlement to and calculation of housing benefits, income support, family credit, child benefit, unemployment benefit, sickness benefit and disability benefits.

Where either the legal problem is too complex for the housing adviser to solve or, in spite of preventive measures, rent arrears accumulate and eviction action appears to be probable, specialist legal advice or representation should be obtained and referral to a legal advice centre of solicitor is recommended.[25] In the latter case it is important that housing advisers should have a knowledge of the legal advice and assistance and the civil legal aid scheme to enable them to explain the financial implications of those schemes to their clients.

---

20. Ss. 27-31 Housing Act 1988; ss. 36-38 Housing (Scotland) Act 1988.
21. Part II of the Conveyancing and Feudal Reform (Scotland) Act 1970 and Part III of the Law of Property Act 1925.
22. EC A1.13; SC 3.14.
23. Diana Wilkinson, *Rent Arrears in Public Authority Housing in Scotland,* op. cit. Ch. 8.
24. EC A1.5; SC 3.16.
25. EC A1.4; SC 3.3.

3. Housing Aid Centres

In order to facilitate preventive action the English Code of Guidance suggests that housing authorities consider establishing area housing aid centres where advice could be sought by and given to persons in need.[26] Although the Scottish Code does not provide for the development of institutional arrangements similar to area housing aid centres, the Scottish Code does suggest that housing authorities should liaise with voluntary bodies which offer advice on housing matters.[27] Importantly, the Code states that "authorities should ensure that where voluntary bodies are assisting them to carry out their duties they are adequately funded."[28]

The legislation[29] empowers housing authorities to give voluntary organisations financial assistance by way of grant or loan or both and to assist them by permitting voluntary organisations to make use of premises, furniture or goods belonging to housing authorities and the services of their staff. The Secretary of State, subject to Treasury consent, may also provide voluntary organisations with similar financial assistance under this provision.[30]

One related form of assistance which has been provided in the past through social work and social services departments is the payment of sums of money to families under legislation promoting general social welfare and the welfare of children. In Scotland the Social Work (Scotland) Act 1968 lays a duty on every local authority to promote social welfare by making available advice, guidance and assistance in cash or in kind, in a variety of situations.[31] This can either be given to prevent children under 18 being taken into care, or where giving assistance in kind or in cash would avoid the greater expense of giving assistance in another form or in the long term. In England there is parallel legislation which is used in relation to the welfare of children. Under the Child Care Act 1980 (formerly the Children and Young Persons Act 1963) it is the duty of every local authority to make available such advice, guidance and assistance as may promote the welfare of children by diminishing the need to receive children into care.[32]

These provisions have been used to provide cash for bed and breakfast accommodation by social work and social services departments. Provision of or payment for accommodation under the child care

---

26. EC 3.3.
27. SC 7.8.
28. *Ibid*
29. Section 73 of the Housing Act 1985; Section 39 of the Housing (Scotland) Act 1987.
30. Concern has been expressed about the inadequacy of the monitoring of the activities and some voluntary organisations; (1981) *Roof* March/April, p.22 and May/June p. 4.
31. Section 12 of the Social Work (Scotland) Act 1968; see generally J.M. Thomson, *Family Law in Scotland* (Butterworths, London, 1987) pp. 202-203.
32. Section 1 of the Child Care Act 1980; see generally B.M. Hoggett, *Parents and Children: The Law of Parental Responsibility* (Sweet & Maxwell, London, 1987) p.18.

legislation, rather than by the housing authorities under the homelessness legislation, was considered by the Court of Appeal in *R. v. Tower Hamlets London Borough Council, ex p. Monaf.*[33] Child care legislation, it was stated, could lawfully operate to provide housing accommodation for children and their families.the principle behind the 1980 Act was the welfare of the children. This might involve children being taken into care. It might be the judgment of the social services or social work authorities, however, that this should be avoided. This might involve either "provision of temporary or semi-permanent accommodation by extending the provision of the accommodation" provided under the homeless persons legislation.[34]

---

33. *The Independent*, 28 April, 1988, and also *Attorney-General ex rel. Tilley v. Wandsworth London Borough Council* [1981] 1 WLR 854 in which it was said that "assistance" in section 1 of the Child Care Act 1980 includes the provision of accommodation.
34. *R. v. Tower Hamlets London Borough Council, ex p. Monaf, supra.*

Chapter 3
Processing Applications

1. Applications

The duties of a housing authority under the legislation arise only if a person applies to a housing authority for accommodation. An application need not be in writing and, as homelessness is a crisis, will seldom be made in this form.[1] Applicants will often be under considerable stress and may not be able to express themselves logically or coherently. Authorities should, however, afford applicants every opportunity to explain their circumstances fully and to have a friend, representative, or interpreter present with them throughout the interview. It is necessary, however, for an applicant to make clear that he is applying for assistance as a homeless person or person threatened with homelessness. If a person merely enquires about housing the authority are not obliged to provide advice or assistance. Although the distinction between an enquiry and application in the urgent circumstances in which homeless persons find themselves must be regarded as extremely tenuous,[2] it is one that has continuing significance.

In *R. v. Cherwell District Council, ex p. Howkins*,[3] for example, this distinction was crucial to the decision of the High Court to deny redress to a homeless person. In this case, Mr Justice Forbes accepted that an application need not be made in writing but added that "in order to be treated as an application ... an oral application has to be conducted in such a way that it is clear that it amounts to an application." As Howkins' solicitor had merely enquired as to the Council's intentions in respect of his client's housing needs it was held that there had been no application for accommodation and hence there was nothing for the Court to deal with. This is an important decision for housing advisers

---

1. EC 2.1-2.5; SC 2.1-2.5.
2. See 'Homelessness' (*above*) pp.8 - 49.
3. (QED) 14 May, 1984.

who should take note that in their dealings with housing authorities they should make it absolutely clear that their client is seeking assistance under the legislation.

By the same token there can be no challenge by way of judicial review until the authority actually take a decision. In *R. v. Hillingdon London Borough Council, ex p. Tinn* [4] a woman was advised by the Director of Housing that in the event of her having to sell her home because she was unable to meet mortgage repayments she would need to make her own arrangements for rehousing. However, this did not amount to a decision because there had been no application. The authority was merely attempting to assist the individual by advising her what their attitude would be if she decided to sell. In these circumstances judicial review could not be granted because no application had been made and therefore no decision taken.

Authorities should bear in mind, however, that provided an application for assistance has been made and there is *prima facie* evidence that the applicant is homeless or threatened with homelessness, the duty to make inquiries arises, not withstanding the fact that the applicant did not formally apply for assistance under the legislation. It may be noted that failure of an authority to consider whether an applicant was homeless or threatened with homelessness and to make appropriate enquiries has been held to constitute maladministration by the Local Ombudsman.[5]

A housing authority must make adequate arrangements for receiving applications from homeless persons. In *R. v. Camden London Borough Council, ex p. Gillan* [6] the housing authority only opened their homeless persons unit for three hours on weekdays and provided no cover at weekends. Applications could only be made by telephone and applicants were unable to meet officials unless they presented themselves at the unit by 9.30 a.m.. The Divisional Court held these arrangements to be unlawful. Lord Justice May stated that there was a duty on housing authorities to take reasonable steps to hear and adjudicate upon applications by homeless persons and that in heavily populated areas reasonable provision might require 24 hour cover.

(a) Separate applications

An application is at the instance of a *person* not a family.[7] It is open to

---

4. *The Times,* 14 January,1988.
5. See, for example, *North Warwickshire Borough Council* [Inv. No. 305/J/82] and *Portsmouth City Council* [Inv. No. 464/S.83].
6. *The Independent,* 13 October, 1988.
7. *Hynds v. Midlothian District Council* 1986 SLT 54.

each member of a family unit to apply for assistance.[8] However, in certain circumstances the courts will permit a housing authority to consider separate applications jointly provided the authority take into account any additional material which relates to only one of the applicants. For example, in *R. v. Swansea City Council, ex p. Thomas*,[9] where cohabitees each applied for assistance, Mr. Justice Woolf indicated that had the authority not considered the special circumstances of the male cohabitee (who was in prison at the time when the conduct took place on which the authority's decision of intentional homelessness was based) he would almost certainly have overturned their decision. Similarly, in *R. v. Eastleigh Borough Council, ex p. Beattie* [10] where a husband and wife each applied for assistance it was held that the wife had not become homeless intentionally and therefore the authority had a duty to provide accommodation for her and her family, notwithstanding the fact that her husband was found to be intentionally homeless on the basis of his application.[11]

Where members of a family unit each apply to an authority for assistance under the legislation it may be necessary for the authority to interview them separately. For example, in *R. v. West Dorset District Council, ex p. Phillips* [12] Mr. Justice Webster observed that, where as a result of conduct of the applicant it was evident that the authority had a duty to make further inquiries as to whether the applicant had acquiesced in her husband's drinking, it was necessary for them "to make further inquiries as to her own situation and that not in the presence of her husband."

It would appear from these cases therefore that if there are factors which justify the conclusions that the members of the same family should not be treated as having been homeless for the same reason (e.g. where a wife was unable to prevent her husband from spending the rent money on drink or a member of the family was unable to control the anti-social behaviour of other members), then separate applications should be made. For as *Beattie* [13] demonstrates, this may result in a family being rehoused despite the fact that a member of the family unit had been lawfully found to have become homeless intentionally. Conversely, unless such factors are present if a couple separate and one of them subsequently applies for assistance in the absence of such factors, the

---

8. *Lewis v. North Devon District Council* [1981] 1 All ER 27; *R. v. Hillingdon London Borough Council, ex p. Thomas, The Times*, 22 January, 1987; *R. v. East Hertfordshire District Council, ex p. Bannon* (1986) 18 HLR 515.
9. (1983) 9 HLR 64.
10. (1984) 17 HLR 168.
11. *See R. v. West Dorset District Council, ex p. Phillips* (1985) 17 HLR 336 in which the authority failed to appreciate that an application was made by the wife and not the husband.
12. *Ibid.*
13. *Supra.*

housing authority may have regard to the conduct of other members of the previous family unit in determining the outcome of the application.[14]

(b) Joint applications

The legislation is concerned with homeless persons and not homeless families. Therefore, as has been stated, an application for housing must be treated as an application made by an individual.[15] Nevertheless, where a joint application is made to an authority then, in the absence of a request from one or both of the joint applicants for their cases to be treated separately or material which comes to light when considering a joint application which points to the need to consider the circumstances of each of the joint applicants separately, an authority may consider the application as a joint application.[16]

(c) Repeat applications

If an applicant makes a fresh application without putting forward new grounds or additional information, the authority may reject that application on the basis of their previous inquiries because there is no material change in the applicant's circumstances. In *Delahaye v. Oswestry Borough Council* [17] an applicant who had been provided with temporary accommodation because he was judged to have become homeless intentionally reapplied to the authority for assistance. As there had been no *material* change in the appellant's circumstances which would justify further assistance from the Council it was held that the applicant was not entitled to "a second bite of the cherry". However, if in a fresh application an applicant puts forward new grounds or additional information, the housing authority must make further inquiries.[18] For example, in *R. v. Ealing London Borough Council, ex p. McBain*,[19] the Court of Appeal held that the birth of a second child to an applicant who had previously refused an offer of accommodation was a material change in the circumstances of the applicant because it made the accommodation previously offered unsuitable.

---

14. Contrast *Hynds v Midlothian District Council* 1986 SLT 54 with *R. v. Basingstoke and Deane District Council, ex p. Bassett* (1983) 10 HLR 125 where marital breakdown occurred after the giving up of the matrimonial home. See *Lewis v. North Devon District Council* [1981] 3 All ER 27 and *R. v. East Northamptonshire District Council, ex p. Spruce* (QBD) 17 February, 1988.
15. See *Hynds v. Midlothian District Council*, above.
16. See *R. v. Penwith District Council, ex p. Trevena* (1984) 17 HLR 526 and *R. v. Wandsworth London Borough Council, ex p. Lord* (QBD) 8 July, 1985.
17. *The Times*, 29 July, 1980.
18. See *R. v. Hambleton District Council, ex p. Geoghegan* [1985] JPL 394.
19. [1986] 1 All ER 13.

If an authority re-open their inquiries it is possible for them to "purify" an unlawful decision made on the basis of previous inquiries. For example, in *R. v. Hambleton District Council, ex p. Geoghagen*,[20] Mr. Justice Forbes indicated that if the authority's decision that a couple had become homeless intentionally had been based on their original inquiries he would have quashed it on the ground that they had failed to inquire into the couple's reasons for leaving their previous accommodation. However, as in their subsequent inquiries they did not deal with this matter, he held that their later decision could not be challenged and that the Court would not quash their earlier decision because it would be futile to do so.[21]

In addition, Mr. Justice Forbes held that it was open to a housing authority to re-open inquiries without a fresh application being submitted to them:

> "It seems to me also that they are entitled to re-open the matter of their own accord if they take the view that they are no longer satisfied upon the matters which they have to be satisfied and in relation to which appropriate enquiries have been made."

(d) Applications to different authorities

It is open to an applicant to apply to any number of authorities for assistance. For example, in *R. v. Slough Borough Council, ex p. Ealing London Borough Council*[22] two families who had been found to have become intentionally homeless by one authority later applied to another authority which concluded that they had not done so. The decision of the second authority was held to displace the earlier decision of the original authority and that authority were compelled to provide them with permanent accommodation.[23] Moreover, when an applicant applies to a second authority they must make their own inquiries, and not merely apply an earlier decision made by the first authority.[24]

(e) Interpreters

The importance of having an interpreter present when interviewing

---

20. [1985] JPL 394; see also *R. v. Wycombe District Council, ex p. Mahsood* (QBD) 30 August, 1988.
21. See also *R. v. Exeter City Council, ex p. Gliddon* [1985] 1 All ER 493.
22. [1981] QB 801. *R. v. Tower Hamlets London Borough Council, ex p. Camden London Borough Council, The Times*, 12 December, 1988.
23. *R. v. London Borough Council, ex p. O'Brian* (1985) 17 HLR 471.
24. The revised code (EC 2.2) reminds authorities that their inquiries "may also cover the circumstances of any previous application to another authority, but the outcome of a previous application should

applicants whose native language is not English can be seen from *R. v. Surrey Heath Borough Council, ex p. Li.*[25] In this case a housing official stated in his affidavit that he had formed the impression that the applicant was not telling the truth because of inconsistencies in his account of the factors which had led to his homelessness. However, Mr. Justice Hodgson stated that the housing officials when interviewing such applicants must bear in mind that "one very frequently finds there to be inconsistencies caused by a lack of communication or for some other reason and therefore to base findings on such inconsistencies of fact in these circumstances can be ill-advised."[26]

(f) Involvement of councillors

The involvement of local councillors in the allocation of council housing has been widely criticised on the ground that if the allocation of council housing is to be seen to be fair it is better that in general housing allocation is administered by professional housing staff in accordance with detailed and comprehensive house letting regulations.[27] This criticism of the involvement of local councillors in housing decision-making would appear to apply with equal force to the processing of applications under the homeless persons legislation. For example, in *R. v. Preseli District Council, ex p. Fisher* [28] in their anxiety to protect the authority's housing stock from "mutants" and squatters, local councillors moved a resolution:

> "That we do not house them ... on the basis that if we do house people who, I am certain, have lived illegally in the area, because we are told we have no alternative, then we shall be opening the doors of Preseli to any nomad who wants to come into the area."

Although Mr. Justice McCullough stated that he could understand and sympathise with the thinking of the councillors, he held their decision to refuse assistance to the applicant on the ground that "the real cause of [her] homelessness was ... her own long-standing and chosen way of life in communal encampments" to be unlawful, because it was immaterial to the real question to be determined, namely whether she

not be given undue weight in deciding on the present application." See also *R. v. South Hertfordshire District Council, ex p. Miles* (1983) 17 HLR 82. See also *R. v. Basingstoke and Deane District Council, ex p. Webb* (QBD) 6 November, 1987.

25. (1984) 16 HLR 79.
26. See *R. v. Westminster City Council, ex p. Rahman* (QBD) 9 June, 1983.
27. Scottish Housing Advisory Committee, *Allocation and Transfer of Council Houses* (HMSO 1980) paras. 5.43-5.47; Edinburgh SHAC, *Time for a Change? Midlothian's Allocation Policy – A Review* (1983) pp. 10-12.
28. (1984) 17 HLR 147.

had given up accommodation which was available for her occupation and whether it was reasonable for her to continue to occupy it. While he was anxious not to criticise the councillors involved in the decision, Mr. Justice McCullough added:

> "It is, I think, unusual for a decision of this kind to be taken by a committee after a debate such as this. Normally, they are taken by officers familiar with the wording of the Act and the Code of Guidance and who know the questions which have to be asked. One cannot expect, particularly in a highly charged atmosphere, such as understandably was present here, members of the local authority to have the same understanding of the precise question which has to be asked. ... It is not for me to lay down as a matter of law, but I think the next time it would be better if the decision were actually taken, certainly initially, by someone on the local authority staff familiar with the legislation, with the decided cases and the Code of Guidance. .."

In short, local councillors should allow their housing officials to process applications from homeless persons according to the law and the Secretary of State's guidance and should not allow their own prejudices to influence that process.[29]

(g) Onus of proof

Although an applicant must give some information in order that a housing authority can have reason to believe that he or she is homeless or threatened with homelessness, the onus thereafter rests upon the housing authority to make appropriate inquiries to satisfy themselves that the applicant is homeless or threatened with homelessness, has a priority need, became homeless or threatened with homelessness intentionally, and, if they think fit, has a local connection with their area or that of another housing authority. The failure of housing authorities to appreciate that it is for them to satisfy themselves as to these matters, and not for the applicant to establish them to the satisfaction of the authority, has led to the decisions of a number of authorities being held to be unlawful. For example, in *R. v. Woodspring District Council, ex p. Walters* [30] the decision of the housing authority that a woman was not homeless because there was adequate accommodation available to her in married service quarters in Cyprus was quashed because, although there was information before them that the accommodation had been lost, they failed to make appropriate inquiries into this matter:[31]

> "It would have been the simplest possible thing for the council to check with

---

29. See *R. v. Port Talbot Borough, ex. p Jones* [1988] 2 All ER 207.
30. (1984) 16 HLR 73. See also *Wincentzen v. Monklands District Council* [1987] SCLR 712.
31. On this question see also *R. v. Westminster City Council, ex p. Rahman* (QBD) 9 June 1983; *R. v.*

the S.S.A.F.A. [Soldiers', Sailors' and Airmen's Families Association] as to whether the assertion in the Applicant's solicitors letter was correct. No such check was made and the housing officer seemed to have taken the view, wrongly in my judgment, that it was for the applicant positively and by evidence in effect which would have convinced a court to place before the council material conclusively showing that the [married service] quarters had been forfeit. I consider that that is to approach the matter in the wrong way ... *the burden is upon the local authority to make appropriate inquiries* ..." (our emphasis)

2. Inquiries

Where, as a result of an application for accommodation or for assistance in obtaining accommodation, the authority have "reason to believe" that the applicant may be homeless or threatened with homelessness, the legislation requires housing authorities to make appropriate inquiries.[32] The scope of these inquiries is detailed by the legislation. Firstly, the housing authority must carry out such inquiries as are necessary to satisfy them that the applicant is or is not homeless or threatened with homelessness. Secondly, if the housing authority are satisfied that the applicant is homeless or threatened with homelessness, the authority shall make such further inquiries as are necessary to satisfy the authority whether the applicant has a priority need, and whether he became homeless or threatened with homelessness intentionally.[33] Additionally the authority are empowered but are not obliged to make enquiries to establish whether the applicant has a local connection with the area of another authority.[34] As the nature and extent of duties of housing authorities towards homeless persons and persons threatened with homelessness are determined by the results of these inquiries it is proposed to look in some detail at their nature and scope, the unit which is the subject of investigation and the procedural safeguards imposed by the courts on the conduct of these inquiries.

(a) Nature and scope of inquiries

Little guidance is provided as to the scope of inquiries or the manner in which these are to be carried out. Appropriate inquiries are merely

Reigate and Banstead Borough Council, ex p. Paris [1984] 17 HLR 103; *R. v. Wandsworth London Borough Council, ex p. Rose* [1983] 11 HLR 105 and *R. v. West Dorset District Council, ex p. Phillips* (1985) 17 HLR 336.
32. Section 62 of the Housing Act 1985; section 28 of the Housing (Scotland) Act 1987.
33. Sections 58-60 of the Housing Act 1985; sections 24-26 of the Housing (Scotland) Act 1987.
34. Section 61 of the Housing Act 1985; section 27 of the Housing (Scotland) Act 1987.

defined as "such inquiries as are necessary to satisfy" the authority[35] and the Code of Guidance states that "the nature and scope of any inquiries will vary according to the circumstances of each case."[36] The Code, however, defines the normal scope of these inquiries by providing a detailed list of matters which should normally be covered.[37] These are:

(i)   the size and structure of the household;
(ii)   the nature and location of the accommodation last occupied;
(iii)   the reasons for leaving it and the prospect of return;
(iv)   the availability of accommodation elsewhere;
(v)   problems such as illness of handicap;
(vi)   the need for accommodation located some distance from a violent partner;
(vii)   the length of time the applicant expects to stay in the area;
(viii) the place and type of employment;
(ix)   family connections; and
(x)   attendance at hospital and schools.

The revised English Code of Guidance states that in addition to the matters listed above:

> "[T]he Act does not preclude other more general inquiries which may be necessary to enable the housing authority to discharge its powers and duties under ... the Act and those inquiries may include inquiries into matters such as financial hardship and the length of time that an applicant expects to stay in an area."

The inclusion of the reference to financial hardship stems from the view of the D.O.E. that "an applicant facing hardship is likely to require more assistance than an applicant who is not." The only other change to this part of the English Code is that authorities are reminded that their inquiries "may also cover the circumstances of any previous application to another authority under the Act, but the outcome of a previous application to another authority should not be given undue weight in deciding on the present application under the Act."[38]

In relation to the nature of these inquiries the Code merely states that inquiries should be carried out quickly and sympathetically and that where inquiries are of a detailed nature and cannot be completed in a single interview applicants should be kept fully informed of what is happening.[39]

---

35. See fn. 31.
36. EC 2.3; SC 2.4.
37. EC 2.2; SC 2.3.
38. EC 2.2A.
39. EC 2.3; SC 2.4.

In *Miller v. Wandsworth London Borough Council* [40] and *Lally v. Kensington and Chelsea Royal London Borough* [41] the High Court indicated that hard-pressed housing authorities were not obliged to conduct detailed C.I.D-type inquiries. While as a broad statement of principle the correctness of the view may not be doubted, it is possible to draw the erroneous inference that inquiries need not be of a detailed nature. Subsequent case law has emphasised that the duty to carry out inquiries rests *solely* with the authority to which the application is made,[42] albeit, that reliance can be placed on evidence obtained from other authorities,[43] and that the failure of an authority to make sufficiently detailed inquiries into any matter which could affect the outcome of their decision can result in that decision being declared unlawful.[44]

For example, in *Krishnan v. London Borough of Hillingdon*[45] Krishnan requested a transfer from his employers, partly to alleviate the overcrowded conditions in which he and his wife and two children were living with a brother and his family. He was transferred from Birmingham to Uxbridge in Hillingdon Borough but his arrangement to stay with other relatives fell through shortly after the move when his relatives emigrated to Canada. The housing authority decided that his homelessness was intentional as Krishnan had left settled accommodation to improve his career prospects. The health aspects of the move do not seem to have come out clearly in the first interview with Hillingdon's homelessness officer and, despite contacts with the authority in Birmingham, the question of overcrowding was never raised by Hillingdon. The finding of intentional homelessness was rejected by the High Court because of Hillingdon's failure to carry out appropriate inquiries. These should have covered:

(i)   the circumstances which led Mr. Krishnan to leave the Birmingham accommodation;

(ii) whether the Birmingham accommodation was accommodation which it would have bee n reasonable to expect him to continue occupying; and

---

40. *The Times*, 19 March, 1980.
41. *The Times*, 27 March, 1980; see also *R. v. Reigate and Banstead Borough Council, ex p. Henry* (QBD) 16 December, 1982; *R. v. Mole Valley District Council, ex p. Burton* (QBD) *The Independent*, 14 April, 1988; *R. v. Wandsworth Borough Council, ex p. Woodhall* (QBD) 12 July, 1988; *R. v. Gravesham Borough Council, ex p. Winchester* [1986] 18 HLR 207.
42. *R. v. Slough Borough Council, ex p. London Borough of Ealing* [1981] QB 801; *R. v. South Herefordshire District Council, ex p. Miles* (1983) 17 HLR 82.
43. *R. v. Bristol City Council, ex p. Browne* [1979] 1 WLR 1437; *R. v. Warwick District Council, ex p. Wood* (QBD) 15 August, 1983; *R. v. Islington London Borough Council, ex p. Adigun* (QBD) 20 February, 1986; *R. v. South Hams District Council, ex p. Proctor* (QBD) 24 September, 1985.
44. See 'Remedies for the Homeless' *(infra)* pp.208 - 42.
45. (1981) LAG, 137; (1981) SCOLAG 307; see also *R. v. Royal Borough of Kensington and Chelsea, ex p. Cunha, The Independent*, 21 July, 1988 and *Mazzaccherini v. Argyll and Bute District Council* [1987] SCLR 475.

(iii) how temporary the arrangements to stay with the relatives in Uxbridge were.

The view expressed in Krishnan has been followed in a number of subsequent cases. For example, in *R. v. Eastleigh Borough Council, ex p. Beattie* [46] the failure of the authority to consider whether it was reasonable for a family to continue to occupy overcrowded accommodation resulted in the authority's decision that they had become homeless intentionally being set aside and in *R. v. Westminster City Council, ex p. Ali* [47] the failure of the authority to consider whether accommodation was available to the applicant and his family and to assess whether, in view of the increase in the number of children in the household and their advance in years, it was reasonable for them to continue to occupy overcrowded accommodation led to a decision of intentional homelessness being declared unlawful.

From the foregoing, it seems relatively clear that where an issue is crucial to the determination of the nature and level of assistance to be given to an applicant the authority's inquiries must be sufficiently detailed to provide them with adequate factual information on which to base their decision. In *R. v. Wyre Borough Council, ex p. Joyce* [48] a housing authority determined that an applicant had become homeless intentionally because of non-payment of mortgage arrears. This decision was held to be invalid by Mr. Justice Forbes on the ground that they had failed to carry out appropriate inquiries to ascertain if the non-payment of arrears had been wilful:

> "... no question was ever asked of Mrs Joyce as to why she had failed to keep up these payments; there was no specific question addressed to that point."

Where an applicant comes from abroad the inquiries which an authority are obliged to carry out are only those which are within the reasonable ambit which an authority can explore.[49] However, that does not excuse an authority from failing to obtain evidence which is vital to their decision. Thus, in *R. v. Reigate and Banstead Borough Council, ex p. Paris* [50] the decision of a housing authority was quashed because they failed to consider whether the accommodation which a couple occupied

---

46. (1983) 10 HLR 134.
47. (1983) 11 HLR 83.
48. (1983) 11 HLR 73; see also *R. v. Tower Hamlets London Borough Council, ex p. Camden London Borough Council, The Times,* 12 December, 1988.
49. See *De Falco v Crawley Borough Council* [1980] QB 460; *R. v. Westminster City Council, ex p. Rahman* (QBD) 9 June, 1983 and *R. v. Royal Borough of Kensington and Chelsea, ex p. Cunha, The Independent,* 21 July, 1988.
50. (1984) 17 HLR 103.

in Italy was available for their occupation and whether it was reasonable for them to continue to occupy it.[51]

A housing authority cannot deem an applicant to have become homeless intentionally unless the authority is satisfied that he ceased to occupy accommodation which was available for his occupation and which it would have been reasonable for him to continue to occupy. Thus, where an applicant occupied different forms of temporary accommodation over a number of years it was held to be necessary for the authority to go back over that period of time to consider how she first became homeless following the loss of *settled* accommodation.[52]

A good example of the application of this principle is in *R. v. Reigate and Banstead Borough Council, ex p. Paris.*[53] In this case the Paris family returned to Italy to enable Mr. Paris (who was an Italian national) to complete his military service. They lived in Italy for two years, at first with Mr. Paris' grandmother, but later they and their two children lived with a friend in a one-bedroomed flat. Later they returned to Britain where Mr. Paris resumed his former employment and lived in a service flat provided with the job. However, when his wife and children moved in with him they were asked to leave. They therefore approached the authority for assistance. On checking their account of their reasons for leaving Italy, an apparent discrepancy arose. Mr. Paris stated that he had arranged employment at the restaurant prior to returning from Italy but his employer indicated that this was not the case and that Mr. Paris in fact had arrived at the restaurant looking for work. On the basis of the information provided by his employer the housing authority decided that the applicants had become homeless intentionally as they had left Italy without securing permanent accommodation for their family in this country. The decision of the authority made no reference whatsoever to the question whether the accommodation they had left in Italy was available for their occupation and whether it was reasonable for them to continue to occupy it.

The issue before the court was whether it was necessary for the authority to inquire about these matters given the discrepancy which had arisen over the way in which Mr.Paris had obtained employment. On behalf of the housing authority it was argued that in the absence of any assertion on the part of the applicants that accommodation was other than available and reasonable, they were entitled to assume that it was both available and reasonable.[54] The applicants, however, contended that Mrs. Paris had stated at their interview that no reasonable accommodation was available to them in Italy. In the end Mr. Justice

---

51. See also *Re. Islam* [1983] 1AC 688.
52. See *R. v. Preseli District Council, ex p. Fisher* (1984) 17 HLR 147.
53. (1984) 17 HLR 103.
54. See *Brown v. Hamilton District Council*, (1982) SCOLAG 185.

McCullough decided that it did not really matter what version of the facts were accurate as in either case the authority had not discharged the onus of proof:

"Either Mrs. Paris is right and information was provided to the effect that no reasonable accommodation was available in Italy, or alternatively, Mr. Rogers is correct and nothing was said. If the latter, I find it difficult to see how anyone could have correctly concluded that Mr. and Mrs. Paris had ceased to occupy accommodation which was available to them in Italy and which it would have been reasonable for them to continue to occupy ... Alternatively, Mrs. Paris is right and the information was given. If so one does not know whether Mrs. Paris was believed or disbelieved ... the effective cause of their becoming homeless was their ceasing to occupy accommodation in Italy, and the circumstances in which they had ceased to occupy that accommodation in Italy should, in my judgment, have been the subject of express consideration."

The importance of this decision is that it very clearly explains to authorities that the onus of establishing intentional homelessness rests with them and in discharging that onus they cannot make assumptions about vital issues which may affect the nature and level of assistance to be provided to homeless persons.

Two points, however, should be made about the *Paris* decision. First, it would appear that the courts are willing to allow housing authorities to rely on their own knowledge where detailed inquiries would be superfluous. For example, in *R. v. Eastleigh Borough Council, ex p. Evans*,[55] the assumption of a housing authority that the R.A.F. would not immediately seek repossession of married quarters to enable an applicant to make other arrangements for accommodation was challenged on the ground that the authority should have made detailed inquiries to clarify the applicant's position within the R.A.F. It was held that as their general knowledge of the situation of women divorced or separated from servicemen proved to be correct, there was no duty incumbent upon them to make further inquiries. Secondly, where there is a conflict of evidence between housing officials and applicants about whether relevant information was drawn to the attention of the authority the court must decide on the balance of probabilities which account of the facts to accept.[56]

(b) Family unit

In his play *Cathy Come Home* Jeremy Sandford vividly portrayed the

---

55. (1984) 17 HLR 515.
56. See *R. v. Harrow London Borough Council, ex p. Holland* (1982) 4 HLR 108; *R. v. Bath City Council, ex p. Collins* (QBD) 27 January, 1983; and *R. v. Hambleton District Council, ex p. Geoghegen* [1985] JPL 394.

harrowing effects of splitting families in a confrontation between the warden of the hostel and Cathy. The practice of providing "Part III accommodation" for the mother and children of a homeless family and leaving the father to fend for himself or taking children into care rather than providing homeless families with accommodation was also widely criticised by groups such as Shelter, CHAR and SHAC. One of the main purposes of the Housing (Homeless Persons) Act 1977 was to keep the family unit together and thus to end this inhumane practice. The Code of Guidance reinforces this objective and states very clearly that:

"[T]he practice of splitting families is not acceptable, even for short periods. The social cost, personal hardship and long term damage to children, as well as the expense involved in receiving children into care, rules this out as an acceptable course other than in the exceptional case where professional social work advice is that there are compelling reasons, apart from homelessness, for separating a child from his family. The provision of shelter from which one partner is excluded is also unacceptable unless there are social reasons, for example, where a woman is seeking temporary refuge following violence from another member of the household and it is undesirable that she be under pressure to return."[57]

The courts have accepted, in the words of Lord Lowry in the leading House of Lords decision, that "the policy of the Act included the object of bringing and keeping families together."[58] In carrying out inquiries a housing authority therefore may have regard to the conduct and needs of the family unit as a whole. In *Lewis v. North Devon District Council*[59] Mr. Justice Woolf stated:

"The fact that the Act requires consideration of the family unit as a whole indicates that it would be perfectly proper in the ordinary case for the housing authority to look at the family as a whole and assume, in the absence of material which indicated to the contrary, where conduct of one member was such that he should be regarded as having become homeless intentionally, that that was conduct to which the other members of the family were a party". (our emphasis)

However, in *Hynds v. Midlothian District Council*[60] Lord Ross indicated that he did not accept that an application for housing by a homeless person should be treated as being made by the family unit.

This conflict however may be more apparent than real. If the applicant is thought to be "caught" by intentionality but is not directly responsible for the loss of accommodation he has to have his circumstances

---

57. EC 4.2; SC 4.2.
58. Re. Islam [1981] 1 AC 688; see also *Din v. Wandsworth London Borough Council* [1981] 1 AC 657.
59. [1981] 1 All ER 27.
60. 1986 SLT 54.

assessed separately on either approach.

It should be noted that the word "family" in the context of the legislation is intended to include both marriages and other forms of stable relationships and that "dependent children" includes all children under the age of 16, and others under the age of 19 who are either receiving full-time education or training or who are otherwise unable to support themselves. This category is not limited to the children of the applicant or legitimate children but includes grandchildren[61] adopted or foster-children, the children of one-parent families and battered women. The Code states that children need not necessarily be residing with the applicant at the date of application providing that they are in fact dependent.[62]

The fact that children are not subject to a full custody order does not affect whether or not they are "dependent" for the purpose of the legislation. In *R. v. Ealing London Borough, ex p. Sidhu*[63] an attempt was made to argue that whilst children were in the interim custody of Mrs Sidhu it was possible that there might be a change of circumstances which justified delaying making a decision on her application for assistance. Mr. Justice Hodgson rejected this suggestion:

> "Custody can, and frequently does, have nothing whatever to do with dependence and residence. It is a quite frequent order of the Family Division that one party shall have custody and that the other party shall have care and control of the children ... the test of whether or not an applicant wife can be taken out of the Act because she has not got a final custody order ... seems to me not only totally wrong in law but totally wrong in common sense as well."

Despite the objectives of the legislation and the Code and these court decisions, it is evident that families, living apart because of lack of accommodation, have not always been treated as a family unit for the purposes of determining the question of "priority need".[64] The implications of the approach to investigating the circumstances of the member of the family unit are that where there is a recognised family unit the authority's inquiries and subsequent decision are to cover each member of that unit unless there is evidence to suggest: (i) that a new family unit has been created; or (ii) that the applicant had not acquiesced in the conduct upon which their decision of intentional homelessness is based. An authority must not assume in making their inquiries that because an applicant was

---

61. *R. v. Lambeth London Borough Council, ex p. Ly* (1987) 19 HLR 51.
62. EC 2.12a; SC 2.13a.
63. (1982) 2 HLR 45.
64. *The Guardian,* 15 September, 1980, concerning the Jelbert family; 'Apart from the Law', Ros Franey, *Roof* (1980) 172.

a member of a family unit at one time that a previous finding of intentional homelessness against a member of that unit also taints an applicant's subsequent application. It will be necessary therefore for them to make inquiries to establish either that, although a new family unit has been created, the applicant acquiesced in the relevant conduct, in the sense that he or she may be regarded as being party to it, or that the original family unit still persists.

A housing authority, however, are entitled to regard the persistent failure of parents to control the anti-social conduct of their children to be sufficient grounds upon which to found a decision that a couple have become homeless intentionally and spouses and cohabitees may be assumed to have acquiesced in the conduct of other members of their family unit unless they have taken positive steps to dissociate themselves from that conduct.[65]

(c) Procedural safeguards

In *Lally* Mr. Justice Browne-Wilkinson suggested that inquiries should be pursued rigorously and fairly. In this section we wish to examine the standard of fairness to which the courts require housing authorities to adhere when conducting inquiries. These relate to:

(i) the need to provide a fair hearing, and
(ii) the requirement to make decisions on the basis of adequate evidence.

(i) Fair hearing

Housing authorities must afford homeless persons an opportunity to make representations.[66] However, this opportunity does not mean that the authority must treat it as a judicial proceeding and give the parties a right to comment on what they have heard.[67] The opportunity to make representations does not have to be exercised personally and representation before a committee by a housing advice worker has been held to be satisfactory.[68]

It has also been held that if an applicant has been warned of the

---

65. See *R. v. Swansea City Council, ex p. Thomas* (1983) 9 HLR 64; *R. v. Swansea City Council, ex p. John* (1982) HLR 56; *R. v. Eastleigh Borough Council, ex p. Beatie* (1985) 17 HLR 168; *R. v. West Dorset District Council, ex p. Phillips* (1985) 17 HLR 336; *R. v. Penwith District Council, ex p. Trevena* (1984) 17 HLR 526.
66. *Stubbs v. Slough Borough Council* (1980) LAG 16; *Afan Borough Council v. Marchant* (1980) LAG 16.
67. *R. v. Reigate and Banstead District Council, ex p. Henry* (QBD) 16 December, 1982; Smythe HC 17; see also *R. v. Southampton City Council, ex p. Ward* (1984) 14 HLR 114.
68. *R. v. West Somerset District Council, ex p. Blake* (QBD) 10 July, 1986.

importance of accurately setting out the facts leading to his homelessness and informed that the housing authority are to investigate the matter then, provided a new issue does not arise of which he had no notice, the duty to act fairly does not require an authority to afford an applicant an opportunity to challenge the authority's findings.[69]

However, where an authority propose to make an adverse decision, the duty to act fairly may require them to put the matter to the applicant and afford him an opportunity to comment upon it. In *R. v. Wyre Borough Council, ex p. Joyce* [70] a housing authority failed both to ask an applicant specifically why she had not maintained payment of mortgage arrears and to give her an opportunity to deal with that question:

> "[I]t is quite plain that she was never asked the simple straightforward question "Why have you failed to pay these outstanding amounts? " Put another way she was never given the opportunity of dealing with that point ..."

Their failure to do so resulted in their decision being overturned by the Court.

Similarly, where a housing authority based their decision that an applicant had become homeless intentionally on information provided by another authority, without either checking the evidence with the applicant or giving him an opportunity to deal with it, their decision was held to be invalid.[71]

It would seem, however, that where the applicant would not be able to provide an adequate explanation which would negate an adverse decision on the part of a housing authority, the failure of an authority to give him an opportunity to respond to the findings of their investigation will not be sufficient grounds on which to overturn the housing authority's decision.[72]

For example, in *R. v. Hambleton District Council, ex p. Geoghegan,*[73] one of the grounds on which the housing authority's finding of intentional homelessness was challenged was that a housing official had made subjective and damaging observations about the character of applicants without giving them an opportunity to rebut them. They were described as "a very sharp couple" who were "milking" the taxpayers and ratepayers with the support of lawyers, social services and the financial assistance provided by the state. While Mr. Justice Forbes observed that the official had expressed his view of the couple in very forceful

---

69. *See R. v. Vale of White Horse District Council, ex p. Lyle* (QBD) 6 July, 1983.
70. (1983) 11 HLR 73.
71. *R. v. South Herefordshire District Council, ex p. Miles* (1983) 17 HLR 82. See also *R. v. Basingstoke & Deane District Council ex p. Webb* (QBD) 6 November, 1987.
72. *See Brown v. Hamilton District Council* (1982) SCOLAG 185.
73. [1985] JPL 384.

language, he held that the official was entitled to form this view and to communicate it to the Council. As the official had not made any allegations of fact which might be challenged by the applicants, he added, the failure to give them an opportunity to challenge this view did not amount to a breach of the rules of natural justice.

(ii) Adequacy of evidence

Related to the right of a fair hearing is the requirement that, in determining questions of "homelessness", "threatened with homelessness", "priority need", "intentional homelessness" and "local connection", the housing authority should have adequate factual evidence before them to enable them to make a decision. The basic legal test concerning adequacy of evidence was authoritatively stated by Lord Wilberforce in the House of Lords in *Secretary of State for Education and Science v. Tameside Metropolitan Borough Council:* [74]

"If a judgment requires, before it can be made, the existence of some facts to be established ... the courts must enquire whether those facts exist."

Initially, it appeared that provided the housing authority offered an applicant an opportunity to make representations and did not exclude relevant considerations, the courts would not require housing authorities to carry out detailed inquiries to ascertain the circumstances leading to the applicant's homelessness. However, judicial scrutiny of housing authority decision-making subsequently has been a good deal more stringent. In *Krishnan* [75] the High Court rejected the decision of the housing authority that Krishnan had become homeless intentionally on the ground that they had failed to carry out appropriate inquiries. The Court held that before the housing authority reached their decision that Krishnan had become homeless intentionally because he had left his brother's home in Birmingham to enhance his career prospects, the housing authority should have made further inquiries. The failure of the housing authority to carry out these inquiries into the circumstances of Krishnan's homelessness, rendered the inquiries inadequate and this in turn meant that there was insufficient evidence upon which they could have come to a decision of intentional homelessness.

Although in the minority in the Court of Appeal in *Islam*,[76] Lord Justice Ackner also pointed to the fact that before decisions can be made which affect the level of assistance to be offered to applicants, a housing authority must carry out detailed inquiries to ensure that they have adequate factual information upon which to base their decisions. This

---

74. [1971] AC 1014 at 1047
75. (1981) LAG 137; (1981) SCOLAG 307.
76. [1979] 3 All ER 344.

matter was not directly considered by the Law Lords.[77] However, it is clear from the speech of Lord Lowry in *Islam* [78] that housing authorities are expected to conduct inquiries of a sufficiently detailed nature as will enable them to support their decisions – a task which may be quite onerous where, as in *Islam,* the housing authority are expected to assess the adequacy of availability of accommodation located in the Indian subcontinent in determining the level of assistance to be offered to a homeless family.

In *R. v. Wyre Borough Council, ex p. Parr* [79] the housing authority for Fleetwood in Lancashire attempted to arrange for housing for Mr. Parr with Birmingham District Council. There was no indication as to whether or not the accommodation was appropriate as all that Wyre Council did was to write to Mr. Parr stating that "housing accommodation has been secured for you and your family with Birmingham District Council." The housing authority claimed that this discharged their statutory duty to secure accommodation but the Court of Appeal rejected this. The Master of the Rolls, Lord Denning, stated:

> "It was no answer for the authority to say that they had carried out their obligations by the letter of October 19th. The accommodation offered had to be appropriate -- not only as to the house itself, as to which the court had no evidence, but also as to other factors such as the nature of the area and whether employment prospects were suitable for the applicant. The letter of October 19th was not sufficient to manifest an offer of appropriate accommodation -- the circumstances were too uncertain and equivocal."

The crucial issue centres on the need, where an applicant puts forward information which an authority must take into account, to make inquiries to satisfy the housing authority on the matter. For example, in *R. v. Wandsworth London Borough Council, ex p. Rose* [80] a housing authority held that an applicant had become threatened with homelessness intentionally when she left settled accommodation in Jamaica without arranging for similar accommodation in this country. This decision was overturned by the High Court because the housing authority had made an unwarranted assumption about whether she had acted in good faith and in ignorance of a relevant fact:

> "[T]o a very considerable extent, the local authority concentrated their inquiries and their thoughts on the reasons why Miss Rose had left Jamaica. I can well understand them doing so. Normally, perhaps in the vast majority of cases, where a person comes to this country and then claims accommodation

77. *Islam v. Hillingdon London Borough* [1981] 3 A11 ER 901.
78. *Ibid* at pp.911-912.
79. (1982) 2 HLR 71.
80. (1983) 11 HLR 105.

under the Housing (Homeless Persons) Act 1977, these inquiries are the vital ones ... But it seems to me that, from the fact that Miss Rose had made no specific inquiry of her father as to the size of his accommodation or as to how long she would be able to stay with him, [the authority] took it for granted that that meant that she could not properly say that she was in good faith ignorant of a relevant fact. I take the view that in making that assumption, [they were] wrong."

Where an applicant makes the claim that he or she acted in good faith in ignorance of a relevant fact, Mr. Justice Glidewell continued, the authority "are obliged to go and make such inquiries as are necessary to satisfy themselves: (a) whether the applicant was unaware of the fact; (b) whether the fact was indeed a material one; and (c) whether in deciding to give up former accommodation in ignorance of the fact, the applicant was acting in good faith."

It is unnecessary for an applicant specifically to raise a matter with a housing authority before they are obliged to carry out further inquiries where it is evident from the applicant's conduct that further inquiries are necessary. For example, in *R. v. West Dorset District Council, ex p. Phillips* [81] Mr. Justice Webster held that where a wife's violent actions towards her husband pointed to the fact that she had not acquiesced in his conduct it was necessary for them to carry out inquiries. In so finding he stated that the housing authority had failed to appreciate that the onus of proof in these matters rested on the authority and not the applicant and that to approach the question on intentionality on the basis that it was necessary for the applicant to put forward an averment of non-acquiescence before it was necessary for them to conduct further inquiries, was plainly misguided.

Indeed, it may be added that, given that the onus of proof in respect of the key tests of homelessness rests with the authority, it is the duty of the authority to make inquiries about any matters which may materially affect the outcome of an application.

(iii) Possession orders

Whereas the existence of an order of possession against a public or private sector tenant on one of the conduct grounds is a relevant consideration in determining whether he became homeless intentionally, a housing authority must not assume that because a possession order has been granted against him he has rendered himself intentionally homeless. [82]

---

81. (1983) 17 HLR 336; see also *R. v. East Northamptonshire District Council, ex p. Spruce* (QBD) 17 February, 1988

82. See *R. v. Salford City Council, ex p. Devenport* (1984) 82 LGR 89; *R. v. Swansea City Council, ex p. John* (1982) 9 HLR 56; *R. v. Swansea City Council, ex p. Thomas* (1983) 9 HLR 56; *R. v. Croydon London Borough Council, ex p. Webb* (QBD) 14 December, 1983.

This question will need to be looked at particularly carefully in the future with the diminution of security of tenure under the 1988 housing legislation. As Mr. Justice Taylor commented in *R. v. Christchurch Borough Council, ex p. Conway* [83] in connection with the status of those tenants with less than full security of tenure there was a distinction between tenancies where landlords had a right to terminate and ones where the right was in some way restricted. Where the line was drawn between short tenancies and longer ones as far as whether accommodation was "settled" was a matter of degree and judgment for the local authority.

Thus, an eviction decree cannot be regarded as conclusive evidence of intentional homelessness because the issue before the courts is not the same as that determined by the authority. The court will in the discretionary cases be looking at whether it is reasonable in all the circumstances to grant an order. In other cases they will have no choice in whether to grant an order provided the landlord is able to establish the existence of certain facts. In both instances the questions before the court will be different from the test applicable for the determination of intentional homelessness. It follows therefore that it is unlawful for authorities to adopt blanket policies to the effect that tenants evicted from public or private sector tenancies are thereby intentionally homeless, since public bodies which are obliged by statute to carry out their own inquiries in respect of specific matters must carry out that statutory obligation. [84]

The existence of a possession order, however, is an important factor which an authority is entitled to take into account in determining whether an applicant became homeless intentionally. For example, in *R. v. Swansea City Council, ex p. Thomas,* [85] a housing authority determined that a member of a family unit was intentionally homeless despite the fact that he was absent from the family home when the conduct occurred as a result of which his family was evicted for anti-social conduct. Notwithstanding his absence Mr. Justice Woolf opined:

> "... I cannot conceive that it was the intention of Parliament where [as here] a council had obtained an order for possession of premises of which the application was a joint tenant, on the ground of nuisance and annoyance, a proper application of the legislation regarding homeless persons requires the council to then rehouse that person, with the same members of the family who had previously occupied the accommodation in respect of which the council had obtained an order for possession for the reasons I have just referred to."

---

83. (1987) 19 HLR 238.
84. See, for example, *Williams v. Cynon Valley District Council* (1980) LAG 16; *Attorney General ex rel. Tilley v. Wandsworth London Borough Council* [1981] 1 All ER 1162.
85. (1983) 9 HLR 64.

Where an authority has doubts about the reliability of evidence presented to them, they must not reject it out of hand without making further inquiries to test their view. For example, in *R. v. Bath City Council, ex p. Sangermano* [86] the decision of a housing authority that an applicant was not vulnerable because of subnormality was held to be invalid. The authority had doubts about the evidence of subnormality contained in letters from the applicant's solicitor and doctor but they failed to make appropriate inquiries about the nature and degree of her subnormality. Similarly, in *R. v. Eastleigh Borough Council, ex p. Beattie* [87] it was held that it was unlawful for a housing authority to reject affidavit evidence without putting forward cogent evidence as to why they did so. This is not to say, however, that where evidence is implausible the authority must accept it. In *R. v. Gillingham Borough Council, ex p. Loch,* [88] it was held by Mr. Justice Hodgson that in the light of the material before them it would have been astonishing if the housing authority had accepted the submission of the applicant's solicitors that his clients were unaware of the fact that their building society would accept a lesser sum in payment of their mortgage arrears when they had in fact made such an arrangement with their building society.

(iv) Appropriate advice

In order to have a proper basis for assessing the evidence before them it may well be necessary for an authority to seek appropriate advice. In *Sangermano,* the decision of a housing authority that an applicant was not vulnerable was held to be invalid because they rejected medical evidence of subnormality without making any inquiries to establish the nature and degree of the applicant's subnormality. A similar result followed in *R. v. Ryedale District Council, ex p. Smith* [89] in which the housing authority failed to consider the medical condition of the applicant before offering him temporary accommodation in a caravan. In this case the applicant was a 67 year old man who suffered from acute bronchitis, chronic fibrosis and emphysema. Although the authority's housing welfare officer interviewed his wife she had not made any mention of the applicant's poor health in her report. The failure of the authority to make inquiries about the health of the applicant, Mr. Justice Nolan held, meant that their decision to offer him temporary accommodation in a caravan was made in ignorance of a relevant matter which their inquiries should have revealed. He therefore quashed their decision in order that the authority could reconsider the application "in the light of full and fresh appropriate inquiries."

86. (1984) 17 HLR 94.
87. (1984) 17 HLR 168.
88. (QBD) 17 September, 1984.
89. (1983) 16 HLR 66.

On the other hand, if an authority does not seek relevant professional advice it would appear that the courts will usually accept that this amounts to carrying out appropriate inquiries. For example, where an authority allocated a house which did not have a shower unit to a disabled applicant it was held that they had discharged their duty to provide permanent accommodation because they acted on the advice of their senior medical officer that a shower unit was not justified.[90]

Equally, where there is conflicting professional advice it is open to the authority to choose which advice to accept. Thus in *R. v. Tandridge District Council, ex p. Hayman*,[91] where there was a disagreement between a consultant psychiatrist and a senior medical officer about the vulnerability of an applicant, it was not held to be unreasonable for the housing authority to accept the latter's opinion that the applicant was not vulnerable.

The authority, however, must be careful to seek advice from the appropriate sources and must not simply assume that because an issue has a health aspect that medical advice is all that is required. In *R. v. Lambeth London Borough Council, ex p. Carroll*[92] Mr. Justice Webster explained how an authority should assess such an issue:

> "It should always bear in mind that it may not be able in any particular case to decide whether a homeless person is vulnerable without taking into account opinion other than medical ones. For instance, if the decision on the question of vulnerability is not made by or with the assistance of the person or persons with experience of housing or social welfare, it may be necessary depending on the particular circumstances of the particular case to take the opinion of some other person."

The one case in which a decision based on professional advice has been held to be unlawful is *Kelly v. Monklands District Council*.[93] In this case the housing authority argued that two homeless 16 year old girls could not be regarded as being at risk of sexual of financial exploitation because the police had advised them that there had never been any question of exploitation of young people in their area. Lord Ross rejected this argument on the ground that, as the Code referred to risk of sexual or financial exploitation, the applicants could be regarded as being at *risk* "even though the police have not encountered exploitation of this kind before."

---

90. *R. v. Hillingdon London Borough Council, ex p. Oatley* (QBD) 2 October, 1984.
91. (QBD) 29 September, 1983.
92. *The Independent*, 8 October, 1987.
93. 1986 SLT 169.

3. Offences[94]

It is an offence to induce a housing authority to believe on the basis of false information that the applicant is:

(1) homeless or threatened with homelessness; or
(2) has a priority need; or
(3) did not become homeless or threatened with homelessness intentionally.

It is necessary that there should be intent to deceive. This may occur through a statement being made, knowingly or recklessly, which is false in a material particular or where information is knowingly withheld which the authority have reasonably required to be given. This offence applies *not only to applicants but also to their representatives* who can be guilty of providing misleading information. It is also an offence for an applicant to fail to inform the housing authority as soon as possible of any change of facts material to his case between the initial interview and the housing authority's decision. In relation to this offence, however, the legislation requires the housing authority to explain in "ordinary language" the duty imposed on the applicant to keep the authority informed of changes in his circumstances and that if he was not given such an explanation or if he was given such an explanation but has a reasonable excuse for his failure to inform the housing authority, he shall not be guilty of this offence. The penalty for these offences is that an offender shall be liable on summary conviction to a fine not exceeding level 5 on the standard scale.

It should be noted that the offences of knowingly or recklessly making a statement which is false in a material particular or knowingly withholding information both require that guilty intent *(mens rea)* be established and that the Code of Guidance states in relation to the failure to notify the housing authority of material changes in circumstances that:[95]

> "[A]uthorities will appreciate that it may not be obvious to those concerned
> what changes are material or that they ought to be disclosed and thus that it
> is important to implement this part of the Act sensitively."

The Scottish Code also adds that the object of this provision is "to avoid the possibility of the applicant feeling intimidated."[96]

A word of caution may be appropriate in this context. In two criminal law cases[97] arising from the similarly worded section 146(3) of

---

94. Section 74 of the Housing Act 1985; section 40 of the Housing (Scotland) Act 1987.
95. EC 2.7; SC 2.8.
96. SC 2.8.
97. *Clear v. Smith* [1981] 1WLR 399; *Barrass v. Reeve* [1981] 1WLR 408.

the Social Security Act of 1975 and Section 21 of the Supplementary Benefit Act 1976 (now section 53 of the Social Security Act 1986) it was held that it was unnecessary to satisfy the requirements of guilty intent to establish a specific intention to defraud. If the defendant made a false statement which he knew to be false in any material respect he is guilty of an offence under these sections. As these sections appear to have been the model adopted by the parliamentary draftsman it is not inconceivable that the courts would follow these authorities in determining the guilty requirement for these offences also.

The enforcement of these offences tends to be patchy with some authorities adopting an avowedly non-prosecution policy. While detailed figures for prosecution are not readily available, Shelter have noted that there were at least nine prosecutions in 1979 under section 11 of the Housing (Homeless Persons) Act 1977, and that in one case an applicant was fined £150 on each of seven separate accounts.[98] The reasons why a number of authorities have adopted non-prosecution policies range from the view that it would reflect badly on the professional standards expected of their staff, to a lack of necessary resources to police such abuses. The failure of a housing authority to prosecute an applicant for failing to inform them of a change in circumstances (in this case the fact that his wife and children had left him) was commented upon by Lord Bridge in *Eastleigh Borough Council v. Walsh*.[99]

To counter this tendency the second edition of the Code of Guidance reminds authorities that "where it is evident that an offence has been committed, [they] should be ready to consider the case for prosecution."[100]

---

98. 'Homeless Act Bites Back', *Roof* (1980) 8 January.
99. [1985] 1 WLR 525.
100. EC 2.7.

Chapter 4

The Circumstances of Homelessness and Priority Need

The nature and level of assistance which a housing authority are obliged to provide to an applicant depends on the results of the housing authority's inquiries. There are broadly four tests which determine this matter:

1. *Is the applicant homeless or threatened with homelessness?* Only if an applicant falls within one of these two categories are a housing authority *obliged* to provide any assistance.
2. *Has the applicant a priority need?* Only applicants who are homeless and have priority need are *entitled* to accommodation.
3. *Did he become homeless or threatened with homelessness intentionally?* A finding on intentionality substantially reduces the responsibilities of a housing authority towards an applicant. Where an applicant is homeless and has a priority need but did not become homeless intentionally, the housing authority must provide him with permanent accommodation.

   However, where an applicant is homeless and has a priority need *but* became homeless intentionally, the duty of a housing authority is reduced to providing temporary accommodation for such a reasonable period of time as will enable the applicant to arrange for his own accommodation. A finding of intentionality has a similar result for those threatened with homelessness. Where an applicant became threatened with homelessness intentionally the duty of the housing authority is merely to offer advice and assistance. However, if the applicant did not become threatened with homelessness intentionally the authority's duty is to take reasonable steps to avert homelessness – a more positive obligation.
4. *Does the applicant have a local connection?* Even where an applicant

is homeless and has a priority need and did not become homeless intentionally it is possible for a housing authority, if the applicant does not have a local connection with the area of the authority and has a local connection with the area of another housing authority in England, Scotland or Wales, to transfer the responsibility for providing *permanent* accommodation to that housing authority. It should be noted that this provision is not mandatory, i.e. there is no obligation on a housing authority to transfer responsibility for housing on an applicant, and that the provision only relates to the obligation to provide permanent accommodation *not the obligation to provide temporary accommodation.*[1]

1. Homelessness and Threatened with Homelessness[2]

(a) Homelessness

Homelessness is defined in THREE ways:

1. where a person has *no accommodation* in England, Scotland, or Wales.
2. a person is to be treated as having *no accommodation if there is no accommodation which he* (together with any person who normally resides with him as a member of his family or in circumstances which the local authority consider it reasonable to reside with him) –

   (i) is entitled to occupy by virtue of an interest in it or by virtue of a court order.
   (ii) has a right or permission or licence in England and Wales to occupy.
   (iii) occupies as a residence by virtue of any enactment or rule of law.

3. A person has accommodation *but* –

   (i) he cannot secure entry to it
   (ii) violence may result from occupation
   (iii) there is no mooring or pitching place
   (iv) the accommodation is not reasonable to continue to occupy (England and Wales) or is statutorily overcrowded and may endanger the health of the occupants.

---

1. See Ch.7, *infra.*
2. Section 58 of the Housing Act 1985; section 24 of the Housing (Scotland) Act 1987.

(i) No accommodation in Great Britain

For the purposes of deciding whether a person is or is not homeless the availability of accommodation outwith Great Britain is irrelevant.[3] A person who is "sleeping rough" on the streets, such as the groups of people who sleep in cardboard boxes or in makeshift shelters in the centre of London, obviously are homeless under this definition. However, this definition also encompasses persons sleeping in emergency accommodation.

If a homeless person is provided with temporary accommodation, as typically in a refuge for battered women, then the fact that such accommodation has been provided does not remove that person from the category of being homeless. If this were not the case, Judge Norman Francis explained in a county court case, *Williams v. Cynon Valley District Council*,[4] it would be necessary for voluntary agencies to give notice every 28 days in order that persons occupying such occupation might be included within the "threatened with homelessness" category. Judge Francis rejected this and stated that this practice would be "deplorable".

This view was echoed by the Divisional Court in *R. v. Ealing London Borough, ex p. Sidhu*.[5] Mr. Justice Hodgson added that:

> "[I]t was important that refuges be seen as temporary crisis accommodation, and that women living in refuges were still homeless under the terms of the Act. If it was suggested that they were not homeless it would be necessary for voluntary organisations to issue immediate 28-day notices when women came in so that they would be under threat of homelessness. That would be totally undesirable and would simply add stress to stress. If living in crisis accommodation took women out of the "homeless category" then the Act was being watered down and its protections would be removed from a whole class of persons that it was set up to help and for whom it was extremely important."

Subsequently, the Divisional Court in *R. v. Waveney District Council, ex*

---

3. This amendment gives statutory recognition to the "territorial restriction" to the legislation put forward by the Court of Appeal in *R. v. Hillingdon London Borough Council, ex p. Streeting* [1980] 1 WLR 1430; see also *R. v. Hillingdon London Borough Council, ex p. H, The Times*, 17 May, 1988. However, the circumstances in which the person gave up accommodation abroad will be relevant in assessing whether that person became homeless intentionally: see, for example, *De Falco v. Crawley Borough Council* [1980] QB 460; *Lambert v. Ealing London Borough Council* [1982] 2 All ER 394; *R. v. Tower Hamlets London Borough Council, ex p. Monaf, The Times*, 28 April, 1988; *R. v. Hillingdon London Borough Council, ex p. H, The Times*, 17 May, 1988; and *R. v. Kensington and Chelsea Royal Borough Council, ex p. Cunha, The Independent*, 21 July, 1988.
4. *Roof* (1979) 195; (1980) LAG 16.
5. (1983) 2 HLR 45; see also *R. v. Broxbourne Borough Council, ex p. Willmoth* (QBD) 29 July, 1988.

p. Bowers [6] held that a night shelter was not accommodation in terms of the Act and that a person staying in such a shelter was homeless.

The Code indicates that this approach is to be followed where temporary hostel accommodation is provided. Referring to the usefulness of short-term accommodation where it is either not possible or not desirable to arrange a long-term solution immediately, the Code states:

> "If there is a women's refuge in the area this could be a useful source of interim accommodation for women who have been subject to or at risk of violence, but should not be considered as permanent accommodation. The authority will still have a duty to secure permanent accommodation."

A person occupying temporary accommodation therefore may be homeless. However, if the temporary accommodation is provided by a housing authority as a stage in performing their duty to provide permanent accommodation, that accommodation will be regarded as "settled" accommodation and hence the applicant may not be regarded as homeless. In *R. v. East Hertfordshire District Council, ex p. Hunt* [7] a single parent was evicted from temporary accommodation provided by the Council due to her conduct. It was held that the housing authority were entitled to consider whether she had thereby become homeless intentionally because the accommodation could be regarded as "settled" accommodation.

(ii) No right to accommodation

A person is deemed to have no accommodation unless he is entitled or permitted to occupy accommodation for example as owner, tenant, lodger, service occupier or under a court order or statutory protection (e.g. a person retaining possession as statutory tenant under the Rent Acts after his contractual rights to occupancy have terminated or a wife invoking her statutory occupancy rights).

Where an applicant puts forward information that he is homeless because he has no right to accommodation it is for the authority to satisfy themselves if this is the case. In *R. v. Woodspring District Council, ex p. Walters* [8] the applicant's solicitor informed the housing authority that she had lost her married quarters in which she had lived with her husband in Cyprus. However, without checking the accuracy of this information, the authority decided that she was not homeless because accommodation was available to her. It was held that the decision was unlawful because they had failed to make appropriate inquiries to establish if in fact this was the case.

---

6. *The Times*, 25 May, 1982; this issue was not contested in the Court of Appeal; see [1982] 3 WLR 661.
7. (1985) 18 HLR 51.
8. (1984) 16 HLR 73.

Walters may be usefully contrasted with the Scottish case of *McAlinden v. Bearsden and Milngavie District Council* [9] in which a housing authority held that a cohabitee was not homeless because she could have applied to the court for the grant of occupancy rights under section 18 of the Matrimonial Homes (Family Protection) (Scotland) Act 1981. Upholding the decision of the authority, Lord McDonald stated that she had a clear right under section 18 of the 1981 Act to seek a grant of occupancy right and accordingly it could not be said that she was a person who had no accommodation which she had no right or permission, or an implied right or permission, to occupy. We doubt whether this decision was soundly based. It confuses "rights" with "rights to seek declaration of rights".

A recent case, *R. v. Kensington and Chelsea London Borough Council, ex p. Minton*, [10] throws further light on the meaning of this provision. In this case Mrs. Minton had given up her job as a resident housekeeper and with it her right to occupy a small boxroom in her employer's house. She applied to the housing authority to rehouse her as a homeless person but the authority refused to do so as her employer had indicated that she was prepared to re-employ her and for her to occupy the boxroom. Mrs. Minton, however, was unwilling to return to her former employment. As she did not have a tenancy or a statutory right to occupy the premises, the question before the High Court was whether she had an express or an implied licence to occupy the boxroom. Mr. Justice Macpherson held that she did not:

> "The offer of a contract of employment was not a licence at all. One was dependent on the other. The whole arrangement between Mrs Minton and her employer depended on there being consent between them and, in fact, a contractual arrangement that one would serve the other.
> In the absence of such a contractual arrangement there was no permission for Mrs. Minton to return to the flat. If she said that she did not want to be the housekeeper but wanted to live in the boxroom she would not be allowed to return. It could not be said that in law there was a licence in existence at all, either express or implied."

Even if an applicant has a right or permission to occupy accommodation he is to be treated as having no accommodation if he is not entitled to occupy that accommodation with any person who normally resides with him as a member of his family or in circumstances which the housing authority consider reasonable for that person to reside with him. The failure of an authority to have regard to this question can render their decision unlawful. [11]

---

9. (1986) SLT 91; see also *R. v. Dacorum Borough Council, ex p. Taverner* (QBD) 27 October, 1988.
10. *The Guardian*, 4 August, 1988.
11. *R. v. Wimborne District Council, ex p. Curtis* (1985) 18 HLR 79.

The first test is whether the person in question *normally resides* with the applicant. It would appear that this test only applies to persons who are not members of the applicant's family. For example, in *R. v. Westminster City Council, ex p. Chambers* [12] Mr. Justice McCullough accepted that a couple were homeless who had lived apart in the names of their respective parents throughout their marriage because neither set of parents was willing to accommodate them as a couple.

The Code defines family membership to include (i) established households where there is a blood relationship, or (ii) other circumstances where people are living together as if they were members of the same household, e.g cohabiting couples or foster parents and children.

The question whether it is reasonable for a member of the applicant's family to reside with him if he is *in fact* residing with the applicant does not arise[13] but the Code of Guidance indicates that an elderly or disabled person may reasonably be accompanied by a housekeeper or companion and where separation has occurred due only to lack of adequate accommodation in which the parties can live together it is reasonable for the authority to consider the housing needs of the applicant and such other persons.

(iii) Unacceptable accommodation

An applicant may have accommodation but he is nonetheless homeless if, broadly speaking, he is unable to use that accommodation, if occupation of that accommodation would constitute a danger to his safety or health, or if the accommodation is unsuitable.

a. Unable to secure access to accommodation.

Even if a person has the right to occupy accommodation it may be that it is impossible to get into that accommodation. He may have been illegally evicted or there may be other practical reasons why the accommodation is not actually available. In these circumstances the applicant is to be treated as homeless.

The question of proof in respect of an applicant claiming to be homeless because he is unable to secure access to accommodation was raised in *R. v. Purbeck District Council, ex p. Cadney*.[14] In this case a married woman who had left her husband for another man, claimed that she could not return to the matrimonial home, of which she was joint tenant, even if she was successful in an application to oust her husband from it because her husband and his family would harass her. That

---

12. [1983] 81 LGR 401; *R. v. Preseli District Council, ex p. Fisher* (1984) 17 HLR 147; see also D. Hoath, 'Split Families and Part III of the Housing Act 1985' [1987] JSWL 15.

13. *R. v. Lambeth London Borough, ex p. Ly* (1987) 19 HLR 51.

14. (1985) 17 HLR 534.

assertion was rejected by the court on the ground that the applicant had failed to produce any evidence to show that she had made an attempt to secure entry to the matrimonial home:

> "It may seem a hard thing to say, but it must be said that on the evidence produced by the applicant there is nothing to show that any attempt has been made by her to secure entry to the house and there is only the most indirect evidence that if she did enter it and occupy it violence from her husband would result. The evidence she has given is that she considered that if she was successful in any application for the matrimonial home her husband would still come to the house and harass her."

The importance of this case is twofold: first, it further demonstrates the increasing tendency of the courts to reject the subjective fears of applicants about the possibility of violent conduct towards them as sufficient grounds either for leaving secure accommodation or for not returning to accommodation which is considered to be available for their occupation;[15] and second, it would appear from the judgment of Mr. Justice Nolan that applicants who allege that they are unable to secure entry to accommodation must provide clear evidence of attempted entry. If this is the case it places a very heavy burden of proof on tenants and separated spouses who may regard this course of action to be quite unrealistic, if not dangerous.

Other than these two principle points it is also noteworthy that *Cadney* provides further evidence of the practice of some housing authorities of considering applicants who possess legal remedies to secure access to accommodation (such as in this case where the applicant could have applied for an order to oust her husband from the matrimonial home) to be intentionally homeless unless such remedies are invoked, however remote the likelihood of legal action being successful.[16]

b. Violence may result from occupation

The problem of domestic violence has been highlighted in recent years by a number of studies.[17] In particular concern has been expressed in many quarters for the plight of those women and children who are forced to "pay the rent" in cuts, bruises and broken bones simply because they have nowhere else to go.

To overcome the need to remain with a violent partner because of the difficulty of securing alternative accommodation, the legislation

---

15. See 'Intentional Homelessness' below at pp. 103-163.
16. See also *R. v. Eastleigh Borough Council, ex p. Evans* (1984) 17 HLR 515.
17. R.E. Dobash and R. Dobash, *Violence Against Wives,* Open Books, 1979, London; Select Committee Report, *Violence in Marriage,* Parliamentary Papers, (HC 553) 1975; Scottish Law Commission Report No. 60, *Occupancy Rights in Matrimonial Homes and Domestic Violence,* July, 1980.

specifically provides that if it is probable that occupation of accommodation will lead to threats of violence from another person living in the accommodation *and* if it is likely that person will carry out those threats, the applicant is to be treated as being homeless. In spite of criticism of the wording of this provision during the passage of the Bill as imposing an onerous standard of proof on battered women to establish not only violent assault or threats of violence but the likelihood of their repetition or escalation, amendment was resisted.[18]

The Scottish Code asks authorities to respond sympathetically to applications from women in fear of violence. In judging the likelihood of violence the authorities are advised that the woman's fears alone may be sufficient evidence because fear of violence may inhibit women from discussing such matters or taking legal action. The absence of evidence of violence should not by itself result in the application being refused. Even the existence of a protective legal order not to molest the woman or enter the house in the form of an interdict or injunction obviously does not mean that it is safe for a woman to return home.

Legislation provides rights to women to exclude violent spouses from the home or vicinity and provides protective mechanisms, such as matrimonial interdicts, which enable the police to arrest violent spouses in the vicinity of the house without a warrant.[19]

The guidance offered by the Scottish Code[20] can be contrasted with *Cadney* where Mr. Justice Nolan rejected an application for *certiorari* from a homeless woman on the ground that her assertion that domestic violence was the cause of her not wishing to return to her husband was not corroborated.

c. No mooring/pitching place for houseboat/mobile house

The plight of travelling people and persons living in mobile homes in rural areas in Great Britain has long been recognised but very little has been done to tackle the basic problems of poor facilities, insecurity and hardship.[21] The planning laws and the Caravan Sites Act 1968 and the Caravan Sites and Control of Development Act 1960 do enable local

---

18. *Hansard*, HL Debates, Vol. 385 (15 July, 1977) col. 1170; vol 386 (22 July, 1977) cols. 655-660.
19. For the position in Scotland see *The Guide to the Matrimonial Homes (Family Protection) (Scotland) Act 1981*, Fran Wasoff (Scottish Women's Aid and Shelter, 1982) revised edition; and *Matrimonial Homes (Family Protection) (Scotland) Act 1981*, David Nichols and Michael Meston (W. Green & Son Ltd, 2nd ed., 1986). The legislation and practice in England and Wales has been discussed extensively in legal journals, particularly *Family Law*. See generally *Family Law*, P.M. Bromley, and N.V. Lowe (Butterworths, 7th ed., 1987).
20. SC 2.11 and *R. v. Broxbourne Council ex p. Willmoth* QBD 29 July, 1988.
21. *Cripps Report on Accommodation for Gypsies*, (HMSO, 1977); DOE *Survey Report of the Mobile Homes Review* (HMSO, 1977); Scottish Office Central Research Unit, *Residential Mobile Homes in Scotland* (1977); SDD *Housing in Rural Scotland* (1979); Shelter, *Neglected too Long* (1980); National Consumer Council, *Mobile Homes*, (1982).

authorities to regulate land use and site conditions. The Mobile Homes Acts 1975 and 1983 provide limited security of tenure and protection from financial exploitation by site owners. However, many inadequacies and injustices remain.[22]

The legislation attempts to overcome some of these disadvantages by providing that an owner of a mobile home, caravan, houseboat or other moveable structure or vessel which is designed or adapted for human habitation who had no place to put it or moor it and to reside in it is to be treated as homeless.

d. Substandard accommodation

Although the word "accommodation" was not qualified in section 1 of the Housing (Homeless Persons) Act 1977, prior to 1986 the courts appeared to accept that not to do so would be contrary to the intention of the legislature as evinced by the statute as a whole.[23] In a number of cases the question asked by the courts was whether it could be said that the accommodation was inappropriate, unreasonable, unsuitable, or uninhabitable.[24] To take an extreme example, as Lord Wheatley did by way of illustration of this principle in *Brown v. Hamilton District Council*,[25] whereas a pig-sty can be regarded as accommodation it is not accommodation which could be regarded as being suitable for human habitation.

However, the House of Lords in *R. v. Hillingdon London Borough Council, ex p. Puhlhofer* [26] held that accommodation in section 1(1) of the 1977 Act did not mean "appropriate" or "reasonable" accommodation, but accommodation that could be properly described as such within the ordinary meaning of the English language. It followed therefore that although accommodation might be unfit for human habitation or overcrowded, it could still be regarded as accommodation within the meaning of section 1(1) and the applicant would not be homeless. Lord Brightman indicated that what was properly to be regarded as accommodation was a question of fact to be decided by the housing authority, but that if the accommodation was not capable of accommodating the applicant and persons who might reasonably be expected to reside with him and therefore could not be regarded as accommodation from an

---

22. See for example *Tickner v. Mole Valley District Council*, (1980) LAG 187; *Smith v. Wokingham District Council* (1980) LAG 92; Report on Complaint against Sedgemoor District Council, 715/H/78, dated 28 March, 1980.
23. *R. v. Hillingdon London Borough Council, ex p. Puhlhofer* [1986] AC 484.
24. *R. v. Dinefyr Borough Council, ex p. Marshall* (1984) 17 HLR 310; *R. v. Gloucester City, ex p. Miles* (1985) 17 HLR 292; *R. v. Preseli District Council, ex p. Fisher* (1984) 17 HLR 147; *R. v. South Herefordshire District Council, ex p. Miles* (1983) 17 HLR 82; and *R. v. Wyre Borough Council, ex p. Parr* (1982) 2 HLR 71.
25. 1983 SLT 397.
26. [1986] AC 484.

objective standpoint, the applicant would be homeless because he had no accommodation.

This decision which appears to have been taken without reference to the earlier House of Lords decision of *Brown v. Hamilton District Council* [27] in which Lord Fraser stated that "accommodation must be reasonable", caused considerable concern. Successful lobbying of the House of Lords by Shelter, however, resulted in the Government being forced to accept amendments to remove the serious limitations imposed by *Puhlhofer*. These amendments apply different standards to England and Wales and to Scotland.

Where a person has accommodation in Scotland he is homeless if the accommodation is overcrowded as defined by section 135 of the Housing (Scotland) Act 1987 *and* may endanger the health of the occupants. This is an objective test insofar as the first test relating to overcrowding is simple to apply. The statute provides two standards of overcrowding the room standard and the space standard and if *either* of these standards is not satisfied there is overcrowding. The question of danger to health is more complex and it may be that medical evidence will have to be produced. Although overcrowding *per se* is widely regarded as being a danger to health it is clear that the "Scottish test" does not recognise this to be the case.

A person who has accommodation in England or Wales is homeless if it is not reasonable for the applicant to continue to occupy it. [28] In assessing "reasonableness" the housing authority may have regard to the general circumstances relating to housing in their district, including demolition, overcrowding, and homes in multiple occupancy. This test is obviously more open-ended than the "Scottish test" and has the advantage of ending the anomalous situation whereby a person who remained in accommodation might not be regarded as being homeless but if he left the accommodation and became homeless he could not be regarded as having become homeless intentionally or if offered the same accommodation he would be entitled to refuse it. [29] However, in view of *R. v. Blackpool Borough Council, ex p. Smith*, [30] where the decision of a housing authority to refuse to accept that an applicant who lived in accommodation which was a fire risk and unfit for human habitation was homeless was upheld as being lawful, it would appear that the narrower but less subjective "Scottish test" is to be preferred.

---

27. 1983 SLT 397.
28. This is exactly the same test as is laid down for determining if an applicant who has *left* accommodation has become homeless intentionally: see below pp. 107-128.
29. *R. v. Ealing London Borough Council, ex p. McBain* [1986] 1 All ER 13.
30. (QBD) 29 July, 1987; see also *R. v. Westminster City Council, ex p. Tansey* (QBD) 6 March, 1987.

(b) Threatened with homelessness

In order that local authorities may take preventive action it is provided that duties arise not only in relation to those who already are homeless but towards those who are threatened with homelessness. A person is regarded as threatened with homelessness if it is likely that he will become homeless within 28 days.

The Code stresses the desirability of avoiding unnecessary homelessness by urging authorities to take preventive action and points out that the earlier action can be taken the greater the likelihood that measures to avert homelessness will be effective. The House of Lords has now given judicial approval to this approach.[31]

2. Priority Need[32]

If a person is homeless, in order to qualify for accommodation he must have a priority need. The legislation specifies FOUR categories of persons who are considered to have priority need for accommodation. In addition to these categories it should be noted that the Secretary of State has power, after consultation, to specify further categories of persons as having priority need for accommodation.

A person has a priority need for accommodation if (a) he has dependent children who are residing with him or who might reasonably be expected to reside with him; or (b) he is homeless or threatened with homelessness as a result of any emergency such as flood, fire or any other disaster; or (c) he or any person who resides with him or who might reasonably be expected to reside with him is vulnerable; or (d) she is homeless and pregnant or the applicant is homeless and resides or might reasonably be expected to reside with a pregnant woman.

(a) Dependent children

A homeless person or a person threatened with homelessness is regarded as having a priority need for accommodation if he has dependent children residing with him. It is unnecessary to obtain a formal custody order to establish dependency. Ealing Borough Council attempted to argue this point before the Divisional Court in the *Sidhu* [33] case. However, Mr. Justice Hodgson declared that it was not necessary to

---

31. *Din v. Wandsworth London Borough Council* [1983] 1 AC 657 at p.679 per Lord Lowry and at p.686 per Lord Bridge.
32. Section 59 of the Housing Act 1985; section 25 of the Housing (Scotland) Act 1987.
33. *R. v. Ealing Borough Council, ex p. Sidhu* (1983) 2 HLR 45.

obtain a custody order and that this view was "totally wrong in law". If a dependent child *resides* with an applicant it is not open to the authority to find that the child might not reasonably be expected to reside with him.[34]

Children living with relatives on a temporary basis are regarded as being the dependants of the person with whom they might reasonably be expected to reside. Where children are in care of the local authority, they nevertheless should be regarded as part of the family unit except in cases where it is unreasonable that they should live with the applicant.

The legislation does not define "dependent children" but the Code of Guidance states that the Secretary of State considers that authorities should treat as dependent all children under the age of 16, and others under the age of 19 who are either receiving full-time education or training or are otherwise unable to support themselves. The Code also points out that this category is not limited to the children of the applicant or legitimate children, but includes grand-children and adopted or foster-children, and the children of one-parent families and battered women.

Furthermore, the children need not necessarily be living with the applicant at the time of application. The last mentioned provision is aimed at preventing the creation of a situation where applicants are not regarded as having a priority need for accommodation because their children are not living with them and the reason for separation is a lack of suitable accommodation.

The Code states that accommodation is "available" only if it is available for occupation by all those who might reasonably be expected to live together and that the practice of splitting families is not acceptable, even for short periods.[35]

(b) Emergency

A homeless person or a person threatened with homelessness is regarded as having a priority need for accommodation if he becomes homeless or threatened with homelessness as a result of any emergency such as flood, fire or other disaster.[36]

Whereas a person who is homeless or threatened with homelessness

---

34. *R. v. Hillingdon London Borough Council, ex p. Islam*, [1983] 1 AC 688.
35. *Ibid* where the House of Lords criticised Sir Denys Buckley's view that rooms in two continents could provide accommodation for a family at p.708 per Lord Wilberforce at p.716 per Lord Lowry. The mother and children were in Bangladesh, the father in Uxbridge.
36. See *R. v. Westminster City Council, ex p. Tansey* (QBD) 6 March, 1987; Report on Complaint No.157/C/81 against Glanford Borough Council dated 12 November, 1981, which concerned accommodation damaged by fire resulting in homelessness.

because of fire or flood clearly has a priority need the meaning of the words "any other disaster" is unclear. Whether other emergencies are included by this provision was discussed in *Noble v. South Herefordshire District Council*.[37] In this case it was argued that the words "any other disaster" should not restrict the meaning of emergency which could cover property in respect of which a demolition order had been made. This view was roundly rejected by the Court of Appeal:

> "[I]n the phrase any emergency such as fire, flood or any other disaster the words or any other disaster are clearly indicating any other disaster similar to a flood or fire. By no stretch of the imagination can it be said that the fact that there is a demolition order in force for the demolition of this property is an emergency such as fire, flood, or any other disaster."

In this context, however, it is noteworthy that even where an applicant clearly falls within the emergency category some authorities have been reluctant to accept displaced persons as having a priority need. For example, in *Rutland District Council* [38] a referee held that the housing authority had a clear duty to rehouse a family who had lost their home because of a fire and were not entitled to refuse to accept them as having a priority need.

(c) Vulnerability

Of the four categories of priority need vulnerability has emerged as the most contentious category.

If a homeless person or a person threatened with homelessness or any person who resides with him or who might reasonably be expected to reside with him is vulnerable as a result of old age, mental illness, handicap, physical disability or any other special reason, or a combination of these causes,[39] that person has a priority need for accommodation.

The persons who are envisaged by the Code as being vulnerable are those above retirement age who are particularly frail or in poor health, the blind, deaf or dumb or persons who are otherwise "substantially" disabled. Apart from these more obviously vulnerable groups, authorities are urged by the Secretary of State to have particular regard for those who do not come into these categories. The Code singles out as vulnerable applicants for whom accommodation should be secured— battered women without children who are at risk of violent pursuit or further violence if they return home and the homeless young who are at

---

37. (1983) 17 HLR 80, C.A.
38. 26 June, 1981 (Decision No. 35).
39. *R. v. Bath City Council, ex p. Sangermano* (1984) 17 HLR 94.

risk of sexual or financial exploitation.[40]

The Government Report *Single and Homeless* [41] has done much to dispel the popular image of the single homeless as drunken "dossers" and reveals that this group is more heterogeneous than hitherto had been supposed. The report identifies a major cause of homelessness among the single to be the lack of adequate housing, with people moving between institutions, charities, hostels and sleeping rough.

In general two guidelines can be given on the meaning of vulnerability. First, that a person is vulnerable if he is "less able to fend [for himself] so that injury or detriment will result when a less vulnerable man will be able to cope without harmful effects".[42] Secondly, "that vulnerability to be considered is vulnerability loosely in housing terms or in the context of housing".[43]

The general question of vulnerability was initially discussed by the Court of Appeal in *R. v. Waveney District Council, ex p. Bowers.*[44] In that case Douglas Bowers, an alcoholic who suffered serious brain damage as a result of a road accident, applied to Waveney District Council for accommodation as a homeless person. The Council refused to accept his application on the alternative grounds that he was not homeless as he had accommodation in a night refuge or, if the Council were wrong and the applicant was homeless, he did not have a priority need for accommodation. Bowers appealed to the High Court which held that he was homeless because a night shelter could not in any sense be regarded as a home but that the Council were entitled to consider him a non-vulnerable applicant. In upholding Bowers' appeal against this decision Lord Justice Waller explained in the Court of Appeal that vulnerability in terms of the legislation was not to be given its literal meaning:

"[B]ut in the context of this legislation ... meant less able to fend for oneself so that injury or detriment would result when a less vulnerable man would be able to cope without harmful effects."

Following this approach Lord Justice Waller then suggested that there is a fundamental difference between what may be broadly described

---

40. *Kelly v. Monklands District Council* 1986 SLT 165 where exploitation was held to be possible even though the local police had indicated that none had hitherto occurred.

41. HMSO, 1981. See also K. Wells et. al. *The Survivors,* RKP (1980).

42. *R. v. Waveney District Council, ex p. Bowers* [1983] QB 238.

43. *R. v. Bath City Council, ex p. Sangermano* (1984) 17 HLR 94; see also *R. v. Lambeth Borough Council, ex p. Carroll, The Independent,* 8 October, 1987; *The Guardian,* 8 October, 1987; cf *R. v. Wandsworth Borough Council, ex p. Banbury* (1987) 19 HLR 76.

44. [1983] QB 238. The council reluctantly accepted responsiblity for housing Mr. Bowers only after the Campaign for Single Homeless People threatened to take the council back to court, *The Times,* 24 July, 1982.

as involuntary and voluntary vulnerability. If Bowers' vulnerability had been attributed solely to his drinking it would appear that the housing authority would have been entitled to refuse to recognise that he had a priority need for accommodation. However, as his vulnerability was to some degree attributable to the road accident, an involuntary occurrence, Lord Justice Waller stated he must be regarded as a priority need applicant. Whether this distinction will prove to be a useful one remains to be seen.

Whether an applicant is vulnerable is a question of fact.[45] However, there is no yardstick and therefore vulnerability is not easy to measure. It is expected that all the relevant professional advice will be used, normally in the form of joint liaison committees between the housing and social work departments concerned, representatives of Health Boards, and other relevant experts.[46]

There are five possible situations indicated by the legislation which might lead an authority to assess an applicant as being vulnerable. As we shall see in many instances applicants fall into more than one of these categories:

Old Age
Mental illness
Mental handicap
Physical disability
Other special reason

(i) Old age

The Code suggests that authorities should treat as vulnerable people who are above normal retiring age and any others approaching normal retirement age who are particularly frail, in poor health or vulnerable for any other reason. Individuals or couples without dependent children may be treated as being in priority need in terms of this part of the legislation by dint of their advancing years. However, there are no "age limits". Whether a person is vulnerable because of old age is a question of fact.[47]

(ii)Mental illness or handicap or physical disability

The Code of Guidance[48] is misleading on the meaning of vulnerability. Whereas the legislation states that a person may be vulnerable as a result

---

45. *R. v. Wandsworth Borough Council, ex p. Banbury* (1987) 19 HLR 76.
46. *Kelly v. Monklands District Council* 1986 SLT 169; *Steventon v Monklands District Council* [1987] GWD 15-576.
47. *R. v. Waveney Borough Council, ex p. Bowers* [1983] QB 238.
48. SC 2.13(c); EC 2.12(c).

of mental illness or handicap or physical disability the Code, while acknowledging that the blind, deaf or dumb are vulnerable, states that in addition to these groups, those who are *substantially* mentally or physically disabled are also to be regarded as being vulnerable. This advice is misleading because it imparts the idea, contrary to the Act and *Bowers,* and *Carroll,*[49] that persons who are otherwise than substantially disabled may not be regarded as vulnerable.

In this respect it is noteworthy, bearing in mind that there is no test of substantiality in respect of disability, that the Code urges authorities to "take a wide and flexible view of what constitutes 'substantial' disability, recognising that this will depend on individual circumstances."

By including both mental illness and mental handicap, Mr. Justice Hodgson observed in *R. v. Bath City Council, ex p. Sangermano,*[50] the legislation draws a distinction between mental illness, which broadly relates to psychotic illness, and mental handicap, which does not relate to illness but subnormality or severe subnormality. However, he continued, a person is not necessarily vulnerable merely because he or she falls within the category of subnormality under mental health legislation.

Those applicants who are in receipt of disability benefits, such as mobility allowance, attendance, or are registered as disabled under the Chronically Sick and Disabled Persons Act 1970 [51] should qualify as vulnerable because of physical disability. The chronically sick who do not suffer from physical disability or mental illness or handicap, may be able to establish vulnerability for other special reason.

(iii) Other special reason

In addition to being vulnerable as a result of old age, mental illness or handicap or physical disability a person may be vulnerable for any other special reason. The Code of Guidance[52] refers to two categories of persons —battered women without children who are at risk and young people at risk of either sexual or financial exploitation —as falling within this part of the definition of vulnerability. However, it should be noted that difficulties, such as severe language problems, when combined with other disadvantages which may not in themselves be sufficient to make an applicant vulnerable in terms of the legislation, may have the cumulative effect of establishing vulnerability. For example, in *Sangermano*[53] Mr. Justice Hodgson stated that:

"[W]hen you get a lady with her record of incompetence who is subnormal

---

49. [1983] QB 238; *The Independent,* 8 October, 1987.
50. (1984) 17 HLR 94.
51. *R. v. Lewisham London Borough Council, ex p. Turner* (QBD) 11 February, 1988.
52. SC 2.13(c); EC 2.12(c).
53. (1984) 17 HLR 94.

and who is incapable of ... articulating properly either in English or indeed in Italian, then you have someone who, properly instructing itself no local authority could , in the special circumstances of this case, come to any conclusion other than that she is vulnerable within the meaning of section 2(1)(c) [of the Housing (Homeless Persons) Act 1977]."

It is clear therefore that, as with local connection, in some cases priority need will be established under one or other of the limbs of vulnerability but in others housing authorities must consider the cumulative effect of different forms of vulnerability on the applicant.

In *Kelly v. Monklands District Council* [54] a housing authority denied assistance to two 16 year old girls on the ground that they did not have a priority need because of vulnerability. This decision was rejected by Lord Ross. In doing so he stated that while he was not persuaded that every 16 year old girl is vulnerable within the meaning of the legislation in the case of *Kelly* who was 16, had no assets or income, had nowhere to go and who had apparently left home because of violence, no reasonable authority could come to any other decision than that she was vulnerable: "a girl of that age and with her background is bound to be less able to fend for herself than a less vulnerable girl; being less able to cope, such a person is liable to injury or harm."[55] A finding which he regarded as being reinforced by the girl's alleged attempted suicide, albeit that she had not required medical treatment.

In so finding, Lord Ross rejected the proposition put forward by the housing authority that the applicant could not be regarded as being at risk of sexual or financial exploitation because she had not been so exploited and the police had advised them that to their knowledge there had never been any question of exploitation of young people in the area. He did so on two grounds: first, that the fact that exploitation had not occurred did not mean that exploitation could not reasonably be apprehended; and second, that as the Code referred to risk of sexual or financial exploitation the applicant could be regarded as being at risk "even though the police have not encountered exploitation of this kind before."

This case is of importance for two principal reasons. First, although Lord Ross was careful to explain that not every 16 year old is vulnerable, the circumstances in which the applicant found herself homeless are not uncommon. *Kelly* therefore provides a useful precedent for those seeking to persuade authorities to adopt a more humane approach to the problems of the young single homeless.[56] Second, by rejecting the evidence of the

---

54. 1986 SLT 169.
55. See also *R. v. Waveney Borough Council, ex p. Bowers* [1983] QB 238 and *R. v. Bath City Council, ex p. Sangermano* (1984) 17 HLR 94.
56. See, for example, S. Venn, *Singled Out* (CHAR, 1985) and Young Homeless Group, *Moving On Moving In* (YHG, 1985).

police on the possibility of exploitation Lord Ross appears to place a very onerous burden of proof on housing authorities to establish that such a risk does not exist in their areas.[57]

Kelly can be usefully contrasted with the decision of Lord Clyde in *Steventon v. Monklands District Council* [58] which also considers the question of vulnerability of young homeless people. In this case the applicant was an unemployed 16 year old boy who had left the family home after quarreling with his step-father. There was no question of physical violence towards him at that time but he had a disturbed background and had been involved in child abuse hearings two years prior to his application. Enquiries with the social work department who were giving him support revealed that he was able to look after himself even though his social worker regarded him as vulnerable. In view of this evidence, Lord Clyde upheld the decision of the authority that he did not have a priority need because of vulnerability.

(d) Assessing vulnerability

In assessing whether an applicant is vulnerable because of mental illness or handicap or physical disability the Code of Guidance[59] states that in some cases it will be appropriate for authorities to seek the help of district health authorities and social services authorities (in Scotland, area health boards and regional social work departments).

In this context it is noteworthy that the principal reason for the different decisions made by the Court of Session in *Kelly* and *Steventon*[60] arose from the housing authority's failure to have regard to the advice given by the social work department in *Kelly* and the fact that in *Steventon* they did not have regard to the advice offered by the social work department. As Lord Clyde explained in *Steventon*, providing an authority has regard to such advice they are entitled to come to a different conclusion as to the inference to those drawn from the circumstances and personal history of the applicant.

(i) Evidence of vulnerability

In *R. v. Bath City Council, ex p. Sangermano* [61] the applicant was a middle-aged Italian woman of subnormal intelligence who found it

---

57. E. Hunter, 'Victory that Opens the Door for Young Homeless', *Glasgow Herald*, 15 June, 1985.
58. [1987] GWD 15-576.
59. SC 2.13(c); EC 2.12(c).
60. *Kelly v. Monklands District Council* 1986 SLT 169 and *Steventon v. Monklands District Council [1987] GWD 15-576.*
61. (1984) 17 HLR 94.

extremely difficult to understand or communicate in English. Her mental handicap and the severe language difficulties under which she laboured were made clear to the housing authority in letters to them from her solicitor and her doctor. However, the housing authority simply were not prepared to consider her as being vulnerable on the ground that there was no evidence of vulnerability. This finding was declared invalid by Mr. Justice Hodgson who criticised the authority's cavalier approach to the evidence of subnormality provided by her doctor and solicitors:

> "If one reads the solicitors' letter and the medical evidence supplied, it is plain that either they ought to have accepted that this lady was subnormal or, if they were not sure about the degree of subnormality or whether it was present at all, they ought to have made inquiries, which they did not do. It seems to me, therefore, clear that in the ways I have described the local authority did not properly instruct itself in coming to the decision it did and was in error of law in that respect."

It would seem therefore that where medical evidence of vulnerability is presented to housing authorities they must not only take the evidence into account but, if they seek to reject it in whole or in part, they should seek another medical opinion as to the nature and degree of vulnerability. If medical opinions diverge in respect of the vulnerability of the applicant, the authority faces a clear dilemma.

(ii) Conflicting medical opinion

The case of *R. v. Tandridge District Council, ex p. Hayman* [62] established that, where there is a conflict of medical opinion in respect of vulnerability of an applicant, it is for the authority to determine on the evidence before it whether or not the applicant is vulnerable as it is their responsibility and that of doctors to adjudicate in this matter.

In this case the applicant claimed to be vulnerable as a result of mental illness. He had been admitted to hospital in October 1982, having attempted suicide by taking an overdose of tablets. The consultant psychiatrist at the hospital evidently took the suicide attempt seriously and considered him to be vulnerable, adding that she would be very worried if he were homeless. Her opinion, however, was not accepted by the senior medical officer with the community health area authority who examined the applicant on behalf of the housing authority.

The housing authority, faced with conflicting medical opinion about the vulnerability of the applicant, decided that on the evidence before them the applicant was not vulnerable within the meaning of the legislation. The decision was upheld by Mr. Justice McNeill on the

---

62. (QBD) 29 September, 1983.

ground that it was not an unreasonable decision for the authority to make upon the material before them.

Similarly, in *R. v. Wandsworth Borough Council, ex p. Banbury* [63] where the applicant was a 49 year old man who suffered from grand mal epilepsy, the housing authority were faced with a conflict of medical evidence between the applicant's neurologist who supported his claim that he was vulnerable and the Medical Officer of Health who advised the authority that he was not vulnerable because of the infrequency of attacks of epilepsy. Mr. Justice Russell held that on the evidence before them the housing authority were entitled to conclude that the applicant was not vulnerable *provided*, he emphasised, they took the decision themselves and did not merely "rubber-stamp" the decision of the Medical Officer of Health.

However, in *R. v. Lambeth Borough Council, ex p. Carroll* [64] Mr. Justice Webster held that the decision of a housing authority that an applicant was not vulnerable was unlawful as it was based solely upon the advice of the medical officer and proper inquiries had not been made:

> "[I]t was its function, and no one else's, to decide whether an applicant was vulnerable or not and its duty, in order to be able to satisfy itself whether a homeless person has a priority need, to make all necessary inquiries."

In appropriate cases, Mr. Justice Webster added, it may also be necessary for the authority to seek the opinion of experts in housing or social welfare as well as medical experts before making a decision.

Hayman and *Banbury* in effect follow the line developed by the Social Security Commissioners (formerly National Insurance Commissioners) in respect of cases where there is a conflict of medical opinion over a claimant's entitlement to sickness benefit. [65] In contrast *Carroll* follows the well-known administrative law principle that the decision-making body may not delegate decision making to another body or person or body not authorised to make the decision on their behalf. [66]

The decision of a housing authority, or indeed any other statutory body, to reject expert professional opinion, particularly where the opinion is that of a doctor or psychiatrist, or to prefer the opinion of one professional to that of another should not be taken lightly and may be open to challenge if they fail to give adequate reasons for it. [67]

---

63. (1987) 19 HLR 76; see also *R. v. Reigate and Banstead Borough Council, ex p. Di Domenico, The Independent,* 21 October, 1987.
64. *The Independent,* 8 October, 1987.
65. See R(S) 15/54; R(S) 16/54; and R(S) 6/78.
66. See 'Remedies for the Homeless' *below* at pp. 208-242.
67. *Metropolitan Properties Co. (FGC) Ltd. v. Lannon* [1969] 1 QB 577; *Albyn Properties Ltd. v. Knox* 1977 SLT 41.

(e) Pregnancy

A homeless person or a person threatened with homelessness who is a pregnant woman or resides or might reasonably be expected to reside with a pregnant woman, has for the purposes of the legislation a priority need for accommodation. This need arises irrespective of the age of the applicant or length of time of the pregnancy.[68] The *date of decision* is the material point in time when priority need is to be assessed. A subsequent miscarriage or termination of pregnancy therefore does not affect the priority need of the applicant on this ground. However, a miscarriage or termination between the date of *application* and *decision* is relevant and the applicant is obliged to disclose this change of circumstances.[69]

---

68. However, Motherwell District Council sought to avoid their responsibilities towards pregnant women on the grounds that "when other young people see [pregnant women receiving priority treatment] it puts ideas into their heads" and the Council had a "responsibility not to encourage immorality" *Sunday Mail,* 18 November, 1979, "Why Single Girls want Babies", and *The Guardian,* 17 September, 1982.
69. See 'Processing Applications' above at pp. 57-81.

Chapter 5
Intentional Homelessness

This test[1] was introduced at the Report stage of the Bill to allay the fears of some local authorities and M.P.s that individuals would attempt to improve their housing conditions by voluntarily giving up accommodation in order to be housed before others on the council waiting list. The evidence for this practice before 1977 did not point to it being a significant phenomenon[2] nor has the situation altered.[3]

In practical terms a housing authority may restrict their obligations to individuals who are deemed to have become homeless intentionally. It is up to the authority to establish that the applicant became homeless intentionally. An applicant is not required to establish that he became homeless unintentionally.

The major implication for an applicant who is homeless and in priority need but who is deemed to have become homeless intentionally is that the housing authority are only required to provide accommodation for a temporary period to enable the applicant to secure accommodation for himself and his family. The amount of time which is required is not laid down in the legislation and will vary from area to area and family to family.[4]

---

1. Section 60 of Housing Act 1985; section 26 of the Housing (Scotland) Act 1987.
2. See 'Homelessness and the Law' *above* pp.25-45.
3. R. Widdowson, *Intentional Homelessness*, Shelter (1981). The major reasons for homelessness continues to be problems between families (72%) no longer being able to accommodate applicants, or disputes. Rent arrears appear to account for 4.1% of loss of accommodation and court orders for 5.4% of loss of insecure accommodation (*Scottish Housing Statistics*, (HMSO, 1986 at 43).
4. In *Lally v. Kensington and Chelsea Royal Borough, The Times*, 27 March, 1980. Browne Wilkinson J. considered that two weeks to find accommodation in London was quite inadequate and that three to four months might reasonably be required or even longer. These longer periods of time are found in the cases of *Youngs v. Thanet District Council* (1980) 78 LGR 474 and *Dyson v. Kerrier District Council* [1980] 3 All ER 313, although the date from which the period is computed may be at issue as in *Dyson*.

The concept of intentional homelessness continues to exercise an influence out of all proportion to the small number of applicants who each year are assessed by housing authorities to have become homeless or threatened with homelessness intentionally. Having said that, however, it is necessary to examine the legal interpretation of this concept in some detail because of its fundamental importance in determining the response of housing authorities to the needs of the homeless.

Duty to the Ratepayers
In determining whether an applicant is intentionally homeless the courts have emphasised that housing authorities have a duty to ratepayers and persons on the housing waiting list to prevent queue-jumping.[5]

The Onus of Proof
The legislation imposes a duty upon housing authorities to satisfy themselves that an applicant became homeless or threatened with homelessness intentionally and it follows, therefore, that the onus of proof rests with the authority to establish that an applicant became homeless intentionally. It is not for the applicant to establish the negative. The onus is discharged upon the balance of probabilities.[6] Therefore, where a housing authority failed to consider whether accommodation in Italy was available for occupation by a couple and their family or if it was reasonable for them to continue to live there, the court held that they had not discharged the onus of proof.[7]

Before a housing authority may make a finding of intentional homelessness they are required to satisfy themselves as to the following questions:

(1) Was accommodation available?
(2) If accommodation was available was it accommodation which it would have been reasonable for the applicant to continue to occupy?
(3) Did the applicant deliberately do or fail to do anything in consequence of which he ceased to occupy such accommodation?

All these aspects of the test must be satisfied before a housing authority are entitled to make a finding of intentional homelessness.

---

5. See *Din v. Wandsworth London Borough Council* [1983] 1 AC 657; *R. v. Wandsworth London Borough Council, ex p. Nimako-Boateng* (1984) 11 HLR 95; and *R. v. Eastleigh Borough Council, ex p. Evans* (1984) 17 HLR 515.
6. See *R. v. Westminster City Council, ex p. Rahman* (QBD) 9 June, 1983.
7. See *R. v. Reigate and Banstead Borough Council, ex p. Paris* (1984) 17 HLR 103; and *R. v. Wandsworth London Borough Council, ex p. Rose* (1984) 11 HLR 107.

1. Accommodation Must Have Been Available To The Applicant

The authority must investigate whether or not accommodation was available before a lawful determination of intentional homelessness can be made. As we have emphasised, the failure to address this issue will result in the determination being deemed to be invalid.[8]

Accommodation is only treated as available for a person's occupation if it was available both to him and to any other person who might reasonably be expected to reside with him, i.e. it must be available for the "family unit".[9]

Those who might reasonably be expected to reside with the applicant include both members of the family, cohabitees and foster-children as well as housekeepers and companions for elderly or disabled persons.

The accommodation in general must be available to the applicant in one location and be of sufficient size to accommodate the "family unit". Although this might seem self-evident this point was raised in the case of *Islam v. Hillingdon London Borough Council.* [10]

In this case Tafazzul Islam came to England in 1965 and worked and lived in England from that time. In 1968 he married whilst on holiday in Bangladesh and returned to visit his wife on a number of occasions. His wife and children lived in his father's home until he was able to obtain entry certificates for his wife and family. Since he came to Britain before 1973[11] he did not require to show that accommodation was available for the family. He arranged temporary accommodation for his wife and family and when he was evicted he applied for accommodation to the homeless families unit of Hillingdon London Borough Council.

Initially the Court of Appeal suggested that Mr. Islam had accommodation which was available for occupation by his family unit. The House of Lords overturned this decision taking the view that Islam's shared single room in England never had been "available accommodation" and that he had never occupied the Bangladesh accommodation.

Although the facts of this case were rather unusual the same principle would apply to determine whether accommodation is available to a family where the breadwinner worked in one part of Britain and the family resided in another.

An authority must not assume that because accommodation was once available to an applicant that it remains so. The failure of a housing

---

8. See *R. v. Reigate and Banstead Borough Council, ex p. Paris* (above) and *R. v. Wimbourne District Council, ex p. Curtis* (1985) 18 HLR 79.

9. See "Processing Applications" above at pp.57-81 *R. v. Lambeth London Borough Council, ex p. Ly* (1987) 19 HLR 51.

10. [1983] AC 688.

11. *Statement of Changes in Immigration Rules,* 20 February, 1980 (HC 394), para.42.

authority to make inquiries as to whether accommodation was available to a family led to their decision being held to be unlawful in *R. v. Westminster City Council, ex p. Ali.* [12] In this case the housing authority decided that the Alis had become homeless intentionally on the ground that they had voluntarily left available accommodation without securing alternative accommodation. The accommodation in question was a 12ft by 10ft room in which the applicant lived with his wife and five children. One of the factors which led the housing authority to form this conclusion was that some years before when he had occupied this room with his wife and three of his children (then aged 7, 2 and 4 months) the applicant had refused an offer of rehousing. This assumption was held to be unlawful to him, given the increase in the number and ages of his children:

> "...Westminster City Council were under a statutory duty to ask itself whether it was satisfied that the accommodation... was available to Mr. Ali and his family before he gave it up at the end of 1981. It seems to me that either [the housing officer] never considered it at all or he simply assumed that, because the family had been able to stay there in 1976-77 and... 1979-80 that they would be able to do so again. What Mr. Ali gave up at the end of December 1981 was, on the evidence, no more than the right to share one room with another man. There was no evidence at all before the Westminster City Council that accommodation was available for him, his wife and their five children.... I find, therefore, that no reasonable authority could, upon the material before it, have reached the conclusion that there was, at the end of December 1981, accommodation available for the whole family...."

An applicant cannot be held to be intentionally homeless on the ground that he previously refused an offer of permanent accommodation for a housing authority. Before an applicant can be found to be intentionally homeless he has to cease to occupy accommodation which is available for his occupation. [13] Therefore, where a single parent refused an offer of accommodation but later approached the same housing authority for assistance it was held that it was unlawful for the authority to find her to have become homeless intentionally. [14] As Lord Justice Ackner explained:

> "If Parliament had intended section 17 of the [1977] Act to apply to an unreasonable refusal of accommodation made by a Housing Authority, it could simply have so provided by an additional sub-section... there is no proper analogy between the applicant who unreasonably ceases to occupy accommodation which is available to him, thereby causing the accommodation to be lost... and the applicant who is unintentionally homeless and is in priority

---

12. (1983) 11 HLR 83.
13. See *Din v. Wandsworth London Borough Council* [1983] 1 AC 657; *R. v. Westminster City Council, ex p. Chambers* (1983) 81 LGR 401; *R. v. Rydedale District Council, ex p. Smith* (1983) 16 HLR 66; and *R. v. Ealing London Borough Council, ex p. McBain* [1986] 1 All ER 13.
14. See *R. v. Ealing London Borough Council, ex p. McBain* (above).

need, but refuses unreasonably the Council's offer of accommodation. His unreasonable conduct causes no loss of accommodation, it merely causes a waste of administrative time and effort...."

However, it may be the case that by offering appropriate accommodation to the applicant the authority have fulfilled their duty towards the applicant, and are not obliged to do any more[15] unless a material change in the applicant's circumstances makes the original offer unsuitable.[16]

2. Accommodation Must be Reasonable for the Applicant to Continue to Occupy

There are two aspects to this test:

(i) condition of housing, and
(ii) personal circumstances.

(a) Condition of housing

The legislation suggests that there may be circumstances where people justifiably leave accommodation because of the condition of their housing, e.g. there may be overcrowding or a lack of basic amenities. However, no specific guidelines are given by the legislation or the Code such as reference to the "tolerable standard"[17] or unfitness for human habitation to indicate when it would be reasonable to give up unsatisfactory accommodation.

In determining the reasonableness of accommodation authorities may have regard to the general circumstances prevailing in relation to housing in their area. That means they may look to the general housing conditions of the area, e.g. whether there are many people in the area living in worse conditions than the applicants and the number of persons on their housing waiting list.

In addition, the House of Lords have indicated that scarcity of housing is a factor which is relevant in determining whether a person in financial difficulties is entitled to move before their occupation is threatened by court action. The question of whether or not a person had to wait until a possession order was granted before leaving accommodation, depended,

---

15. See *R. v. Hammersmith and Fulham London Borough Council, ex p. O'Brian* (1985) 17 HLR 471.
16. See *R. v. Ealing London Borough Council, ex p. McBain* (above).
17. Section 86 of the Housing (Scotland) Act 1987 defines tolerable standard to cover structural stability; freedom from rising or penetrating damp; satisfactory lighting ventilation and heating and hot and cold water supply to sink; internal w.c. for exclusive use of occupants; effective drainage system; satisfactory cooking facilities, and satisfactory access to all external doors and outbuildings.

in the view of Lord Fraser, in *Din v. Wandsworth London Borough Council,* [18] on overall housing conditions and prevailing demand for accommodation in the areas of the housing authority. In this case the Din family quit accommodation attached to a failing take-away food business and moved in with relatives to avoid incurring further rent and rate arrears. Observing that accommodation in the area of Inner London is very scarce the House of Lords suggested that it was not reasonable for the Dins to quit their accommodation. However Lord Fraser stated that if the same issue had arisen in another part of the country where accommodation was under less pressure the position might have been different.

A recent example of how this "balancing exercise" can operate to the detriment of homeless persons is *R. v. Peterborough City Council, ex p. McKernan.* [19] This case arose from the decision of two families — one Protestant and one Roman Catholic — to flee from intimidation in Northern Ireland. Notwithstanding the very real predicament in which these families found themselves Mr. Justice Mann held that, taking into account the housing scarcity in their area, the authority were entitled to conclude that it was reasonable for them to continue to live in Northern Ireland.

In assessing whether it was reasonable for an applicant to continue living in available accommodation, it is also necessary for an authority to consider the condition of the housing which he left. For example, the failure of a housing authority to consider whether it was reasonable for a family of six to continue to live in a two-bedroomed house led to their decision being quashed in *R. v. Eastleigh Borough Council, ex p. Beattie.* [20]

However, if an authority take into account the condition of the housing vacated by an applicant they are entitled to have regard to the statutory definitions of unfitness and overcrowding. This follows from the decision of the High Court in *R. v. Eastleigh Borough Council, ex p. Beattie* [21] where the housing authority in assessing whether the Beatties' home was in fact overcrowded had regard to the standards of overcrowding laid down by the Housing Act 1957[22], a practice later approved by Mr. Justice Webster:

---

18. [1983] AC 637 at p.671. Lord Fraser in fact observed that the scarcity of accommodation in Inner London was a matter "within judicial knowledge". The implication of this observation is that no evidence needs to be led on this issue since it is assumed the judiciary are aware of the situation, Walker A.G. and Walker N. *The Law of Evidence in Scotland* (1964) at p.47 and *Cross on Evidence* (5th ed.) 1979, p.154, refer to "facts judicially noted without inquiry". See also *Tickner v. Mole Valley District Council* (1980) LAG 187; and *R. v. Hammersmith and Fulham London Borough Council, ex p. Duro-Rama* (1983) 81 LGR 702.

19. (QBD) 17 July, 1987; *R. v. Hillingdon London Borough Council, ex p. H, The Times,* 17 May, 1988 and *R. v. London Borough Council Tower Hamlets, ex p. Monaf, The Times,* 28 April, 1988.

20. (1983) 10 HLR 134. See also *R. v. Preseli District Council, ex p. Fisher* (1984) 17 HLR 147 and *R. v. Reigate and Banstead Borough Council, ex p. Paris* (1984) 17 HLR 103.

21. (1984) 17 HLR 168.

22. See now section 324 of the Housing Act 1985; section 135 of the Housing (Scotland) Act 1987.

"Although I take into account the fact this legislation relates not to homeless persons but to the relationship between landlord and tenant, and the fact that if the maximum permitted number of units is exceeded a criminal offence is committed, nonetheless those figures do seem to be figures which must be regarded as having some relevance to this question and certainly something the... Authority was entitled to take into account."

The question of whether it was reasonable for an applicant to continue to live in overcrowded or unsatisfactory accommodation was also discussed in *Ali* [23] and *R. v. Bristol City Council, ex p. Lester.* [24]

In *Ali* the second issue before the Court was whether, if as the authority had assumed, the 12 ft by 10 ft room in which the applicant's family lived was available for their occupation, it was reasonable for them to continue to live in that overcrowded accommodation. The authority's view on this question was, as has already been stated, that as they had previously refused an offer of housing when there were only three children, it was still reasonable for them to continue to live there. Mr. Justice McCullough rejected this view on the grounds that since the date of their refusal of that offer two other children had been added to the family and that the ages of the five children had increased:

"At the end of 1981 there were children of twelve, seven, four and four months. By the time he applied in August 1982 these were nearly thirteen , nearly eight, five, two and one. Even if one starts from the premise that it was reasonable for husband, wife, seven year old, two year old and baby to live in one room [in 1977], it does not follow that it was reasonable for husband, wife, twelve year old, seven year old, four year old, one year old and baby all to live in one room."

Indeed, Mr. Justice McCullough expressed the view that it was astonishing that anyone should regard it as reasonable that a family of that size should continue to live in one room measuring 12ft by 10ft and added that in the absence of the evidence that the general housing circumstances in the area were so desperately short that it was reasonable to accept such gross overcrowding he was driven to the conclusion that the question of reasonableness was not properly determined.

In *Lester* a couple decided to terminate their tenancy of damp council premises and to move in with relations despite being warned by a housing official of the possible consequences of their action. In taking this course of action the Lesters were influenced by three main factors; the unwillingness of the council to grant them a housing transfer, mounting rent arrears, and a deterioration in the health of their family. Of the three factors, it would appear that the most influential was the deterioration of

23. (1983) 17 HLR 168.
24. (QBD) 22 February, 1984.

the health of their baby son, who had been admitted to hospital on two occasions — on the first occasion because of a respiratory infection and on the other occasion because he had contracted pneumonia — and whose poor health, their doctor stated, was partly attributable to the severe dampness in the house.

Four months after terminating their tenancy, the Lesters applied to the housing authority for assistance. Notwithstanding the damp condition of the house and a letter from their doctor explaining that the dampness was a cause of the baby's ill health, the housing authority found the Lesters to have become homeless intentionally on the ground that their decision to leave was prompted by their failure to clear their outstanding rent arrears and their resulting inability to obtain a housing transfer, adding that they did not believe that the dampness of the premises was their genuine reason for leaving the accommodation or, if it was their genuine reason, that it gave them sufficient reason for leaving. Mr. Justice Hodgson, while upholding the housing authority's decision on the grounds that the authority had considered whether in the circumstances it was reasonable for them to remain in accommodation and that their decision was not a perverse one, suggested that the authority reconsider the position of the applicants:

> "In February of 1983 Mr. and Mrs. Lester, on any view of the matter, were behaving in a rash and foolish fashion, the local authority, as they have been for some months, were extremely considerate of them and gave them every opportunity to step back from their foolish decision and not to place themselves in the position in which they now find themselves. Since the decision there has been evidence which tends to show that the flat was somewhat more damp than perhaps appeared from the evidence before the Committee and also it is now clear that the doctor, whose short letter was before the Committee, did in fact go to the premises. In those circumstances, I can perhaps not without impropriety express the hope that this local authority might look again at the position of the Lesters."

All of which seems to suggest that whilst removing their six month old baby form the source of his pneumonia may have been "foolish", the Lesters should not be penalised for taking that action.

In terms of housing conditions there is clearly an overlap between the questions of the availability of accommodation and the reasonableness of continuing to occupy accommodation. For example, accommodation may be so grossly overcrowded that it is *both* unavailable for occupation by an applicant and his family and not reasonable for him to continue to occupy it.[25]

---

25. *R. v. Westminster City Council, ex p. Ali* (1984) 11 HLR 72; *Krishnan v. London Borough of Hillingdon* (1981) SCOLAG 307; *R. v. Reigate and Banstead Borough Council, ex p. Paris* (1984) 17 HLR 103.

Similarly, problems caused by unemployment may be relevant in determining whether it is reasonable for a person to continue to occupy accommodation available for occupation. In *R. v. Hammersmith and Fulham London Borough Council, ex p. Duro-Rama,* [26] the applicants were Spanish nationals with a right of abode in this country. They had lived in the UK from 1964 until 1979 when they returned to Spain to care for a relative. In Spain they built a house but were unable to obtain a mains water supply. The husband's entitlement to unemployment benefit lapsed in early 1981 and being without any means of support the family returned to Britain where the husband obtained work and a flat to rent. Later the family were evicted from their accommodation and applied for housing. The Council, however, held that they were intentionally homeless because they voluntarily left accommodation in Spain which it would have been reasonable to continue to occupy. This finding was challenged in the High Court on the ground that the Council should have taken into account that the family had left Spain because of the lack of employment prospects and social security benefits. In rejecting the Council's contention that only the applicant's housing circumstances were relevant, Mr. Justice Woolf, observed that section 17(4)[27] of the Housing (Homeless Persons) Act 1977 was couched in permissive language and was not to be regarded as exhaustive. Hence, the housing authority in deciding on intentionally, had to have regard to the applicant's employment prospects and the lack of social security benefits available in the country he left.

While the principle laid down in *Duro-Rama* that employment prospect is a relevant matter to be considered by a housing authority in determining if it was reasonable for an applicant to continue to occupy accommodation has been accepted as valid, later cases do not show that this principle is rigorously applied. For example, in *Mazzaccherini v. Argyll and Bute District Council* [28] Lord Jauncey rejected the submission that it was incumbent on the authority to make exhaustive inquiries into the labour market in Glasgow as compared to Dunoon for a person with the applicant's qualifications and in *R. v. Kensington and Chelsea Royal London Borough Council, ex p. Cunha* [29] Mr. Justice Otton stated that to require the housing authority to inquire into employment conditions in Brazil would be to place an unwarranted burden on them.

(b) Personal circumstances of applicant

Apart from the question of the physical condition of the housing viewed

---

26. (1983) 81 LGR 702.
27. See now section 60(4) of the Housing Act 1985 and section 26(4) of the Housing (Scotland) Act 1985.
28. 1987 SCLR 475.
29. *The Independent,* 21 July, 1988; *The Times,* July 18, 1988.

in the context of the overall housing conditions in the area, there are circumstances where applicants will not be expected to remain in accommodation which is available to them because of personal factors. The Code envisages that where conditions have degenerated to such a point that they are causing severe emotional stress it would not be reasonable to expect someone to stay on in the property. The physical condition of the housing here is material but what is crucial is the physical or emotional state of the applicant.[30]

Related to this is the special position of women who have been the victims of domestic violence. The Code states that battered women should never be regarded as having become homeless intentionally in such circumstances because it would clearly not be reasonable for a woman to remain with a violent partner.[31] Two areas of concern which have been highlighted in litigation in recent years are non-violent marital difficulties and non-domestic violence or intimidation.

(i) Non-violent marital difficulties

Where there are marital difficulties of a non-violent nature, whether or not it is reasonable for an applicant to leave the matrimonial home would appear to turn on her personal circumstances and the availability of legal redress in respect of occupation of the matrimonial home.

In *R. v. Wandsworth London Borough Council, ex p. Nimako-Boateng* [32] a pregnant mother left her husband in Ghana and returned to this country where she stayed in temporary accommodation with relatives. Later she applied to the housing authority for housing as a homeless person but the authority determined that she had become homeless intentionally because she had come to this country without ensuring that settled accommodation was available to her. One of the reasons given by the applicant for leaving Ghana was that her marriage had broken down because her husband had been treating her badly, although he had not been violent towards her. The Court therefore had to consider whether in these circumstances the authority were entitled to find that it was reasonable for the applicant to continue to live in the matrimonial home. Mr. Justice Woolf held that they were entitled to reach that conclusion:

"In considering the matrimonial home, what was relevant was the marital conduct to which the applicant was subjected by her husband whilst she was living there. Of course, there could be conduct on the part of the husband, who could not be prevented from entering the home, which could make it quite impossible for the wife to continue to occupy that accommodation.... The

---

30. SC para.2.17; EC para.2.16.
31. *Ibid.*
32. (1984) 11 HLR 95.

conclusion that [the housing officer] came to was that there was no fear of any violence and, on that basis, he formed the opinion that it would be reasonable for the applicant to remain in the accommodation provided by the matrimonial home... that is a conclusion to which the authority were fully entitled to come."

In effect this disposed of the application, but Mr. Justice Woolf added that in this country where "there is all sorts of protection that a woman can get if her husband misbehaves" it is reasonable for an authority to take the view that it is reasonable for a wife to continue to live in the matrimonial home with her husband and to rely on the wife to seek legal redress:

"The local authority could perfectly properly in many cases in this country take the view that it would be reasonable for the wife to continue to occupy accommodation and to say to a wife, if she thinks it right: 'If you are having trouble with your husband, go to the appropriate authority, be it a magistrates' court or the Family Division, and get protection against your husband'. If the woman does not then take that course and choose to leave, the authority could then take the view that it was reasonable for the lady to remain."

This sweeping *obiter* remark should not be interpreted by authorities as justifying decisions of intentional homelessness in all cases where a woman refused or fails to exercise her legal remedies in respect of the matrimonial home. Indeed, it would be quite wrong to apply it to the case of battered women and in other cases it might be quite unrealistic to leave it to the woman to take court action where there is severe marital stress.[33] For, as *R. v. Basingstoke and Deane Borough Council, ex p. Bassett* [34] demonstrates, it is also necessary for a housing authority to consider the human situation in which applicants may find themselves. In this case a couple whose marriage was foundering decided that it would be best for them to make a fresh start in Canada. They therefore gave up the tenancy of their council flat and went to stay with an aunt in Canada while the husband sought employment. However, their application to stay in Canada permanently was refused and some months later the family were deported.

On their return to England they stayed with the husband's sister but their marriage rapidly deteriorated and the following month they separated. Divorce proceedings were initiated and a year later Mrs. Bassett obtained a decree nisi against her husband on the ground of his unreasonable behaviour. Little more than a month afterwards the friends with whom Mrs. Bassett was staying decided to move and gave her notice to quit. The applicant therefore approached the authority for assistance under the legislation. However, the authority, as they had done on a previous

33. *R. v. Eastleigh Borough Council, ex p. Evans* (1984) 17 HLR 515, and *R. v. Purbeck District Council, ex p. Cadney* (1985) 17 HLR 534.
34. (1983) 10 HLR 125.

occasion, decided that the applicant had become homeless intentionally when she and her husband voluntarily terminated the let of their council house to go Canada. That finding was deemed unlawful by Mr. Justice Taylor on the ground that the authority had failed to consider the personal circumstances of the applicant at the time when the accommodation was given up:

> "[The authority] failed in this case to take into account the human element; the human situation of a marriage which was in danger of foundering and the human situation of a wife doing her best to follow her husband and hold the marriage together. I find it quite impossible to say that any reasonable authority could have regarded what she did as being unreasonable, or would have regarded it in the circumstances as reasonable if she had continued to stay whilst her husband departed for Canada."

The *Bassett* case, therefore, establishes that in some circumstances it is reasonable for an applicant to give up available accommodation in an attempt to deal with marital difficulties such as, in this case, the avoidance of marital breakdown. However, it is thought that these cases will turn on their special circumstances. For example, in *R. v. Eastleigh Borough Council, ex p. Evans* [35] where a woman left her husband following an unsuccessful reconciliation attempt because they were not able to live together, Mr. Justice McNeill upheld the decision of a housing authority that she had become homeless intentionally. Describing the *Bassett* case as a high watermark in the sympathetic treatment of women applicants, he stated that, in the absence of matrimonial violence or severe emotional stress as outlined in the Code, the authority were entitled to find that she became homeless intentionally because she failed to accept their advice and exercise her legal remedies in respect of the matrimonial home. This, we believe, appears to penalise the applicant for attempting a reconciliation and follows the tenuous line developed in other cases that where legal remedies exist in respect of the matrimonial home an applicant will be expected to exercise them. This is a view which in some cases may be wholly unrealistic.

(ii) Non-domestic violence or intimidation

In *R. v. Hammersmith and Fulham London Borough Council, ex p. Duro-Rama,* [36] Mr. Justice Woolf held that, in assessing whether it was reasonable for an applicant to continue to live in available accommodation, housing authorities are entitled to take account of non-housing circumstances, such

---

35. (1984) 17 HLR 515; see also *Hynds v. Midlothian District Council* 1986 SLT 54.
36. (1983) 81 LGR 702. *Mazzaccherini v. Argyll and Bute District Council* 1987 SCLR 475 and *R. v. Royal Borough of Kensington and Chelsea, ex p. Cunha, The Times,* 18 July, 1988; *The Independent,* 21 July, 1988.

as, in that case, the lack of employment prospects and the non-availability of social security benefits. Although *Duro-Rama* in removing these obvious impediments to labour mobility represents a major breakthrough, its impact in other areas appears to be limited. For example, in *Fezoui v. Torbay Borough Council*[37] an applicant gave as her reason for leaving her flat in Algeria the very unpleasant living conditions in that country and, in particular, the Moslem attitude to women, which she found to be totally alien to the way in which women are treated in the Western world. She later expanded on this statement, explaining that there had been threats of violence or violence from local children; no facilities for women, such as theatres and cafes, and that the beaches there were mainly for men. Notwithstanding the difficulties which living in a Moslem culture posed for a Western woman, the housing authority found that she and her husband had become homeless intentionally because they deliberately chose to give up their flat in Algeria to come to this country without ensuring that there was settled permanent accommodation for them here.

When this case was heard before the Court of Appeal it was argued on the basis of *Duro-Rama* that in these circumstances the authority were wrong to conclude that it was reasonable for them to continue to live in Algeria because of the intolerable conditions in which they lived. This submission was rejected by the Court of Appeal. While they did not deal directly with the question of whether *Duro-Rama* had been correctly decided, it was held that the authority were entitled to reach the conclusion that they did on the evidence before them at the date of the application:

> "...the duty of assessing the weight to be attached to the evidence and the weight to be attached to other considerations relevant to the decision is for the Council and not for this Court. It is only when circumstances are such that this Court can say that the decision is so wholly unreasonable that no Council directing itself properly to relevant considerations could have arrived at such a conclusion that this Court interferes. I find myself quite unable to say that in evaluating the weight to be attached to that letter and taking into account that no attempt had been made to ascertain the state of housing in Torbay or the chance of getting accommodation in Torbay no reasonable council could conclude that these applicants gave up their accommodation in circumstances which made them intentionally homeless."

The same conclusion was reached by Mr. Justice Glidewell in *R. v. Hertsmere Borough Council, ex p. Sedaghat.*[38] In this case the applicant was an English woman who had married an Iranian and had lived with him and his parents in Tehran. Their marriage was not a happy one and there was a brief separation in 1980 when she, and later her husband, were housed in a caravan by the housing authority. Some months later her

---

37. (CA) 27 July, 1983.
38. (QBD) 7 March, 1984.

husband decided to return to Tehran and in order to keep their marriage together she accompanied him. Unfortunately, although the present political regime had been established at the time of her first visit to Tehran, when she returned she found that there was even greater hostility towards Europeans:

"On the first visit to Tehran, before my marriage, life was reasonably tolerable, but when I returned to Tehran in August 1981 the attitude to Europeans had deteriorated markedly and I found very considerable prejudice against Europeans on my second visit. Whenever I went out into the street I was spat at by Iranian women and stones were thrown at me by students. Frequently, if accompanied by my husband in his car, the car would be stopped and searched because I was Western in appearance.... On one occasion when I was walking in the street I was stoned by a student who shouted 'death to American women'."

In view of the violence and intimidation she had experienced the applicant decided to leave Tehran with her children and return to this country to stay with her parents. However, her parents' house was already overcrowded and she therefore approached the housing authority for assistance. Her application was refused on the ground that she had become homeless intentionally. As a result of her first application to the High Court, Mr. Justice Woolf asked the authority to reconsider her application for assistance. However, having reconsidered the matter, they did not alter their determination because, in their view, she had settled accommodation in Tehran which was available for her occupation and which was reasonable for her to continue to occupy. In so finding the authority relied on the fact that she had lived in Tehran on an earlier occasion and had knowledge of the conditions there and therefore should have known the problems faced by Western women in that country. In short, they concluded that when she returned to Tehran she knew what she had let herself in for. Counsel for the applicant argued on her behalf that her knowledge of the general situation there was an irrelevant consideration to the assessment of whether it was reasonable for her to continue to live in her husband's parents' house. This submission was rejected by Mr. Justice Glidewell as was another submission that their decision was so unreasonable that no reasonable authority could have come to it. While he had some sympathy for the applicant he stated that he was not convinced that their decision came into this category:

"...I am not sitting as a Court of Appeal. It is not for me to say what I would have found if I were the Council's Committee, or if I had the task of saying whether I thought the Council's Committee decision was right or wrong. Clearly, there was material upon which the Council could have found that a decision to leave was reasonable and not unreasonable, and thus that it would not have been reasonable for her to continue to occupy, but they found the opposite."

"The question is: Can I say, faced with the evidence which was properly before them, advised as they were properly as to the matters, they had to take into account, that no sensible council could properly come to the decision to which they came? I regret to say I cannot."

Both *Fezoui* and *Sedaghat* show that whereas the *Duro-Rama* principle may be accepted in relation to employment prospects and the non-availability of welfare benefits it does not appear to stretch as far as living conditions which are unpleasant because of cultural differences or which for similar reasons are made difficult because of general hostility towards and intimidation of groups of people (such as Western women in Moslem countries).

There is some doubt, however, if this principle is also inapplicable to non-domestic violence and intimidation within the United Kingdom. Three cases may be cited to illustrate the point that it is inapplicable: *R. v. The Vale of White Horse District Council, ex p. Preen* [39] and *R. v. Warwick District Council, ex p. Wood,* [40] both of which concerned applicants fleeing from threatened violence in Glasgow, and *R. v. Peterborough City Council, ex p. McKernan* [41] which concerned families fleeing from intimidation in Northern Ireland. In *Preen* the threat of violence came in the form of a letter from the applicant's estranged wife who wrote to the applicant informing him that he should leave the council flat of which she was tenant and warning him of the repercussions if he did not do so:

"I don't care where you go but don't stay in Glasgow and don't come back or you will be *sorry.*
P.S. If you are not out by 28th January I will put you out by force."

The applicant took his wife's threat seriously and requested Glasgow District Council to grant him a housing transfer. This request was refused and the applicant and his three children decided to leave Glasgow and return to his home town of Shoreham in the Vale of White Horse. After staying briefly with his parents he was asked to leave and thereafter approached the housing authority for assistance. The housing authority contacted Glasgow District Council and were informed by them that they were willing to make arrangements for housing the applicant, either by way of a temporary tenancy of his wife's flat or in their homeless family unit, pending the grant of alternative accommodation. The applicant, however, was reluctant to return to Glasgow because of his wife's threat and refused Glasgow's offer. Notwithstanding the threat of violence and the fact that when the applicant had left Glasgow he was not aware of his

39. (QBD) 18 April, 1983.
40. (QBD) 15 August, 1983; see also *R. v. Croydon London Borough Council, ex p. Toth* (1986) 18 HLR 493.
41. (QBD) 17 July, 1987.

legal rights, the housing authority concluded that he had become homeless intentionally. The issue before the court was whether it was reasonable for an authority to conclude that it was unreasonable for Mr. Preen to leave his home in Glasgow in these circumstances. While accepting that Mr. Preen's position was an extremely difficult one, Mr. Justice Woolf held that the decision of the housing authority was a lawful one:

> "...it seems to me that on the information that was put before Mr. Wood [the Director of Housing of Vale of White Horse District Council] he was equally entitled to take a different view. He was entitled to say that a father of three children being put in a position where he received a letter of this nature should make full enquiries before he vacates the matrimonial home with his three children... if he had done that he would have learnt that Glasgow were perfectly content to ensure that he had permanent accommodation, as they are, and that it was quite unreasonable for Mr. Preen to leave Glasgow in these circumstances."

The *Wood* case is an even more extreme example of threatened violence. In this case the Woods lived in Easterhouse in Glasgow until May 1982. However, on 24th May Mrs. Wood's brother-in-law, with a gang of ten or twelve men wielding knives and other weapons, came to their home and threatened them with violence. The Woods reported the incident to the police but no action was taken. They therefore decided to take flight to London where they applied to the London Borough of Chiswick for accommodation, but were advised to return to Glasgow. The Woods therefore returned to Glasgow and requested a housing transfer but the District Council were not prepared to grant a transfer to an area outside Easterhouse. In June the Woods again left Glasgow, on this occasion for Leamington Spa where they applied to the housing authority for assistance. The housing authority also contacted Glasgow District Council and as a result of their inquiries were informed that the Woods had accommodation available to them in Easterhouse and, if they returned to Glasgow, they might be considered for a housing transfer to an area outwith Easterhouse. The authority therefore found that they were not homeless as they had the tenancy of a council house in Easterhouse and advised them to return to Glasgow.

The Woods returned to Glasgow, formally gave notice terminating the tenancy of their house in Easterhouse, and later returned to Leamington Spa where they re-applied to the housing authority for assistance under the legislation. The housing authority on this occasion concluded that they had become homeless intentionally because of their voluntary surrender of their tenancy in Easterhouse. Later explaining that a "strong factor" in reaching their decision was the advice given by Glasgow District Council that despite their problems it would be reasonable for them to resume occupancy of their home in Easterhouse and that as the type of violence of which the applicants complained was not in their view the kind envisaged by the legislation, the Woods' remedy was to seek assistance from the police.

The finding of intentional homelessness was attacked on the ground that the authority had unlawfully reached the conclusion that it was reasonable in these circumstances for the Woods to continue to live in their home in Easterhouse; and, in particular, that the housing authority had failed to regard the violent threats made to the applicants as being material (i.e. that they had failed to take account of a relevant consideration) and that they had not made their own inquiries about the threats of violence but had wrongly accepted the decision of Glasgow District Council on this matter. This submission was rejected by Mr. Justice Glidewell who held that the authority had taken the threats of violence into consideration and that, while housing authorities must make their own inquiries, they were entitled to rely on the advice tendered to them by Glasgow District Council[42]:

> "[W]here a housing authority in the Midlands of England is confronted with a couple who had come from Glasgow, who had just given up a tenancy of Glasgow council accommodation, it seems to me to be manifest that the main source of information for the Warwick Council would be bound to be Glasgow District Council, and having received information from Glasgow District Council they were wholly justified in relying on it."

In addition, Counsel argued that, given the threats of violence that had been made to the couple and their ignorance of the fact that Glasgow District Council were willing to consider them for a housing transfer to an area outwith Easterhouse, no reasonable authority could have formed the conclusion that they were unjustified and unreasonable in giving up their accommodation. This submission was also rejected by Mr. Justice Glidewell. Indeed, he went on to say that:

> "[T]he prime responsibility for ensuring their safety must lie in the first place, on the police force in Glasgow and, in the second case, the responsibility for moving them, if they were to be moved, would seem to me must lie on the responsibilities of the Glasgow District Council."

The third case, *McKernan,* arose from the flight of two families — one Protestant and one Catholic — from intimidation in Northern Ireland. The head of the first family had served in the armed forces during the Falklands War and both he and his family had experienced considerable hostility from the Roman Catholic community in which they lived, culminating in the family being evacuated from their home due to a bomb scare. The second family was a Roman Catholic family living in a

---

42. See also *R. v. Bristol City Council, ex p. Browne* [1979] WLR 1437.

119

Protestant community who had been advised by the police to leave the area for their own safety. Despite the hostile environment in which they lived Mr. Justice Mann held that it was lawful for the housing authority to conclude that it was reasonable for the families to continue to live in Northern Ireland.

These cases, however, must now be contrasted with the decision of Mr. Justice Kennedy in *R. v. Hillingdon London Borough Council, ex p. H.*[43] In this case the applicant, an ex-soldier, left Northern Ireland because he and his family were being harassed and intimidated by the I.R.A. One of the grounds on which the housing authority found the applicant to have become homeless intentionally was that the harassment and intimidation being of a non-domestic nature was not relevant to the determination of the question whether it was reasonable to continue to occupy accommodation in Northern Ireland. Mr. Justice Kennedy, however, held that their decision was unlawful as there was nothing in the legislation which would entitle the authority to disregard harassment in assessing whether it was reasonable for the applicant to continue to occupy accommodation simply because it was not of a domestic nature.

Although the majority of these cases make depressing reading, and it could be said demonstrate the insensitivity of both councils and the judiciary to the reality of violence and intimidation, further support for the view that non-domestic violence or threats of violence may make it reasonable for a person to leave available accommodation can be gleaned from the judgement of Mr. Justice Woolf in *R. v. Wandsworth London Borough Council, ex p. Nimako-Boateng.*[44] While in this case the decision of the housing authority that the applicant had become intentionally homeless when she left Ghana without first ensuring settled accommodation was available to her in this country was upheld, Mr. Justice Woolf did envisage that persons fleeing from political persecution or oppression might reasonably leave available accommodation without becoming homeless intentionally[45]:

"Where for some political reason, perfectly satisfactory accommodation in Ghana becomes accommodation which a particular person cannot reasonably be expected to continue to occupy, that is something which, in my view, the housing authority would be entitled to take into account when considering the obligations and duties it owes when executing its functions under s.17 of the Housing (Homeless Persons) Act [1977]."

It would appear from the case of *R. v. Crawley Borough Council, ex p. The Mayor and Burgesses of the London Borough of Brent* [46] however, that

---

43. *The Times,* 17 May, 1988.
44. [1984] 11 HLR 95.
45. Now section 60 of the Housing Act 1985; section 26 of the Housing (Scotland) Act 1987.
46. (QBD) 24 March, 1983.

the courts place great weight on whether an applicant has acquired political refugee status. In this case one of the issues before the court was whether a Ugandan family was entitled to permanent accommodation under the Act. In their application they had represented that they had to flee from Uganda because they feared for their lives. Although they had been allowed by the Foreign Office to stay on in this country beyond the time period for temporary residents they had not been granted the status of political refugees. Following the view expressed in *R. v. Hillingdon London Borough Council, ex p. Streeting* [47] that only persons who were lawfully in this country are persons within the meaning of section 1(1) of the 1977 Act, Mr. Justice McNeill held that as the applicants had not acquired the status of political refugees the authority were not under a duty to provide them with accommodation:

> "Although the Kavuma family deliberately left their house in Uganda, if it were established that they had refugee status in the United Kingdom it could be reasonably inferred that they could not return to that home and they would therefore be homeless and unintentionally homeless in England. Until then, however, it is plain to my mind that they did not qualify as persons to whom the Act applied. If this refugee status were not established, the departure from the home in Uganda would have been not only deliberate but intentional within the meaning of the Act."

In our view this is an unfortunate decision because it places undue emphasis on whether the applicant has been awarded refuge status by the Foreign Office, a decision which is not always clearly based on non-political considerations, rather than whether or not there was a risk of violence abroad. Nonetheless, its practical implications for those advising homeless immigrants are important and should be carefully considered.

In addition to non-violent marital difficulties and non-domestic violence and intimidation the question whether the personal circumstances of an applicant make it unreasonable for him or her to continue to occupy available accommodation has also been raised in other contexts. For example, in *R. v. Hillingdon London Borough Council, ex p. Wilson* [49] the question before the court was whether it was reasonable for a pregnant woman to continue to occupy accommodation in Australia when it would have been contrary to their immigration laws for her to remain there. In this case the applicant had been informed that when her temporary visa expired permission to stay there would not be granted. At this time she was nearing the date of her confinement and therefore decided to return to her parent's home in England rather than wait to be deported. However, when she approached the authority for assistance, the authority decided that she had

47. [1980] 1 WLR 1430.
48. Now section 58(1) of the Housing Act 1985; section 24(1) of the Housing (Scotland) Act 1987.
49. (1984) 12 HLR 61.

become homeless intentionally because she had deliberately left accommodation in Australia which was available to her and which it would have been reasonable for her to continue to occupy. Mr. Justice Woolf quashed this decision on the ground that this decision was one which no authority could reasonably have made. Distinguishing this case from *De Falco* [50] he stated:

> "This lady is an English national, who had no right to remain in Australia and was coming back to this country. What is more, having regard to the fact that she was in Australia, it really would have been difficult for her to make arrangements for her accommodation in this country. In any event, it does not seem to me that the failure to make those arrangements can detract from my conclusion that she could not reasonably remain in Australia when it would have been contrary to the assurance that she had given to the immigration authorities that she would not make a further application for leave to remain." [51]

The other context in which the question of whether it was reasonable for an applicant to continue to occupy available accommodation has been discussed relates to circumstances where an applicant voluntarily relinquishes occupancy of accommodation without forcing his landlord to obtain an order of possession or physically to evict him. In circumstances where there would be no defence to an action of possession the revised Code of Guidance[52] advises that "it is counter-productive and may cause hardship to treat as intentionally homeless [an occupier]... who leaves before a court order has actually been obtained."

As the case law on this question is discussed elsewhere it is sufficient to state that the courts have held that it is unlawful for an authority to treat an applicant as being intentionally homeless if he has no defence to possession proceedings and vacates premises without putting his landlord to the needless expense of obtaining an order of possession or evicting him on the ground that in these circumstances it was not reasonable for the applicant to continue to occupy the accommodation.[53]

A final area which must be considered in the context of reasonableness to continue to occupy accommodation surprisingly is the "lifestyle" of the applicant. In *R. v. Tower Hamlets London Borough Council, ex p.*

---

50. *De Falco v. Crawley Borough Council* [1980] QB 460.
51. *R. v. Wandsworth London Borough Council, ex p. Wells* (QBD) 23 November, 1983.
52. EC A 1.3; but see the problem encountered when Maureen Archibald had to get a court order before South Hertfordshire would provide her with accommodation. Her husband, Hibs striker Steve had stopped paying rent some four months before and there were arrears of £4,336, *Daily Record*, 22 October, 1988.
53. See *R. v. Mole Valley District Council, ex p. Minnett* (1984) 12 HLR 49; *R. v. Portsmouth City Council, ex p. Knight* (1983) 82 LGR 184; *R. v. Surrey Heath Borough Council, ex p. Li* (1984) 16 HLR 79; *R. v. Exeter City Council, ex p. Gliddon* (1985) 1 All ER 493; *Din v. London Borough of Wandsworth* [1983] 1 AC 657.

Monaf [54] the housing authority decided that it was reasonable for Bangladeshi families to continue to live in Bangladesh because the applicants who had indefinite leave to remain in the U.K. had lived for long periods with their families in Bangladesh. In upholding this decision Lord Donaldson M.R. opined that the authority were entitled to have regard to "the lifestyle of members of the Bangladeshi community in London who have come here to earn a living and then return to Bangladesh every few years for a prolonged period on each occasion in order to marry and to raise a family."

3. Deliberately Doing or Failing to do Something in Consequence of Which the Applicant Ceases to Occupy Accommodation

An authority must satisfy themselves on three distinct matters before they can proceed to make a finding of intentional homelessness. If they are not satisfied on any one of these issues then they cannot make an intentional homelessness finding. The matters which they must consider are:

(a) deliberate acts or omissions;
(b) acts or omissions in good faith and ignorance of any relevant fact; and
(c) homelessness in consequence of deliberate acts or omissions.

(a) Deliberate acts or omissions

Before an applicant can be deemed homeless intentionally or threatened with homelessness intentionally the housing authority must establish that the acts or omissions in question are deliberate.

In recent cases the view that the word deliberate qualifies acts or omissions only and that it is therefore unnecessary for an authority to establish that the applicant had intended to induce his homelessness would appear to have been accepted by the courts. [55]

R. v. Salford City Council, ex p. Devenport [56] is authority for the view that the word "deliberate" qualifies acts or omissions only and therefore it is unnecessary for a housing authority to go on to establish that the act or omission was intended to bring about eviction. In this case the

---

54. *The Independent,* 28 April, 1988.
55. (1984) 82 LGR 89.
56. See also *Robinson v. Torbay Borough Council* [1982] 1 All ER 726; *Zold v. Bristol City Council* (1981) LAG 287; *Jones v. Bristol City Council* (1981) LAG 163; *R. v. Croydon London Borough Council, ex p. Webb* (QBD) 14 December, 1983; *R. v. Slough Borough Council, ex p. London Borough of Ealing* [1981] QB 801.

children of the tenant had been guilty of extreme acts of vandalism and violence, including assaults on neighbours. In spite of warnings from the Council that eviction would take place if the Devenports did not control their children, their anti-social behaviour continued and the family eventually was evicted. When the Devenports applied to the Council for accommodation the Council held them to be intentionally homeless on the ground of their persistent failure to control their children. This finding was upheld by the Court of Appeal.

Likewise, in *R. v. Penwith District Council, ex p. Kevern,* [57] Mr. Justice Woolf stated that:

> "[C]learly, if a person consciously fails to make payments under a mortgage they must appreciate that a likely result of this conduct is that the person to whom mortgage repayments should have been made will bring proceedings for possession and will seek to enforce the mortgage."

(i) Involuntary acts or omissions

Where an act or omission is involuntary or largely attributable to external factors then the Code of Guidance[58] states that the act or omission should not be regarded as being deliberate:

(i)   where a person was obliged to sell his home because he could not keep up the mortgage repayments, or got into rent arrears, because of real personal or financial difficulties or because he was incapable of managing his affairs on account of old age or mental illness;

(ii)   where homelessness is the result of serious financial difficulties arising, for example, from loss of employment or greatly reduced earnings;

(iii)   an owner-occupier inescapably faced with foreclosure who sells before the mortgage recovers possession through the courts;

(iv)   a battered woman who has fled the marital home;

(v)   a woman who becomes pregnant;

(vi)   people who have been driven to leave their accommodation, e.g. because of a drop in income;

(vii)   people who have been driven to leave their accommodation, because conditions have degenerated to the point where they could not in all the circumstances be expected to remain — perhaps because of overcrowding or lack of basic amenities or severe emotional stress;

(viii) a person who loses tied accommodation because the employment

---

57. (QBD) 14 December, 1984; see also *R. v. Gillingham District Council, ex p. Loch* (QBD) 17 September, 1984; *R. v. Eastleigh Borough Council, ex p. Beattie* (1984) 17 HLR 168; and *R. v. West Somerset District Council, ex p. Blake* (QBD) 10 July, 1986.
58. SC 2.16-2.17; EC 2.15-2.16.

has ended through no fault of his own; and

(ix)   a person who has voluntarily resigned from the job in circumstances where it would not have been reasonable for him to continue in that employment.

As most of these examples of non-deliberate homelessness are dealt with elsewhere we propose to discuss only the most salient examples here.

a. Real personal or financial difficulties

Whereas the Code stresses that it would be inappropriate to treat persons who get into rent arrears or do not keep up their mortgage repayments because of real personal or financial difficulties as being intentionally homeless it is necessary to locate this advice within the overall context of rent or mortgage arrears.

The first point which can be made is that, provided an authority are satisfied that "the person has taken the action which has led to the loss of his accommodation with full knowledge of the likely consequences,"[59] a person who chooses to sell his home, or who has lost it because of *wilful and persistent refusal* to pay rent, will in most cases be regarded as having become homeless intentionally.[60] Although the view has been expressed that the non-payment of rent or mortgage arrears need not be wilful and persistent[61] that view has not been followed in other cases. In *R. v. Wyre Borough Council, ex p. Joyce,* [62] for example, both parties accepted the proposition that where a person loses his accommodation due to non-payment of rent or mortgage instalments it is right that the person has become homeless intentionally if the failure to make those payments can be regarded as wilful default by him. On this basis Mr. Justice Forbes overturned the decision of the housing authority on the ground that they had failed to ascertain the applicant's reasons for default and therefore were not in a position to establish if the default had been wilful; a matter which he believed was necessary to establish intentional homelessness:

"It must be wilful default because you have got to be homeless intentionally."

Secondly, the existence of real personal or financial difficulties may not be sufficient in itself to displace a finding of intentional homelessness because it is also necessary to examine the way in which people respond to such difficulties and their capacity to deal with them. In *R. v. Cannock*

---

59. EC 2.15.
60. See *Tickner v. Mole Valley District Council* LAG (1980) 187; *Robinson v. Torbay Borough Council,* [1982] 1 All ER 726; and *R. v. Penwith District Council, ex p. Kevern* (QBD) 14 December, 1984; *R. v. Eastleigh Borough Council, ex p. Beattie* (1983) 10 HLR 134 and (1984) 17 HLR 168.
61. See *Zold v. Bristol City Council* LAG (1981) 287.
62. (1984) 11 HLR 73; see also *R. v. Gillingham Borough Council, ex p. Loch* (QBD) 17 September, 1984; *R. v. Croydon London Borough Council, ex p. Webb* (QBD) 14 December, 1984.

Chase Borough Council, ex p. McIlhatton [63] a mother of six children was evicted from council accommodation for non-payment of rent. Her rent arrears arose from the failure of her taxi business which became insolvent due to the decision of the Council not to renew hackney-cab licences for two of the three taxis which she owned. Faced with financial difficulties from the insolvency of her business, costly appeals against refusal to renew the licences, and the birth of two children with a year, she argued that she could not be regarded as wilfully failing to pay rent and hence that the decision of the housing authority that she was intentionally homeless was unlawful. While the court expressed sympathy towards the applicant in the "sad situation" in which she found herself, it was held that the decision of the housing authority was lawful. During the period when she was experiencing financial difficulties, it was stated, she had made no real endeavour either to reduce her arrears or to make alternative arrangements with the housing authority; a response which was regarded as being inadequate, given the applicant's obvious knowledge of business affairs and her dealing with the Council, and the fact that she was receiving legal advice concerning her appeals over the refusal of the hackney-cab licences:

> "The applicant, throughout 1981 and 1982 until, at any rate, 20th July, had not made any real endeavour to reduce the arrears of rent or to make some alternative arrangements with the Council. Moreover, this was after repeated warnings.... She could not have been in ignorance of the fact that her continued failure to deal with the arrears of rent was likely to render her liable to eviction... the applicant was apparently in touch with solicitors who had been acting for her in relation to the taxi business during the relevant period. She was not a person who was without knowledge of business affairs and of dealing with the Council."

b. Leaving accommodation early where there is no effective alternative
Both the courts and the Code of Guidance[64] recognise that where an occupant has no defence to possession proceedings and therefore faces the inevitability of losing his accommodation, he should not be treated as being intentionally homeless because he did not remain in the property until an order of possession was obtained or he was physically evicted. This is not to say that owner-occupiers or tenants who are facing financial difficulties will be justified in voluntarily relinquishing their homes to ease those problems. In *Din v. Wandsworth London Borough Council* [65] the House of Lords held that, despite the fact that the applicant would have been homeless by the date of his application, a housing authority were entitled to find that an applicant had become homeless intentionally, when, in the face of repeated advice from the authority that his family

---

63. (QBD) 9 February, 1983; *R. v. Rushmoor Borough Council, ex p. Lloyd* (QBD) 15 April, 1983.
64. SC 3.5; EC A 1.3.
65. [1983] 1 AC 657.

could not be evicted from their accommodation unless their landlord obtained an order for possession, he voluntarily relinquished the let of the dwelling to ease his financial problems.[66]

However, a finding of intentional homelessness will not be held to be lawful where the loss of accommodation is inevitable even if the applicant ignores advice from the housing authority that he should stay. In *R. v. Mole Valley District Council, ex p. Minnett* [67] the decision that an applicant had become homeless intentionally when she left her accommodation one day before a possession order took effect was held to be unlawful. Mr. Justice McCullough stated that the reasoning of the authority that she was intentionally homeless because she did not stay on until the bailiffs actually turned her out was plainly wrong.

In the case of licences or service occupancies, where the occupiers have very limited rights of security, the position adopted by the courts would appear to be that it is unreasonable for an authority to insist that the full course of the legal process should run before the applicant vacates the property.

In *R. v. Portsmouth City Council, ex p. Knight* [68] the applicants were formerly employed to managed a shop in Blackheath and had been granted a licence to occupy the flat above it. The licence specifically provided that they should not be entitled to exclusive possession of the premises. In October 1982 their employment was terminated and they were paid four weeks' salary in lieu of notice. Wishing to avoid any "hassle" with their employers, the Knights vacated the property voluntarily and went to live with Mrs. Knight's parents. Her parents' accommodation was grossly overcrowded and in January 1983 they applied to the authority for assistance. Relying on *Din* and the considerable pressure on council accommodation in their area, the authority decided that the Knights had become homeless intentionally. Mr. Justice Woolf held this decision to be unlawful on the grounds that the authority had failed to distinguish between tenants, who have extensive rights to remain in occupancy, and licensees, whose rights are of a much more restricted nature, and had failed to have regard to the position of their employers who would be forced to seek a possession order against them and the applicants who would then be in the position of a trespasser:

---

66. See, for example, *R. v. Penwith District Council, ex p. Hughes* (1980) LAG 188, and *R. v. Bristol City Council, ex p. Lester* (QBD) 22 February, 1984.

67. (1984) 12 HLR 49.

68. (1984) 82 LGR 184. On the importance of the nature of company rights in respect of the property vacated and, in particular, the importance of "settled accommodation" see also *De Falco v. Crawley Borough Council* [1980] QB 460; *Dyson v. Kerrier District Council* [1980] 1 WLR 1205; *Lambert v. London Borough of Ealing* [1981] 1 WLR 550; *R. v. South Hams District Council, ex p. Proctor* (QBD) 24 September, 1986; *Mazzaccherini v. Argyll and Bute District Council* 1987 SCLR 475; and *R. v. Tower Hamlets London Borough Council, ex p. Monaf, The Times,* 28 April, 1988.

"I am bound to say, that for myself, I would have regarded a service licensee who, at the end of his employment, leaves the accommodation, as doing something in consequence of which he ceases to occupy the accommodation, but would have, in normal circumstances, the greatest difficulty in regarding him as leaving accommodation which it would have been reasonable for him to occupy."

"When an employee has a service occupancy, then on the termination of that licence, he becomes a trespasser if he remains in the accommodation. Unlike the service tenant or other tenant, he does not have the right to remain in occupation provided by the Rent Act."

In reaching this decision Mr. Justice Woolf also took the opportunity to remind authorities that *Din* was not, as had been suggested in a number of cases, authority for the proposition that whenever a person occupying accommodation leaves the accommodation without forcing the owner to obtain a possession order, he is rendering himself intentionally homeless. *Din,* he stated, does not go "anywhere as far as that".

The same principle was followed in *R. v. Exeter City Council, ex p. Gliddon.* [69] The facts of this case are somewhat complex even by the standard of complexity of homelessness cases but can be stated briefly. The applicants obtained a tenancy through deception. When their landlord discovered the deception he agreed to allow them to remain in the premises provided they surrendered their tenancy in exchange for a licence which consequently resulted in a reduction in their rights of security of tenure. At this stage the applicants sought advice from the housing authority and were advised not to surrender their tenancy without taking legal advice. However, the applicants ignored their advice and surrendered the tenancy. Subsequently, the landlord obtained an order of possession in respect of the premises and the applicants were evicted. The applicants therefore approached the authority for assistance but the authority found them to be intentionally homeless because of their surrender of the tenancy. The issue before Mr. Justice Woolf was whether, in view of their deception, it would have been reasonable for them to continue to occupy the accommodation. Mr. Justice Woolf held that it would not:

"Where you have a situation where a person has only obtained accommodation... by deception, and the landlord on discovering that deception requires the person concerned to surrender their lease, the consequences must be that that person has no possible justification for refusing to do so. In my view, it is almost inevitable that if this is required by the landlord, it would be unreasonable for him to continue to occupy the accommodation against the wishes of the landlord. He would have no defence in law to a claim for possession by the landlord. It would be adding to the harm which has already

69. [1985] 1 All ER 493.

been done to the landlord to require the landlord to bring proceedings to obtain possession in those circumstances...."

Similarly, in *R. v. Surrey Heath Borough Council, ex p. Li* [70] an authority found that applicant had become intentionally homeless when, contrary to the advice of the authority, he voluntarily left shared accommodation. In this case Mr. Li had lived and worked as a waiter in the authority's area for over ten years prior to going to the North East of England to start a business. The business failed and he returned to the area of the authority as his former employer had found him accommodation. The accommodation provided, however, was extremely cramped. Mr. Li lived in one room (11ft by 16ft) with his pregnant wife and two year old son and his elderly grandmother slept in the sitting room. They shared a kitchen, bathroom and toilet with two other families.

In September 1983 he applied to the authority for housing stating that when the baby was born it would be intolerable for them to continue to live in such conditions. The baby was born in October 1983 so that at this time there were four persons (two adults, a young child, and a baby) living in one small room. In January 1984 he found work as a waiter in a Chinese restaurant and was asked by the owner to leave the shared accommodation. Although he had been advised by the housing authority on a number of occasions not to leave the accommodation because it was necessary for the owner to obtain a court order to evict him, Mr. Li voluntarily left the shared accommodation. On the ground that he did so in the face of their advice that a court order for possession must be obtained against him and no threat of "strong-arm tactics" had been made, the housing authority held that the applicant had become homeless intentionally. Mr. Justice Hodgson quashed their decision as the advice given to Mr. Li was erroneous and contrary to the case law[71] and the Code of Guidance:[72]

"Where it is clear from the facts that tenants [and it follows mere licensees] have no defence or counterclaim to an application for possession, authorities should not insist that an order [for possession] is obtained, and a date for eviction set, before agreeing to help the tenant. It is counterproductive or may cause hardship to treat as intentionally homeless a tenant who is in such a position but who leaves before an order has actually been obtained."

These cases establish three important points. First, where an occupier has no legal right of occupation (viz he is in virtually the same position as a trespasser) there is no accommodation which is available for his occupation

---

70. (1984) 16 HLR 79.
71. See *Din* and *Knight* (above).
72. EC para. A 1.3.

and it is not reasonable for him to continue to occupy it. The alternative, of course, would be to force applicants or the State to incur legal costs in defending actions for possession which would be doomed to failure. Secondly, housing authorities cannot rely on an applicant's failure to comply with erroneous advice as grounds for finding an applicant to have become homeless intentionally. Thirdly, it demonstrates that *Din* is not authority for the proposition that when an applicant voluntarily relinquishes accommodation without a court order having been obtained or in the face of housing authority advice he necessarily becomes intentionally homeless. In addition, it must be said, that *Li* demonstrates once again the difficulties which housing authorities have in determining the legal status of occupancy and the need for housing authorities to develop expertise in this area.[73]

c. Failure to make arrangements before leaving settled accommodation
Where a person leaves accommodation in circumstances where it would be unreasonable to expect him to arrange for alternative accommodation prior to his departure, it would be wrong for an authority to find that he became homeless intentionally. The most obvious example is a woman who flees the matrimonial home because of domestic violence.[74] However, in general the position appears to be that unless an applicant makes such arrangements prior to leaving available accommodation he is very likely to be found to be intentionally homeless.[75]

Since 1983 a large number of cases have been heard in which the question of whether it was reasonable to leave available accommodation without first arranging that *settled* accommodation would be available was central to determining whether findings of intentional homelessness were lawful. As many of these cases have been discussed elsewhere it is only proposed to outline the law on this subject.

d. Non-domestic violence or intimidation
As we have seen in general the courts have been loathe to accept that applicants are entitled to leave their homes when faced with non-domestic violence or intimidation without first making arrangements for settled accommodation in another place.[76] In *Preen*,[77] for example, where the applicant left Glasgow after receiving a threatening letter from his estranged wife without making arrangements for settled accommodation

---

73. See [1984] JSWL 372-373; *Street v. Mountford* [1985] AC 809. *Hadjilucas v. Crean* [1987] 3 All ER 1008; *A.G. Securities v. Vaughan; Antoniades v. Villiers, The Independent,* 11 November, 1988.
74. SC 2.17; EC 2.16.
75. See *De Falco v. Crawley Borough Council* [1980] QB 460; *Dyson v. Kerrier District Council* [1980] 1 WLR 1205 and *Lambert v. Ealing London Borough Council* [1982] 1 WLR 550.
76. See *Fezoui; Sedaghat; Preen; Wood; Nimako-Boateng; The Mayor and Burgesses of the London Borough of Brent; Toth; McKernan; ex p. H* (above).
77. (QBD) 18 April, 1983.

it was held that his action was precipitate and that the authority were entitled to find that he became homeless intentionally:

> "[I]t seems to me that on the information that was put before Mr. Woods [the Director of Housing of Vale of White Horse District Council] he was equally entitled to take a different view. He was entitled to say that a father of three children being put in a position where he received a letter of this nature should make full enquiries before he vacates the matrimonial home with his three children... if he had done that he would have learnt that Glasgow were perfectly content to ensure that he had permanent accommodation, as they still are, and that it was quite unreasonable for Mr. Preen to leave Glasgow in the circumstances."

e. Returning from abroad

It would also appear that persons coming or returning from outwith Great Britain will normally be expected to arrange for settled accommodation before leaving accommodation there. *R. v. Westminster City Council, ex p. Rahman* [78] echoes the findings of the Court of Appeal in *De Falco*. In this case the applicant was a Bangladeshi with citizenship of the United Kingdom and Colonies. He lived in England from 1963 to 1973 but then returned to Bangladesh where he lived for ten years. Having obtained entry certificates in October 1982, he returned to England with his wife and family in April 1983, one week before the certificates' expiry date. On 14 April, some eight days after his arrival, he approached the authority's Homeless Persons Unit for assistance under the Act, explaining that his friend from whom he rented accommodation had asked him to leave and that he was now staying in overcrowded temporary accommodation with another friend in London who had also asked him to leave. The crux of the matter was whether the housing authority were entitled to find that he became homeless intentionally because he voluntarily gave up the accommodation he occupied in Bangladesh. In essence this required the authority to consider (i) whether the accommodation was available for his occupation in Bangladesh, and (ii) if so, whether it was unreasonable for him to give it up.

On the question of the availability of accommodation Mr. Justice McNeill stated that:

> "That accommodation was available and only ceased to be available because he left, but would have been available to him until he chose to accept, if he did choose to do so, the opportunity of returning to this country... he chose when to make no longer available to him accommodation which was, and would have continued to be, available for him, if he had not taken his air flight to England.... While I am prepared to recognise that that accommodation might not have been as attractive as accommodation in either London W1 or London

---

78. (QBD) 9 June, 1983. *R. v. Hillingdon London Borough Council, ex p. H, The Times,* 17 May, 1988.

E1, that of itself does not mean it was not available to him. It was accommodation available for him which he chose to leave when he did leave."

Having decided that the authority were entitled to find that the accommodation in Bangladesh was available for his occupation, the second question to be considered was whether it was reasonable for him to continue to occupy it. This required the authority to weigh up three factors: his desire for resettlement in England, his exercise of choice of date of return, and his failure to make satisfactory arrangements for accommodation on his return. Of these three factors, Mr. Justice McNeill stated, the last was the most significant:

"He had at least 5 1/2 months in which to make arrangements for accommodation here. It would, to my mind, be wholly unreasonable for him not to make any arrangements at all...."

This decision is not unsupportable but it gives rise to some anxiety as it appears from the court transcript that there was scant information on the nature and adequacy of the accommodation occupied in Bangladesh. Moreover, although the applicant had not made any arrangements for accommodation in this country, the plight of a family saving against time to make use of entry certificates which they had waited for a long period to obtain was a matter which might have figured more prominently in the deliberations of the authority and the court. Nevertheless, this general approach to the question of leaving settled accommodation abroad appears to have found favour with the Court of Appeal in their now notorious decision in *R. v. Tower Hamlets London Borough Council, ex p. Monaf.* [79]

A similar finding was also made in *R. v. Wandsworth London Borough, ex p. Wells.* [80] In this case the applicant decided to return from Australia to this country in the hope of improving his job prospects. His father had offered to accommodate the applicant and his family but the applicant did not enquire about the size of his father's accommodation or how long they could remain there.[81] The accommodation proved to be inadequate for his family and he approached the authority for assistance. However, the authority held that he had become homeless intentionally because he left settled accommodation in Australia without making any provision for settled and secure accommodation.

That finding was upheld by Mr. Justice Nolan who stated that as the authority had taken account of all the relevant considerations, including the very tentative arrangements made for accommodation in this country, they had not erred in law.

---

79. *The Times,* 28 April, 1988.
80. (QBD) 23 November, 1983.
81. *R. v. Wandsworth London Borough Council, ex p. Rose* (1984) 11 HLR 105.

It would seem from *Rahman, Monaf* and *Wells* that in general before leaving available accommodation abroad it is essential that settled accommodation in Great Britain is secured. However, these cases can be usefully contrasted with *R. v. Hillingdon London Borough Council, ex p. Wilson* [82] in which it was held that the failure of a pregnant woman (who risked contravention of the Australian immigration laws) to arrange settled accommodation in this country before returning was not sufficient to justify a finding of intentional homelessness:

> "This is not a situation of the sort that existed in... *De Falco...*, where Italian nationals left Naples to come to England to look for work. This lady is an English national, who had no right to remain in Australia and was coming back to this country. What is more, having regard to the fact that she was in Australia, it really would have been difficult for her to make arrangements for her accommodation in this country."

(ii) Voluntary acts or omissions

The legislation talks of acts being deliberate rather than voluntary so that it can be suggested that for acts or omissions to be termed deliberate they must be both the product of the free will of the individual and the consequence of a calculated decision. So how does one judge whether a decision is calculated or not? As the subsections dealing with those who are homeless and those threatened with homelessness employ different wording, these need to be examined separately:

a. Homeless

For those who are already homeless the relevant provision[83] reads:

> "...a person becomes homeless intentionally if he deliberately does or fails to do anything in consequence of which he ceases to occupy accommodation."

In assessing whether or not a person's acts or omissions can be termed deliberate, two possible lines of approach have been put forward — a subjective and an objective approach. The issue was discussed in an *obiter* statement by Lord Denning in *R. v. Slough Borough Council, ex p. London Borough of Ealing* [84] who favoured a subjective approach. Talking of the conduct of tenants evicted for non-payment of rent and arrears over a number of years, Lord Denning stated:

> "Their non-payment of rent was deplorable, but it may not have been

---

82. (1984) 12 HLR 61.
83. Section 60(1) of the Housing Act 1985; section 26(1) of the Housing (Scotland) Act 1987.
84. [1981] QB 801.

'deliberate' in the sense required by s.17(1)[of the Housing (Homeless Persons) Act 1977]. The family did not do it deliberately so as to get turned out."[85]

The subjective test, however, was rejected in a later case involving arrears of rent by His Honour Judge Goodall as follows:

"I think that if a man has been evicted then... he became homeless intentionally, if the fair-minded bystander could say to himself, 'He asked for it,' ...if his conduct is such as to drive his landlord to evict him, and if the fair-minded bystander can say of the person evicted, 'Well, I'm very sorry but he asked for it.'"[86]

The argument here is between a subjective test and an objective one - what consequences the homeless applicant himself may have intended his acts or omissions to have, as opposed to the view which the "reasonable man" might take as to what consequences are likely to flow from the same acts or omissions. In our view the subjective test would seem to be more in keeping with the spirit of the legislation, but the weigh of authority now clearly favours the objective test.

In *R. v. Salford City, ex p. Devenport*, [87] for example, the Court of Appeal dealt with a case where tenants who persistently failed to take any steps to control their children were evicted by Salford City Council. When they applied for assistance as homeless persons they were deemed intentionally homeless. The failure to exercise control over their children was stated to amount to deliberate acts in consequence of which they ceased to occupy accommodation.

Two distinct questions were involved here. Firstly did the Devenports deliberately do or fail to do something? If they did, then, was their ceasing to occupy the accommodation a consequence of these deliberate acts or omission?

As far as the acts or omissions being deliberate was concerned Lord Justice Fox looked at the various grounds in Salford City Council's possession action — (i) acts of vandalism by the children; (ii) threats and actual use of physical violence by Mr. and Mrs. Devenport against persons living in the neighbourhood; (iii) Mr. Devenport's threat to stab a neighbour and members of her family; (iv) the daughter's physical attack on a neighbour's son; (v) an attack by Mrs. Devenport and two of her children on a neighbour and her daughter; and (vi) the Devenport family repeatedly shouting abuse at neighbours. He concluded that:

"There was ample evidence on which the council could conclude that Mr. and

85. *Ibid.* at p.810.
86. *Robinson v. Torbay Borough Council* [1982] 1 All ER 726 at p.730.
87. (1984) 82 LGR 89.

Mrs. Devenport had deliberately failed to take any steps to control their children, and that would be quite sufficient to justify the council's resolution [that the Devenports were intentionally homeless] whatever the position as to the acts of the parents themselves."

b. Threatened with homelessness

The wording varies slightly between subsections (1) and (2) dealing with those already homeless when the authority make their decision about intentionally and those only threatened with homelessness.[88]
Subsection (2) states:

> "[A] person becomes threatened with homelessness intentionally if he deliberately does or fails to do anything *the likely result of which* is that he will be forced to leave accommodation..."

The insertion of the words "the likely result" has meant that some judges have seen a clear distinction in the tests to be applied to determine if acts or omissions are to be judged deliberate. In a case involving a tenant with a long history of rent arrears *Zold v. Bristol City Council,*[89] the court took the view that acts or omissions were only caught by subsection (2) if being forced to leave accommodation has a certain degree of likelihood. This, Judge Fallon suggested, should be judged by an objective test — would a reasonable council in such circumstances take steps to force the person to leave?

In *Jones v. Bristol City Council*[90] Judge Fallon reiterated this test. Here he was dealing with a tenant who had withheld rent because of the appalling state of the homeless accommodation which the Council had provided. Applying the "reasonable council" test to the question of whether or not eviction was likely, he decided that no reasonable council would have said that the likely result of withholding rent to get repairs carried out by the council would be that the family would be forced to leave the accommodation.

Later in 1981 Judge Goodall took a somewhat different view of the matter in *Robinson v. Torbay Borough Council.*[91] Judge Goodall, sitting as a judge of the High Court, rejected the idea that the tests for those who were homeless should be different from those threatened with homelessness. However, whilst he was of the opinion that the same test should be applied, the test which he wished to apply was on much the same lines as Judge Fallon in *Zold* and *Jones* — namely the objective test of a reasonable landlord or as he also expressed it, the fair-minded bystander. Judge

---

88. Section 60(2) of the Housing Act 1985; section 26(2) of the Housing (Scotland) Act 1987.
89. 26 February, 1981 (Smythe CC7); (1981) LAG 287.
90. 30 April, 1981 (Smythe CC7); (1981) LAG 163.
91. [1982] 1 All ER 726.

Goodall rejected the subjective test put forward by Lord Denning by reference to the intentions of the person threatened with homelessness.

"In my judgement if a person deliberately does an act the reasonable result of which is his eviction, and the act is in fact the cause of his eviction, then he becomes homeless intentionally even though he did not appreciate that it would be the cause. Similarly, if a person does an act and eviction is the likely result of what he deliberately does, then he becomes threatened with homelessness intentionally, even though he may not have appreciated that it would be the likely result."[92]

The importance of whether the subjective view of the applicant or the objective view of the fair-minded bystander is applied to determine whether acts or omissions are deliberate may be more apparent than real. Housing authorities are not entitled to take into account acts or omissions made in good faith and in ignorance of relevant facts and are obliged, as a consequence of *Robinson,* to assess the nature of acts or omissions and their likely consequence. If these requirements are fulfilled there should be few cases where the view of an applicant as to the deliberateness of his actions and that of the fair-minded bystander should differ.

(b) Intentional homelessness and the family unit

In general, acts or omissions which are not those of the applicant should not be relied upon by an authority in determining their statutory obligations. For example, the rent arrears of one spouse as sole tenant of a council house should not affect his estranged wife's application. However, as the courts have noted, the Act aims to bring and keep families together and therefore the applicant's needs for housing include those of his family and as a corollary of this view it has been widely accepted that the acts or omissions of a member of the applicant's "family unit" can lawfully be examined when considering an application.[93]

It should not be assumed, however, that the deliberate acts or omission of one member of the family unit *automatically* affect the other. Everything depends on the particular circumstances of each case. The case which established this principle is *R. v. North Devon District Council, ex p. Lewis.*[94] In this case a farm labourer gave up his job and as a result was evicted from tied accommodation. He applied to the housing authority for assistance under the 1977 Act but was refused permanent accommodation on the ground that he had become intentionally homeless. Later his cohabitee, who was pregnant and therefore had a priority need, applied to

---

92. *Ibid.* at p.730.
93. See "Family Unit", above at pp.69-72.
94. [1981] 1 All ER 27. But see *R. v. Swansea City Council, ex p. Thomas* (1983) 9 HLR 64.

the housing authority for assistance. She did not deny that she would share any accommodation which the authority provided with the original applicant. The housing authority determined that, as she was a member of his family unit and had acquiesced in him terminating his employment, she was also intentionally homeless. In these circumstances Mr. Justice Woolf held that the authority were entitled to reject her application. However, he added, where it is clear that a member of the family unit was not party to the act or omission which resulted in a finding of intentional homelessness that person should not be regarded as having acquiesced:

> "The fact that the Act requires consideration of the family unit as a whole indicates that it would be perfectly proper in the ordinary case for the housing authority to look at the family unit as a whole and assume, in the absence of material which indicates to the contrary, where the conduct of one member of the family was such that he should be regarded as having become homeless intentionally, that that was conduct to which the other members of the family were a party."[95]

There are two problems inherent in this approach. The first is, as Lord Ross explained in *Hynds v. Midlothian District Council,* [96] the legislation deals with homeless persons and not homeless families and the application is at the instance of a person and not a family. The second is to determine whether there is material which indicates that a member of a family was not a party to such conduct. In *Lewis* Mr. Justice Woolf gave as an example of non-acquiescence a woman who had tried but was unable to prevent her husband from spending money on drink instead of paying the rent. In these circumstances, he indicated that the legislation required the housing authority to provide her with accommodation, albeit that her husband would benefit from their decision to treat her as not having become homeless intentionally.

A later case which demonstrates circumstances in which a member of a family unit is not to be regarded as intentionally homeless because of the act or omission of another member is *R. v. Ealing London Borough Council, ex p. Sidhu.* [97] In this case a woman had been subjected to violent assaults by her husband throughout their marriage and had been thrown out of the family home by him in January 1981. However, a reconciliation was effected and she returned to him. In March 1981, the family were evicted because of rent arrears. At this time they approached the housing authority for assistance as homeless persons and were provided with temporary accommodation for one month. Thereafter they lived in a privately rented room. However, relations between them deteriorated again following further assaults she left him and obtained accommodation

---

95. *Sub. nom. Lewis v. North Devon District Council* [1981] 1 All ER 27, at 31.
96. 1986 SLT 54.
97. (1983) 2 HLR 45.

in a battered women's refuge. Mrs. Sidhu approached the housing authority for assistance in her own right. The housing authority declined to treat her as a separate unit for the purpose of her application until she obtained legal separation and custody orders. The effect of this ruling was that her application remained tainted until then by the previous finding of intentional homelessness against the original family unit. Referring to *Lewis*, Mr. Justice Hodgson emphatically stated that this was totally unacceptable:

> "[T]here was no doubt that on the evidence and surrounding circumstances the applicant's case should have been considered as separate from that of her husband and no reasonable local authority could have come to any other conclusion but that she was not intentionally homeless."

In terms of subsequent case law this problem has been viewed in terms of establishing that an applicant did not acquiesce in the conduct of a member of his family unit.

Three cases which may be cited as examples of acquiescence in the conduct of other members of a family unit are *R. v. Swansea City Council, ex p. Thomas* [98]; *R. v. Swansea City Council, ex p. John* [99]; and *R. v. Croydon London Borough Council, ex p. Webb.* [100]

In *Thomas* the applicant was the joint tenant of a council house in Swansea where he lived with his cohabitee and their two children. While he was in prison neighbours complained to the housing authority of anti-social conduct and as a result eviction proceedings were initiated against them. As their tenancy was a joint one the county court offered to postpone the date of the hearing to enable Thomas to file a defence or to attend the hearing if he so wished. However, he declined to do so because the prison authorities informed him that it would be necessary for him to pay his own expenses for attending the hearing. An order of possession was granted against him but before it took effect he applied to the authority for assistance.

The housing authority considered his application and a previous application made by his cohabitee jointly as they took the view that the purpose of each application was to obtain a home which they could share with their two children. Whilst accepting that he was not guilty of causing annoyance or nuisance to their neighbours, the housing authority found that he had become homeless intentionally because he was a member of the family unit. This finding was challenged in the High Court on the basis that as the authority had accepted that he was not guilty of the conduct

---

98. (1983) 9 HLR 64; see also *R. v. Southhampton City Council, ex p. Ward* (1984) 14 HLR 114.
99. (1982) 9 HLR 58; *R. v. East Hertfordshire Borough Council, ex p. Bannon* (QBD) 21 March, 1986.
100. (QBD) 14 December, 1984; *R. v. Vale of Whitehorse District Council, ex p. Lyle* (QBD) 6 July, 1983; *R. v. Wandsworth LBC, ex p. Lord* (QBD) 8 July, 1985; and *R. v. Hillingdon LBC, ex p. Thomas* (1987) 19 HLR 196; *Stewart v. Monklands District Council* 1987 SLT 630.

which resulted in their eviction, he could not be regarded as having become homeless intentionally.

However, the High Court accepted that the authority were entitled to form this conclusion, despite the fact that he was in prison at the time, on the ground that he had acquiesced in the conduct of his family unit because he had been aware of the complaints about the conduct and the court proceedings but had neither filed a defence in those proceedings nor sought to contend that he disapproved of the conduct or did not feel responsible for it.

In some respects this case is quite unremarkable. It reaffirms the accepted family unit approach determining applications under the legislation and warns housing authorities against assuming that merely because a person may be regarded as a member of a family unit at one time he is to be regarded as intentionally homeless because of the acts or omissions of another member of that unit. In such cases therefore it will be necessary for authorities to make detailed inquiries to satisfy themselves that a member of a family unit can in fact be regarded as being a party to the act or omission which resulted in homelessness. Where this case differs from earlier cases on the family unit is that it accepts that a person who is absent from the family home may be regarded as intentionally homeless because of the deliberate acts or omissions of another member, unless he takes positive steps to disassociate himself from the conduct which forms the basis of the finding of intentional homelessness.

Whereas in *Thomas* the applicant may have disassociated himself from the conduct of the members of his family unit either by showing that he disapproved of it by taking steps to convince them to desist from their anti-social conduct or filing a defence to the eviction for possession, in *John* it is plain that to establish non-acquiescence the applicant was expected to sever her long-standing relationship with her partner. In this case the applicant was 67 year old woman who had cohabited with a man for some 18 years in the council flat of which she was the tenant. Her cohabitee was younger and was considerably larger and stronger than she was and suffered from alcoholism. When she was absent from their home he became drunk and caused nuisance and annoyance to her neighbours. As a consequence of complaints from neighbours about anti-social conduct the housing authority instituted eviction proceedings against her and obtained an order of possession. The applicant applied for assistance as a homeless person but the housing authority found that she had become homeless intentionally because of her continued breach of tenancy conditions. An application for judicial review was made by the applicant but it was dismissed by Mr. Justice Woolf on the ground that, although it was hard to expect her to sever her long-standing relationship with this man, the authority's decision that she had become homeless intentionally was a lawful one:

"It seems to me that faced with those alternatives [the woman severing the relationship and the order of possession being rendered meaningless by providing her with permanent accommodation] there are circumstances where the council can properly come to a conclusion... that the persons had rendered themselves intentionally homeless... where a woman can only be said to have acquiesced in the conduct complained of by not taking action to terminate the man's right to remain in the accommodation."

In the final case in this section, the conduct relied upon the authority to establish acquiescence was not anti-social conduct but non-payment of rent. In *Webb* the applicant argued that he did not acquiesce in his wife's non-payment. Although the applicant was not the tenant of the house from which they were evicted it was accepted on the evidence that he knew that her rent arrears were mounting and, although he had the means to do so, he had not taken the opportunity to pay off some of the arrears. In these circumstances the court held that the authority were entitled to conclude that he had acquiesced in his wife's intentional homelessness and therefore they had no duty to provide him with permanent housing.

However, these decisions must be treated with caution in light of other cases decided on the question of non-acquiescence. *Beattie No.2*, [101] as the suffix suggests, followed from the decision of Mr. Justice Woolf in *R. v. Eastleigh Borough Council, ex p. Beattie* [102] in which the decision of the housing authority was quashed because of the failure of the authority to consider whether it was reasonable for the Beatties to continue to occupy allegedly overcrowded accommodation. As a consequence of that finding and the suggestion made by Mr. Justice Woolf that the applicants should make fresh applications the applicants each submitted a separate application. In her application Mrs. Beattie stated that she did not acquiesce in her husband's decision not to pay mortgage instalments but:

"[O]n the contrary I did seek to persuade my husband to pay the mortgage when I found out that it was not being paid because I was afraid if [the house] was sold by [the council] as Mortgagees, we would not, in fact, be rehoused. I was afraid that the children would be taken into care and that was unacceptable to me."

In her application she also made it clear that she wished to live with her husband and children. [103] The authority found that they had become homeless intentionally as their house was not overcrowded and that in these circumstances it was reasonable for them to remain in occupation of it.

The principal issue before the court as far as Mrs. Beattie was

---

101. (1984) 17 HLR 168; see also *R. v. East Northamptonshire District Council, ex p. Spruce* (QBD) 17 February, 1988.
102. (1983) 10 HLR 134.
103. See *R. v. North Devon District Council, ex p. Lewis* [1981] 1 All ER 27.

concerned was whether she had acquiesced in her husband's conduct and, if she had not, whether it followed that Mr. Beattie could benefit from the decision that his wife had not become homeless intentionally. In the earlier case, *Beattie No.1*, [104] Mrs. Beattie had sworn an *affidavit* that when she found out that her husband was not discharging their liability to repay the mortgage she questioned him as to what he was going to do about it and on a later occasion she discussed the matter with her husband again:

"I was very angry and there was a big argument. I pleaded with my husband to pay off all the arrears and to make sure that he kept up the mortgage repayments. My husband told me that he would get in touch with [the authority] immediately and sort something out."

In short, on at least two occasions over an eight month period she had questioned her husband about the payment of the mortgage and had unsuccessfully attempted to persuade him to pay off their arrears and to maintain the mortgage repayments. This evidence was before the authority when dealing with her application but they had rejected it because they regarded it as being too unreliable on the ground that there was no corroborating evidence to establish that she had not acquiesced in her husband's decision. Mr. Justice Webster held that in the unusual circumstances of this case the authority were not entitled to brush aside the applicant's *affidavit* evidence without giving cogent evidence for their decision to do so:

"There is no doubt that her *affidavit* constitutes very material evidence and, if it is to be believed, detailed evidence that she had not merely acquiesced in her husband not paying the mortgage but that she had repeatedly, or at least more than once, protested about it. In my view, if that evidence is to be rejected by the...Authority they must put before this court, when the decision is challenged, evidence to the effect that they have rejected it and evidence as to why they have done so... I am very far from convinced that they have sufficient reasons to entitle [them] to come to that conclusion. Mrs. Beattie's evidence is, as I have said, detailed and circumstantial... I am satisfied that on the material before them the...Authority was not entitled to be satisfied that Mrs. Beattie had acquiesced in her husband's conduct, and that the decision she had done so was one which no reasonable authority, properly directing itself on the material before it, would have reached."

In effect, this decision follows the dictum of Mr. Justice Woolf in *Lewis* that where a wife has no control over her husband and has done what she could to prevent him from getting into difficulties which might result in their homelessness, it is not lawful to regard her as acquiescing in his conduct. It followed from this that as Mrs. Beattie had not become

---

104. (1983) 10 HLR 134.

homeless intentionally it was the duty of the authority to provide accommodation for her and her family notwithstanding the fact that her husband would benefit from it.

Interestingly, *R. v. West Dorset Council, ex p. Phillips* [105] puts flesh and bones on to the example of the uncontrollable drunken husband given by Mr. Justice Woolf in *Lewis*. In this case a young couple fell into arrears due to "the fact that the money was going down the throat of the... husband in the form of alcoholic refreshment." The wife applied to the housing authority for assistance as a homeless person and they were interviewed by a homeless persons officer who explained that he was of the opinion that they had become homeless intentionally because of their failure to pay rent. When he did this the wife forcibly demonstrated her non-acquiescence in his indulgence:

> "Mrs. Phillips lost her temper and began to strike her husband with such violence that she knocked him off the chair on which he was sitting. She shouted at him that she had always been telling him that his drinking would only result in trouble and now it appeared as if they would be homeless."

Despite this violent outburst, the officer made no further inquiries to establish whether the applicant had acquiesced in her husband's conduct. The failure to make further inquiries into this matter resulted in their finding of intentional homelessness being overturned by Mr. Justice Hodgson who strongly condemned the authority's attempt to shelter behind the fact that the applicant had not specifically raised the problem of her husband's drinking with them as justifying their failure to make further inquiries:

> "It seems to be astounding that anyone, faced with a 26 year old woman behaving in that way and saying that she had always been telling him that his drinking would only result in trouble, should come to the conclusion that no further enquiries were necessary.... The demonstration of her attitude towards her husband before [the homeless persons officer] showed with enormous certainty what her attitude was towards her husband's drinking and could hardly have been construed as acquiescence by the most hard-hearted of officers."

R. v. Penwith District Council, ex p. Trevena [106] also demonstrates the perspicacity, if not clairvoyance, of Mr. Justice Woolf in *Lewis*. In that case, he drew attention to the situation where a husband is tenant and surrenders his tenancy in circumstances where he is properly to be regarded as having become homeless intentionally. In normal circumstances, he added, the wife could also be regarded as having

---

105. (1985) 17 HLR 168.
106. (1984) 17 HLR 526.

become homeless intentionally as their decision to surrender the tenancy would be treated as a joint one:

> "If, however, at the end of the day, because of evidence put before the authority by the wife, the housing authority is not satisfied that she was a party to the decision, it would have to regard her as not having become homeless intentionally."

Although in *Trevena* it was the wife who was the tenant and surrendered the tenancy, the outcome was exactly as envisaged by Mr. Justice Woolf. In this case the wife surrendered her tenancy of a council house in St. Ives after she had left her husband to go and live with another man in Northampton. Her husband refused to leave the family home and the housing authority evicted him. Shortly afterwards the couple reconciled their differences and for a period occupied 'out-of-season' lets or shorthold tenancies. The husband later applied to the authority for housing but was found by them to be intentionally homeless because he was party to his wife's decision to deliberately surrender the tenancy of the accommodation.

This decision was held to be unlawful by Mr. Justice McNeill on the ground that there was no evidence to support the conclusion that he had been party to the surrender of the tenancy:

> "It seems to me that on the material here there was nothing which could have led a local authority, exercising its function reasonably, to conclude that the present applicant [Mr. Trevena] was party to the surrender of the tenancy.... Plainly the wife had left her husband. There is no question of consent to that. She had gone to live with another man in Northampton. She surrendered her tenancy for the purpose of enabling her to obtain accommodation in Northampton. The correspondence indicates not that he was a party to that but at that time there was a marked degree of hostility."

A final example of the "non-acquiescence" principle in action is *R. v. East Northamptonshire District Council, ex p. Spruce.* [107] In this case a couple had accumulated substantial rent arrears over a number of years and, despite numerous attempts by the housing authority to encourage them to pay their debt, were eventually evicted from the council house of which they were joint tenants. It would appear that the husband had deceived his wife for some time about their position concerning the payment of the rent arrears and that until a fairly advanced stage she believed that no arrears were outstanding. After separating from her husband the applicant applied to the housing authority for assistance. The authority found that she had become homeless intentionally because of the rent arrears accumulated when she was joint tenant with her husband of their council house. Mr. Justice Kennedy, while accepting that the applicant

---

107. (QBD) 17 February, 1987.

143

latterly became aware of the existence of the rent arrears, was of the view that that knowledge did not show that she could be regarded as having become intentionally homeless:

> "By way of example...I put forward the case of a wife who only finds out that her husband has failed to pay the rent or instalments at a time when the debt has become so substantial that the couple simply cannot cope with it. In that situation, in my judgement, it would be very hard to say that simply because the wife was aware of the debt before the situation of homelessness arose that she should be regarded as being intentionally homeless."

In failing to consider the applicant's circumstances separately from those of her husband he held that the decision of the authority was unlawful.

The importance of *Spruce, Trevena, Phillips* and *Beattie No.2* cannot be over-emphasised as they provide a 'life-line' to innocent spouses and cohabitees against being found to be intentionally homeless because of the actions of other members of the family unit. Where there is evidence that those actions were carried out in the face of opposition from the other members of the family unit or that they were in no position to control the conduct of the other person or that the other members of the family unit were ignorant of the act or omission in question until it was effectively too late to do anything about it they are not to be held to be intentionally homeless. Thus, as members of the family unit who are not party to such conduct are not intentionally homeless, the housing authority has an obligation to house them and the other member of the family unit whose deliberate conduct resulted in him or her becoming homeless intentionally.

The implications of these cases for housing advisers are that when advising members of the family unit in similar circumstances it will be necessary to point out that if the innocent member(s) of the family unit apply separately to a housing authority, they will be obliged to house the family as a whole. Therefore, without creating a new family unit, the obligation to rehouse can exist notwithstanding that a member of the existing unit became homeless intentionally.[108]

(c) Acts or omissions made in good faith in ignorance of any relevant fact

Where acts or omissions are made in good faith by a person who is unaware of any relevant fact, such acts or omissions are not to be treated as being deliberate. This qualification was introduced at the Report stage of the Bill in the House of Lords to protect persons who were not attempting to

---

108. *R. v. Wandsworth LBC, ex p. Lord* (QBD) 8 July, 1985.

manipulate the system but who nevertheless might be caught by the very wide ambit of the intentional homelessness clause. The Code of Guidance does not provide examples of what might be regarded as acting or failing to act in good faith. However, a fairly straightforward example would be a person acting on bad legal advice providing that the advice given was not aimed at putting unfair pressure on the housing authority to rehouse the applicant.[109] The Code gives as examples of persons acting or failing to act in ignorance of relevant facts as being:

> "[T]hose who get into rent arrears being unaware that they are entitled to rent allowances or rebates or other welfare benefits and those who left rented accommodation on receipt of notices to quit being unaware of their legal rights as tenants."

It should be borne in mind, however, that Lord Fraser in *Brown v. Hamilton District Council* [110] did indicate that there might be a restriction on this exception. Discussing the claim that Mrs. Brown was unaware that rent was payable since the family were on supplementary benefit he stated:

> "[T]he matter of which she alleges she was in good faith unaware was a question of law and not one of fact."

This appears to draw a distinction between matters which people may or may not know about, such as rights to welfare benefits. This distinction does not seem to us to be particularly helpful, since as we have seen in discussing *Zold, Jones and Robinson,* matters of tenants' evictions turn on less precise grounds such as the "likely result" of a determination by a "reasonable council". Conversely an act or omission made in the face of housing authority advice may be sufficient to form the basis of a finding of intentional homelessness, provided the advice is good advice.[111]

This point arose in *Din v. London Borough of Wandsworth.* [112] In this case Mr. Din, who had got into considerable difficulties with the payment of rent and rates, sought advice from Wandsworth Housing Aid Centre. He was advised on two separate occasions that he could not be evicted until his landlord obtained a possession order. Until then the housing authority would not assist his family under the 1977 Act. However, following the service of a distress warrant for rates, the Dins voluntarily terminated the let of their accommodation in Wandsworth and moved in with a relative who occupied a small flat in Uxbridge. Later tensions between the Din family and their relative became so great that they were

---

109. See *R. v. Eastleigh Borough Council, ex p. Beattie* (1984) 17 HLR 168.
110. 1983 SLT 397.
111. *R. v. Surrey Heath Borough Council, ex p. Li* (1984) 16 HLR 79.
112. [1983] 1 AC 657.

asked to leave. At this stage Mr. Din once again approached Wandsworth for assistance.

The housing authority determined that the Dins were homeless and had a priority need for accommodation but that they had become intentionally homeless because they had voluntarily terminated the let of their former accommodation in Wandsworth despite repeated advice from the housing aid centre that they must remain there until their landlord had obtained a possession order. The Dins challenged this finding in the courts. Although concerned that housing authorities should not adhere to a rigid policy of refusing assistance until possession orders were granted and should not incur the costs of time-consuming and futile litigation,[113] the House of Lords upheld the decision of the housing authority. Lord Wilberforce stated that it did not follow from this decision that in every case where occupants moved before a notice to quit took effect a finding of intentional homelessness would be justified.[114] In this case the Dins, in voluntarily terminating their let had so clearly set their faces against housing authority advice that the housing authority were entitled to be satisfied that they had become homeless intentionally.

Further clarification of what constitutes ignorance of relevant facts on which a finding of intentional homelessness may be challenged was given in R. v. Eastleigh Borough Council, ex p. Evans. [115] In this case the applicant sought to challenge a finding of intentional homelessness on the ground that when she left service quarters which she shared with her husband she was unaware of the fact that the housing authority considered "any time spent by an applicant in accommodation which he is entitled to occupy as being of greater importance as it helps to relieve the pressure of applications for accommodation borne by the council in circumstances of general housing shortage." This submission was rejected by Mr. Justice McNeill who stated that this fact was in no way analogous to those examples given by the Code of Guidance.[116]

In R. v. Penwith District Council, ex p. Kevern [117] the applicant argued that she should not be treated as being intentionally homeless because she believed that the DHSS was paying her mortgage instalments direct to the Council. This submission was also rejected on the ground that as the DHSS had informed the housing authority by letter that they had not discussed this matter with the applicant the authority had sufficient material on which to base their decision of intentional homelessness.

It is also the case that a claim by an applicant that he was ignorant of a relevant fact may fail if the danger of eviction was so obviously

---

113. *Ibid* at 679 and 686.
114. See, for example, *R. v. Exeter City Council, ex p. Gliddon* [1985] 1 All ER 493; and *R. v. Portsmouth City Council, ex p. Knight* (1984) LGR 184.
115. (1984) 17 HLR 515.
116. SC 2.18; EC 2.17.
117. (QBD) 14 December, 1984; *R. v. West Somerset District Council, ex p. Blake* (QBD) 10 July, 1986.

apparent that it may be inferred that the applicant must have appreciated it. In *R. v. Rushmoor Borough Council, ex p. Lloyd* [118] a woman applicant stated that she had been ignorant about the position of rent arrears and that a possession order had been granted against the property in which she was living. That claim was rejected by the housing authority on the basis of evidence of their housing welfare officer that at least six months prior to her application for assistance he had made it clear to her that there was a possession order in respect of the property and that there were rent arrears which had to be paid off. In upholding the authority's decision Mr. Justice Woolf stated:

> "Whether or not [the applicant] was precisely aware of the fact of the possession order...is not important to my consideration of this matter, because clearly she must have appreciated...that there was a considerable danger, if the rent was not paid, that a possession order would be made. Notwithstanding that she...continued to occupy the premises without paying the rent or the arrears, so that the arrears were increasing rather than reducing...."

It follows therefore that, even if the applicant had been ignorant of the existence of rent arrears and the possession order, that the authority was entitled to find that she had become intentionally homeless because of the obvious danger of eviction for non-payment of rent.

Two cases which illustrate when ignorance of a relevant fact renders an act or omission non-deliberate are *Wincenzen v. Monklands District Council* [119] and *R. v. Christchurch Borough Council, ex p. Conway.* [120] In *Wincenzen* a 16 year old girl who wished to take up a college place was warned by her father that if she went to live with her mother and step-father on a temporary basis until she completed her college course, he would not allow her to return to his home. The applicant nevertheless decided to go and lived with her mother and step-father for the duration of her course. After completing her college course she sought to return to her father's home but he refused to allow her to do so. The applicant therefore turned to the housing authority for assistance explaining to them that she had not taken her father's threat seriously. The housing authority, however, found that she had become homeless intentionally on the ground that her father had made it clear to her that he would not allow her to return to live with him if she left home to live with her mother. Lord Clyde, however, held that she had acted in good faith and in ignorance of a relevant fact:

> "The fact she founds upon is the fact that she was unaware that he [her father] meant what he said. Of that fact she was unaware. She was aware of his stated

118. (QBD) 15 April, 1983; *R. v. Gillingham Borough Council, ex p. Loch* (QBD) 17 September, 1984; *R. v. Wandsworth LBC, ex p. Henderson* (1986) 18 HLR 522.
119. 1987 SCLR 712.
120. (1987) 19 HLR 238.

intentions. She was unaware that he was serious in stating them.... If she did not believe he was serious, she cannot have been aware of the fact that he was serious."

Lord Clyde's judgement needs to be interpreted carefully. For example, two implications of his judgement are that a fact includes a factual consequence which may or may not occur at some future date and that awareness comprises knowledge *and* belief. However, the Inner House upheld his decision noting the close bond of affection between "the [applicant] and her father", and on the ground that the "fact" she was unaware of was the seriousness of her father's threat. In doing so, however, the Inner House pointed out that the decision would not be helpful to a person who takes a course of action which is likely to result in the loss of accommodation and cite as an example of such a situation "the young person who persists in a course of anti-social conduct in the face of parental warning that if he did so he would be put out of the family home."

In *Conway* the question at issue was whether an applicant was aware of the significance of a deadline for taking up the offer of an extension to the period of a short tenancy. On the evidence before them Mr. Justice Taylor concluded it was difficult to understand how any interpretation of the conduct of the applicant other than that she was unaware of the deadline's significance could be put upon the facts. He therefore quashed the authority's decision that the applicant had become homeless intentionally.

In *Brown v. Hamilton District Council* [121] Lord Fraser suggested that ignorance of law was not the same thing as ignorance of fact and that an applicant could not rely upon ignorance of law to displace a finding of intentional homelessness. In *R. v. Eastleigh Borough Council, ex p. Beattie* [122] the applicant attempted to step around this distinction by arguing that notwithstanding that there was an error of law (in this case, that the authority would rehouse him if he ceased to maintain repayment of his mortgage) there was a relevant fact of which he was unaware, namely the fact that because of that error of law he would be found to have become homeless intentionally. This argument was rejected by Mr. Justice Webster on the ground that:

"[I]f that submission is correct... almost any error of law is to be regarded as an error of fact because it is always likely to have factual consequences."

Whether or not an applicant can be said to be entitled to act in good faith in ignorance of a relevant fact, as we have seen in *Wincenzen,* [123] may turn

---

121. 1983 SLT 397; *White v. Exeter City Council* (1981) LAG 297.
122. (1983) 10 HLR 134.
123. Inner House, Court of Session, 7 July, 1988.

on the relationship between the applicant and the person on whom he relied. In *R. v. Wandsworth London Borough Council, ex p. Rose* [124] Mr. Justice Glidewell held that a daughter was entitled to assume that her father's accommodation was adequate for her and her daughter and that she would be able to stay with him on more than a temporary basis without specifically enquiring if this would be so. In reaching this conclusion he sought to distinguish *De Falco* [125] on the basis that:

> "[T]here seems... to be a practical difference between the situation of an adult brother who comes with his wife to this country to stay with another adult brother and his wife, where the relationship is one where no doubt the brother who came here can expect some assistance from his brother but cannot expect indefinite accommodation, and the situation which stems from the relationship of father and daughter.... I take the view that a daughter, and indeed a son for that matter, of that sort of age [the applicant in this case was 21 years old], is entitled to expect that a father who says: 'Yes, come and join me' is doing so with the intention that at least for a reasonable period of time, until a son or daughter can secure accommodation for him or herself, he will be able to provide the necessary accommodation."

It would appear therefore that in assessing whether an applicant acted in good faith in ignorance of a material fact housing authorities will have to inquire into the relationship of the applicant and the person on whom he relied and the age of the applicant. For *Wincenzen* and *Rose* establish that in this respect the parent/child relationship and that of adult siblings are to be treated differently. [126]

(d) Homelessness in consequence of deliberate acts or omissions

Before a person can be found to have become homeless intentionally it is necessary for the housing authority to establish a causal connection between the deliberate act or omission in consequence of which it is said that the applicant became homeless or threatened with homelessness. [127] Thus, while an authority are entitled to look at events prior to those which occurred immediately prior to an applicant's homelessness, [128] before they can do so there must be a "continuous unbroken chain of causation" between that earlier act or omission and the applicant's homelessness or the applicant being threatened with homelessness. Thus, if there is a fresh

---

124. (1984) 11 HLR 105; See also *R. v. Wandsworth LBC, ex p. Woodall* (QBD) 12 July, 1988.
125. *De Falco v. Crawley Borough Council* (1980) 1 QB 460.
126. *R. v. Wandsworth LBC, ex p. Wells* (QBD) 23 November, 1983 (adult son/father).
127. See *Din v. Wandsworth LBC* [1983] 1 AC 657.
128. See *De Falco v. Crawley Borough Council* (1980) QB 460 and *Dyson v. Kerrier District Council* [1980] 1 WLR 1205.

event *(novus actus)* which breaks that chain of causation, such as the applicant obtaining settled accommodation or the formation of a new family unit, the original act or omission cannot be regarded as the effective cause of the applicant's homelessness or the applicant being threatened with homelessness.

R. v. Basingstock and Deane Borough Council, ex p. Bassett [129] is a prime example of this principle in operation. In an attempt to salvage their foundering marriage a couple decided to terminate the tenancy of their council house and go to Canada. They were refused permission to stay there permanently and returned to this country, where their marriage finally broke up. The wife then applied to the housing authority for assistance under the Act. They found that she had become homeless intentionally on the ground that she had made a joint decision with her husband voluntarily to terminate the let of their council house and to go to Canada. As she had lived in temporary accommodation with friends and relatives since that date there was no question of the applicant having broken the chain of causation by obtaining settled accommodation. However, it was successfully argued that the effective cause of her homelessness was not the termination of their council let but the breakdown of their marriage. As this factor was a *novus actus* which broke the chain of causation between the termination of their tenancy and the applicant's subsequent homelessness, she could not be regarded as having become homeless intentionally.

Bassett, however, can be usefully contrasted with *Hynds v. Midlothian District Council.* [130] Whereas in *Bassett* it was accepted that the effective cause of homelessness was marital breakdown and that the applicant's reason for terminating the let was her desire to save a foundering marriage, in *Hynds* it would seem that the absence of such a reason for terminating the let of Mrs. Hynds' council tenancy meant that the effective cause of Mrs. Hynds' homelessness was the voluntary termination of the let. It was irrelevant therefore that their marriage broke down after they terminated the tenancy.

Difficulties have also arisen as to when a test of causation should be applied. These two questions are closely related and raise the problem of how far back in time it is permissible for a housing authority to go in an attempt to discover the cause of an applicant being homeless or threatened with homelessness.

(i) When to apply a test of causation

The importance of when a test of causation is to be applied may be illustrated by examining the decision of the House of Lords in *Din v.*

---

129. (1983) 10 HLR 125.
130. 1986 SLT 54.

Wandsworth London Borough Council. [131] Mr. Din, contrary to advice which he had been given by the local housing aid centre, voluntarily relinquished the let of accommodation in Wandsworth and moved in with a relative in Uxbridge. After a time, however his relative asked them to leave. Mr. Din then approached Wandsworth L.B.C. for assistance under the 1977 Act. Wandsworth however, held him to be intentionally homeless because he had voluntarily terminated his let in spite of their advice that he should remain there until his landlord obtained a possession order. Mr. Din challenged this finding in the courts.

Judge White in the county court held the housing authority's decision to be invalid because the family did not apply for assistance until about four months after they had voluntarily terminated their let by which time they would have been homeless in any event. In other words it was irrelevant that the Dins had not heeded the advice of the housing aid centre to remain in occupation and had voluntarily relinquished their let because in those four months the landlord would have been evicted them. Hence, in Judge White's view, the housing authority had failed to establish a causal connection between the deliberate act of the Dins in giving up their accommodation and their subsequent homelessness. This decision was appealed to the Court of Appeal which, by a majority, upheld the decision of the housing authority. [132] The Dins had become intentionally homeless, in the majority view, when they had given up their accommodation in Wandsworth to move into accommodation with a relative on a temporary basis. The fact that they would in any event have become homeless therefore was irrelevant. Lord Justice Donaldson, as he then was, dissented from this view on the ground that the intention of section 17 of the Housing (Homeless Persons) Act 1977 was to prevent queue jumping and self-induced homelessness. In his view as the Dins had not jumped any queue but had in fact postponed the time when they joined the housing queue, the housing authority had not established a causal connection and hence the Dins were not intentionally homeless.

Because of the fundamental importance of the question of when a test of causation is to be applied this decision was appealed to the House of Lords which by a majority of 3 to 2 upheld the decision of the Court of Appeal. The majority held that the material test was why the applicant had become homeless not why he was homeless at the date of the inquiry. This, they agreed, led them to the same conclusion as that of the majority of the Court of Appeal, viz. that the Dins had become homeless when they voluntarily relinquished their accommodation in Wandsworth and that it was irrelevant that by the date of their applicant they would have been homeless anyway.

---

131. (1983) 1 AC 657.
132. *The Times,* 30 June, 1981.

The minority view was based on the question of when a test of causality was to be applied. In their view such a test should be applied at the date of the application and not the date when the applicant became homeless. It followed from this that there was no causal connection between the Dins giving up their accommodation and their subsequent homelessness. Lord Bridge put the matter well:

> "[I]t would be absurd to hold that the housing authority were at liberty to rely on any past act or omission on the part of the applicant which satisfies the section 17 formula but which is not causally related to the applicant's present state of homelessness."[133]

While the decision of the majority of the House of Lords has been followed by the English courts and by the Scottish courts[134] it is worth commenting that it neither coincides with the intention of the legislature nor with the advice on this matter contained in the Scottish Code of Guidance.

It should not be thought that *Din* cannot operate in favour of homelessness applicants. For example, in *R. v Gloucester City Council, ex p. Miles* [135] the issue in contention was whether an applicant had become homeless when she left the home of which she was joint tenant to stay with friends in Gloucester or at a later date when her estranged husband vandalised the premises to such an extent that they were rendered uninhabitable. The housing authority argued that she had become homeless intentionally at the earlier date when she left her home in Bristol which was available for her to occupy and which it was reasonable for her to occupy. However, at that time the applicant had not surrendered her tenancy or instructed the Department of Health and Social Security to stop paying rent on her home and had not sought to make any alternative arrangements for accommodation in Gloucester. Therefore, if she had approached the housing authority for assistance at this time they would have been entitled to find that she was not homeless. However, prior to approaching them the applicant's husband vandalised their home and had rendered it uninhabitable.

If follows then that the cause of homelessness was the vandalisation of her home. Applying *Din,* as the cause of her homelessness was her husband's act of vandalism, she could not be held to be intentionally homeless. The importance of this case is twofold. It illustrates the way in which applying a test of causation at the date of homelessness can work to the benefit of homeless applicants. In addition the Court of Appeal in *Din* and *Dyson* the deliberate act relied on was the voluntary surrender of the tenancy and not leaving or ceasing to occupy accommodation,

---

133. [1983] 1 AC 657 at 681.
134. See for example *Lambert v. Ealing LBC* [1982] 2 All ER 394 and *Mazzaccherini v. Argyll and Bute District Council* SCLCR 475.
135. (1985) 17 HLR 292.

which was merely the consequence of the surrender. As the tenancy in this case was not surrendered the applicant was not homeless until her husband vandalised their home and left it uninhabitable.

(ii) How to test causality

The causes of homelessness, as we have seen, are complex and multi-dimensional.[136] Thus in order to allow housing authorities to implement the legislation without interminable debate, the Code of Guidance provides housing authorities with practical advice on how to determine whether or not an applicant has become homeless or threatened with homelessness intentionally. The Scottish Code of Guidance suggests that in assessing the link between deliberate acts or omissions and homelessness:

> "[O]ne of the prime considerations to be taken into account should be the immediate cause of homelessness rather than events which may have taken place previously."

The English Code of Guidance is differently worded stating that:

> "[I]n assessing whether a person has become homeless intentionally, it is open to an authority to look beyond the most immediate cause of that homelessness."

However, it is clear that both forms of wording point to the pre-eminence of the immediate cause in assessing intentional homelessness. For example, both Codes specifically state that it would be inappropriate to treat a person who gave up accommodation to move in with relatives or friends who then decided that they could no longer accommodate him, as being intentionally homeless.

It can also be noted that in *Brown v. Hamilton District Council* [137] Lord Fraser appeared to suggest in an *obiter* statement that, where there were several causes of homelessness, provided one of these causes included a deliberate act, then that allowed the intentional restriction to apply:

> "It is clear that the respondent [Brown] deliberately failed to pay over the allowance to the appellants [Hamilton District Council] that that in consequence of that he ceased to occupy the accommodation in question. That may not have been the only reason why he ceased to occupy it, but provided it was one of the causes... then the requirements of the sub-section [s.17(1) of the Housing (Homeless Persons) Act 1977] are satisfied."

---

136. See 'Homelessness and the Law', *above,* at pp.8-49.
137. 1983 SLT 397 at 417; *Roughead v. Falkirk District Council* (1979) SCOLAG 188.

The first case in which the Court of Appeal rejected the immediate cause test was *De Falco v. Crawley Borough Council.* [138] This case arose from the housing difficulties of two immigrant families, the De Falcos and the Silvestris. The De Falcos had left Naples to come to England in order to obtain employment. Initially they had stayed with Mrs. De Falco's brother while they searched for work. Both husband and wife were successful in obtaining employment. However, their host's wife became pregnant and they were asked to leave. Thereafter they were accommodated by another relative in Crawley. However, he eventually asked them to leave and at this stage they approached Crawley Borough Council for assistance.

The history of the Silvestris was in many ways similar to that of the De Falcos. The one important difference was that the Silvestris' accommodation had fallen through prior to them leaving Italy but they nevertheless decided to go to England where they were put up on a temporary basis by a number of relatives and friends. As with the De Falcos, the Silvestris eventually approached the housing authority for assistance under the 1977 Act. As a result of their inquiries the housing authority determined that each family was homeless and had a priority need for accommodation but that the De Falcos and Silvestris were intentionally homeless because they had come to England without having ensured that they had permanent accommodation to come to. With the assistance of Shelter both families challenged these findings.

Laying the basis of the approach of the courts to testing causality Lord Denning, the then Master of the Rolls, stated that if the immediate cause test contained in paragraph 2.18 of the original English Code of Guidance "were to be treated as a binding statute, the council ought not to have looked at the position of the families when they left Italy. They ought to have looked at the position when their relatives or friends in England threw them out." However, Lord Denning was of the opinion that the Code of Guidance was not to be treated as a binding statute:

> "The council, of course, had to have regard to the Code... but, having done so, they could depart from it if they thought fit. This is a case in which they were perfectly entitled to depart from it. That paragraph [paragraph 2.18] may be all very well for people coming from Yorkshire or any other part of England. (sic) But it should not, or, at any rate, need not be applied to people coming from Italy, or any other country of the Community. There is a great difference between the two position." [139]

Lord Denning did not explain why a difference exists and it is difficult to reconcile with Community Law that nationals of Member States covered

---

138. [1980] QB 460.
139. *Ibid.* at p.478.

by the freedom of mobility of labour provisions[140] should be treated differently. That point aside however, this general approach has been followed in other decisions.

Fuller consideration of the question of causality was given in *Dyson v. Kerrier District Council.* [141] The applicant in the case, Fiona Dyson, was a single parent. Prior to the birth of her child she had shared a council flat with her sister in Huntingdon. Her sister moved to Cornwall shortly after the birth of the child and the tenancy of the local authority accommodation was transferred to Ms. Dyson. She shortly followed her taking a winter off-season let of the flat next door to her sister and near to other members of her family. Prior to the landlord gaining repossession of the flat Ms. Dyson applied to Kerrier District Council for assistance. Following eviction the Council determined that she was homeless intentionally as she had voluntarily terminated the let of her council flat in Huntingdon. The applicant challenged this finding in the courts on the grounds that the housing authority were only entitled to have regard to acts or omissions immediately before she became homeless and therefore were not entitled to have regard to what happened in Huntingdon.

The Court of Appeal, upholding the decision of the county court, dismissed Ms. Dyson's appeal. Although subsections 17(1) and 17(2) of the Housing (Homeless Persons) Act 1977 were drafted in the past tense the Court of Appeal stated that the housing authority were entitled to look beyond the immediate cause of homelessness:[142]

"This subsection [subsection 17(1)] is dealing with cause and effect. The subsection states the effect first. The specified effect is the state of being homeless. The subsection specifies that effect and then describes a particular cause which, if it exists, requires the effect to be treated as intentional. The subsection therefore means 'a person becomes homeless intentionally if he deliberately has done or failed to do anything in consequence of which he has ceased to occupy accommodation which was available for his occupation and which it would have been reasonable for him to occupy.'"

A later Court of Appeal case concerning causality, *Lambert v. Ealing London Borough Council,* [143] demonstrates that this approach may lead to inequitable, if not bizarre, results. René Lambert had been forced to sell his business as a bookseller in Grenoble to alleviate financial difficulties. In July 1978 he travelled with his three daughters to England in a motor-caravan, arranged for their education and placed his name on the housing

---

140. Articles 48-51 of the Treaty of Rome and Articles 2-18 of EEC Regulation No. 1612/68, October 15, 1968. See too the judgement of Sir David Cairns, ibid at p.479 who points out that homeless immigrants from Member States of the Community must be treated as favourably as UK nationals.
141. [1980] 3 All ER 313.
142. *Ibid.* at p.319.
143. [1982] 2 All ER 394. *Krishnan v. London Borough of Hillingdon* (1980) LAG 137.

waiting list. He entered into a series of "holiday" letting agreements and obtained employment, appropriately enough, with a French patisserie. When his rental agreements expired, M. Lambert unsuccessfully attempted to obtain alternative accommodation. He applied under the 1977 Act to Ealing Borough Council. They considered that he had become intentionally homeless and were prepared to provide him with temporary accommodation. M. Lambert appealed against this decision. The Court of Appeal, following *De Falco* and *Dyson* stated that:[144]

> "When M. Lambert sold up and left France, he became homeless. He was intentionally homeless here because he had given up his home in France. That intentional homelessness was the effective cause of his becoming homeless in England. The intervening 18 months do not alter the fact that he was intentionally homeless."

In this case Lord Denning stressed that the only kind of accommodation which counted for the purposes of avoiding a finding of intentional homelessness was "permanent accommodation".[145] However, in *Din v. Wandsworth London Borough Council* [146] the House of Lords approved the view expressed by Lord Justice Ackner that what amounts to 'settled' accommodation is "a question of fact and degree depending on the circumstances of each case" and more recently, in *R. v. Christchurch Borough Council, ex p. Conway* [147] Mr. Justice Taylor stated that:

> "At which point one draws the line between short-tenancies and longer ones and says that on one side of the line, the accommodation is temporary and on the other side it is settled is a question of degree and judgement."

Whether accommodation is settled and therefore will provide a break in the chain of causation is to be determined objectively rather than on the subjective view of the applicant. Thus, in *R. v. Purbeck District Council, ex p. Cadney* [148] the fact that the applicant regarded the home to which she moved after leaving her husband to be a settled one was irrelevant and the authority were entitled to find her to have become homeless intentionally:

> "...the proposition that the accommodation...was a new settled and secure home seems to me to be too subjective. Possibly the applicant at the time may have so regarded it, but looked at objectively it appears to me to be a situation in which...[the housing authority] were entitled to take the view that it was a transient or at any rate, precarious arrangement.... It follows that, even if I

---

144. *Ibid.* at p.398 per Lord Denning M.R.
145. *Ibid.* at p.399. See also *R. v. Harrow LBC, ex p. Holland* (1982) 4 HLR 108 where "bed and breakfast" accommodation is dealt with.
146. [1983] 1AC ER 657 at 668.
147. (1987) 19 HLR 238; see also *Mazzaccherini v. Argyll and Bute District Council* 1987 SCLR 475.
148. (1985) 17 HLR 534; *Krishnan v. Hillingdon LBC* (1980) LAG 137.

could accept that the applicant is homeless within the meaning of the Act, I would be forced to conclude that the homelessness she suffered was caused by her departure from the matrimonial home, which in the circumstances the [housing authority] are entitled to regard as an intentional departure."

It should be stressed that an applicant may only be regarded to be intentionally homeless if as a result of a deliberate act or omission he *ceases* to occupy accommodation which is available to occupy and which is reasonable for him to *continue* to occupy. Thus, the refusal of an offer of accommodation cannot be regarded as amounting to intentional homelessness as the applicant cannot be said to have *ceased* to occupy accommodation which he has never occupied.[149] Moreover, the accommodation which is relevant is the last "settled accommodation" not the accommodation which he last occupied. For example, in *R. v. Preseli District Council, ex p. Fisher* [150] it was held that where an applicant had lived in temporary forms of accommodation for a number of years it was necessary for the housing authority to identify the "settled accommodation" which the applicant last occupied and to consider why she lost that accommodation. On the other hand if the reasons for the loss of "settled accommodation" are sufficient to justify a finding of intentional homelessness the length of time which an applicant lives in non-settled accommodation is regarded as being irrelevant to the question of causation.[151]

Other than obtaining "settled accommodation" the only occurrence which the courts appear to be willing to accept as breaking the chain of causation is the formation of a new family unit.[152] As we have already discussed the question of intentional homelessness and the family unit in some detail this matter can be dealt with briefly. For example, in *Sidhu* [153] and *Bassett* [154] it was held that although the applicants in those cases had in the past acted in a way which may have justified a finding of intentional homelessness there was not "a continuous chain of unbroken causation"[155] between that act or omission and their subsequent homelessness. However, as *Hynds* [156] and *Stewart* [157] both illustrate separation alone is not sufficient to displace an earlier act or omission such as termination of a let

---

149. *R. v. Ealing LBC, ex p. McBain* [1986] 1 All ER 13. However, the authority may be justified in considering that they have fulfilled their duty to the applicant: see 'The Duties of Housing Authorities' (below) pp.182-207.
150. (1984) 17 HLR 147; *R. v. Christchurch Borough Council, ex p. Conway* (1987) 19 HLR 238; cf. *R. v. East Hertfordshire District Council, ex p. Hunt* (1986) 18 HLR 51.
151. *Lambert v. Ealing LBC* [1982] 2 All ER 394.
152. See above at pp.69-72; 136-144.
153. (1982) 2 HLR 45.
154. (1983) 10 HLR 125.
155. *Ibid.* at 131.
156. 1986 SLT 54.
157. 1987 SLT 630.

or non-payment of rent which can form the basis of a finding of intentional homelessness.

(iii) Tied accommodation

Related to the problem of insecurity of tenure faced by persons living in accommodation under limited occupancy agreements is the vulnerability to eviction of employees occupying tied accommodation. It is not our purpose in this section to attempt to explain the complexities of the law which distinguish tied accommodation from other forms of occupancy or the employment law problems which arise where an employer is also landlord but to focus on the relationship between the loss of tied accommodation and intentional homelessness.[158] The primary question which arises in determining whether or not homelessness is intentional in such cases is whether the employee's dismissal was attributable to some culpable act or omission or if the employee resigned whether it was reasonable for him to do so.

Before turning to examine this problem in detail however, it might be helpful to identify a number of principles which should guide housing advisers and housing authorities when determining whether the circumstances in which an employee lost tied accommodation amounts to intentional homelessness or being threatened with homelessness intentionally:

1. The Scottish Code of Guidance specifically states that "[a] person who becomes homeless or threatened with homelessness as a result of losing accommodation tied to his job should not necessarily be considered as intentionally homeless nor should a person be expected to continue in employment where it would not be considered reasonable for him to do so simply in order to retain his accommodation."[159]

2. Where an employee voluntarily terminates his employment for some extraneous reason, viz. a reason which is not directly connected with the job itself, such as a desire to improve his job prospects, the housing authority may be entitled to find that he became homeless or threatened with homelessness intentionally.[160]

---

158. On the problem of tied accommodation in general see Shelter (Scotland), *Tied Housing in Scotland: The Forgotten One Hundred Thousand* (1976); E.Ramsay, *Caught in the Housing Trap: Employees in Tied Housing* (1979); S. Schifferes, *The Forgotten Problem,* Shelter (1980). See generally on the law *MacGregor v. Dunnett* 1949 SC 510; *Smith v. Seghill Overseers* (1875) LR 10 QB 422.
159. SC 2.20.
160. See A. Arden, "The Loss of Tied Accommodation", (1982) LAG 8; *R. v. Thurrock Borough Council, ex p. Williams* (1982) LAG 8.

3. The fact that an employee has been found to be intentionally homeless or threatened with homelessness intentionally does not necessarily prevent a member of his family unit from applying for accommodation in her own right.[161]

4. If there is adequate evidence before a housing authority to enable them to determine whether in the circumstances an employee has become homeless or threatened with homelessness intentionally the courts will be reluctant to interfere with that finding.[162]

The revised Code of Guidance for England and Wales[163] contains advice on the loss of tied accommodation on similar lines to that contained in the Scottish Code. This is, that a person who loses tied accommodation because the employment has ended through no fault of his own or resigned in circumstances where it would have been unreasonable for him to continue in employment, should not be treated as intentionally homeless. However, if the loss of employment arises from the employee's misconduct or where the employee resigns in circumstances which do not justify resignation[164] it may be that the authority are entitled to treat him as having become homeless intentionally.

For example, in *R. v. Vale of White Horse District Council, ex p. Lyle* [165] an applicant allegedly gave up his part-time employment as a gardener because he had received intimidation that if he continued with his part-time work he would no longer be eligible for unemployment benefit. As a consequence his employer became entitled to repossess the tied accommodation in which he lived with his wife and family. As the information in respect of unemployment benefit proved to be highly suspect, it was held that the authority were entitled to conclude that he had become homeless intentionally.

From the cases on tied accommodation and intentional homelessness which have been heard by the High Court thus far two principal difficulties have emerged. These relate to the reasonableness of the action of the applicant and the adequacy of the evidence upon which a housing authority have based their finding of intentionality. The High Court has upheld the finding of a housing authority that an applicant had acted unreasonably and hence had become homeless or threatened with homelessness intentionally where the applicant had given up his job

---

161. *R. v. Eastleigh Borough Council, ex p. Beattie* (1984) 17 HLR 168.

162. *R. v. North Devon District Council, ex p. Lewis* [1981] 1 All ER 27; *Jennings v. Northavon District Council,* (1982) LAG 9; *Goddard v. Torridge District Council, ibid.*

163. EC 2.16.

164. See Ogus and Barendt, *The Law of Social Security* (above) pp.106-112.

165. (QBD) 6 July, 1983; see also *R. v. Gravesham Borough Council, ex p. Winchester* (1986) 18 HLR 207.

166. *R. v. North Devon District Council, ex p. Lewis* [1981] 1 All ER 27 at p.29.

simply because he was unhappy,[166] where an employee's homelessness had arisen because of his desire to improve his job security[167] and where a couple resigned as manager and manageress of a club because family commitments made it impossible for them to fulfil their duties.[168]

In these High Court decisions it was reiterated that housing authorities are to conduct inquiries of such a nature as will provide them with adequate evidence on which to base their decisions.[169] This point was most clearly articulated in *R. v. Thurrock Borough Council, ex p. Williams.*[170] In this case a manager of a pub threatened with dismissal for financial and stock irregularities agreed to resign in exchange for a reference from his employers. As a result of his resignation he was threatened with the loss of tied accommodation and therefore applied to the housing authority for assistance. The housing authority found him to be threatened with homelessness intentionally and subsequently intentionally homeless because he had voluntarily resigned. They added that their decision would be the same even if he had not resigned because he would have lost his accommodation due to misconduct. The applicant denied that the allegations against him were true and challenged the finding of the housing authority on the ground that it was based on inadequate evidence. The High Court in upholding his objection observed that the onus of establishing that an applicant was homeless or threatened with homelessness intentionally rests on the housing authority and where there is doubt or uncertainty following their inquiries, that doubt or uncertainty must be resolved in favour of the applicant.

Similar doubts over the machinery and powers of housing authority investigation under the legislation were expressed in *Jennings v. Northavon District Council*[171] and *R. v. Thanet District Council, ex p. Reeve.*[172] The court added in those cases that its function is not to investigate the facts and merits of a dismissal or resignation but merely to scrutinise the decision-making of the authority to ensure that they have remained within the four corners of their discretion.[173]

The only recent major development in the case law on homelessness and tied accommodation is the emergence of the principle that, in the absence of misconduct, it is unreasonable for a housing authority to expect an employee to continue to live in tied accommodation after the termination of his employment and force his employer to obtain a possession order or evict him from the premises. Thus, in *R. v. Portsmouth City Council, ex p.*

---

166. *Jennings v. Northavon District Council* (1982) LAG 9.
167. *Jennings v. Northavon District Council* (1982) LAG 9.
168. *Goddard v. Torridge District Council* (1982) LAG 9.
169. See "Processing Applications" above at pp.64-79.
170. (1982) LAG 8.
171. (1982) LAG 9.
172. (1981) 6 HLR 31.
173. See "Remedies for the Homeless" below at pp.208-242.

Knight [174] it was held that the decision of a housing authority that former employees had become homeless intentionally when they voluntarily left premises in respect of which they held a non-exclusive occupancy agreement was unlawful because they were licensees with limited rights of security of tenure and it was unreasonable with regard to the position of the applicants and their former employer to stay on.

4. Local Authority Review of Intentional Homelessness

Where an authority makes a determination that an applicant is intentionally homeless, it is still possible for this decision to be reviewed or reversed by another authority or by the same authority where there are material changes in the applicant's circumstances.

(a) Changes in personal circumstances of the applicant

The Scottish Code states that people should not be judged to be intentionally homeless for all time. Where there is a change in behaviour of tenants evicted for anti-social behaviour or where those evicted for rent arrears are making genuine efforts to reduce outstanding rent arrears, these are sufficient grounds to merit a review of the earlier decisions. The timing of this review will depend on individual circumstances but there should not be a fixed period of disqualification and all cases should be subject to periodic review.[175]

It is clear from the decision of the High Court in *R. v. Westminster City Council, ex p. Ali* [176] and *R. v. South Herefordshire District Council, ex p. Miles,* [177] that an increase in the size of an applicant's family, the ages of his children, or the addition of children of different sexes which have implications for overcrowding and suitability of accommodation are material changes in the personal circumstances of applicants which can lead them to becoming homeless or accommodation ceasing to be available for their occupation. In our submission such changes would also justify a housing authority reviewing decisions of intentional homelessness. Likewise, where a new family unit is formed this can be enough to displace an earlier finding of intentional homelessness, particularly if coupled with domestic violence.[178]

---

174. (1983) 10 HLR 115; see also *R. v. Surrey Heath Borough Council, ex p. Li* (1984) 16 HLR 79.
175. SC 2.21.
176. (1983) 11 HLR 83.
177. (1983) 17 HLR 82.
178. See 'Intentional Homelessness and the Family Unit' *(above)* pp.136-144.

(b) Changes in housing circumstances of the applicant

Where an applicant is judged intentionally homeless at one time but later finds 'settled accommodation' which he ultimately loses, he should not be treated as homeless intentionally. In *Youngs v. Thanet District Council*, [179] for example, a family was evicted from their council house for rent arrears. They moved into a house with a resident landlord and were given notice to quit the accommodation. The Divisional Court decided that the finding of intentional homelessness stemming from the original rent arrears was spent with them finding accommodation in the private rented sector.

(c) Decision of a different authority on intentionally

If authority A makes a determination about an applicant which indicates that he is homeless intentionally, this determination may be altered by authority B.

Briefly if authority B finds an applicant homeless, in priority need and not intentionally homeless but that the applicant has no local connection with them but has a local connection with authority A, they may refer the applicant back to authority A. What is significant here is that the later decision by authority B on intentional homelessness binds authority A.

The Court of Appeal decision which established the principle that a second authority may overturn the decision of another authority is *R. v. Slough Borough Council, ex p. Ealing London Borough Council.* [180] A family deemed by Slough to be intentionally homeless on account of being bad neighbours was provided with temporary accommodation in the nearby borough of Ealing. When the applicant approached that authority Ealing made a different finding as to intentionality and referred the family back to the area where there was a local connection, namely Slough. The other family in the same case had gone to live with relatives in nearby Hillingdon, after being evicted by Slough for rent arrears and deemed intentionally homeless. They were evicted from the Hillingdon accommodation by the Council who proceeded to make a different intentionality finding from that of Slough. Hillingdon also referred the family back to Slough. Thus as we can see, authorities will accept applications from those temporarily in their areas but who may be referred elsewhere where they have a local connection and the notified authority must accept the duty permanently to rehouse them.

Whereas the decision of authority B binds authority A on the question of intentional homelessness an authority must do more than

---

179. (1980) 78 LGR 474.
180. [1981] QB 801; *R. v. Tower Hamlets LBC, ex p. Camden LBC, The Times,* 12 December, 1988.

rubber stamp a decision of intentional homelessness made by another authority. Thus, in *R. v. South Herefordshire District Council, ex p. Miles* [181] where the decision of an authority that an applicant had become intentionally homeless was made on information supplied by another authority without checking whether the applicant had any explanation or giving him an opportunity to deal with it, it was held that their decision was unlawful.

The decision by authority B that an applicant did not become homeless intentionally cannot be challenged by authority A when they refer a local connection dispute to arbitration. Thus, for example, in *Slough Borough Council,* [182] the referee categorically stated the question of whether the applicant had become homeless intentionally could not be reviewed by him.[183]

---

181. (1983) 17 HLR 82. See also *R. v. Basingstoke and Dean District Council, ex p. Webb* (QBD) 6 November, 1987.
182. 5 January, 1980 [Referees Decision No.22].
183. See LBA, Digest of Referees Decisions for England and Wales (November, 1980) No.22; see also Referees' Decisions Nos. 5, 37 and 40.

Chapter 6
Local Connection and Transfer of Responsibility

1. Local Connection[1]

Housing authorities have a discretionary power under the legislation to inquire whether applicants have a local connection with the area of another authority and in certain circumstances to transfer responsibility for the *permanent* housing of homeless persons to other authorities.

The legislation provides that a housing authority are not obliged to take positive steps to ensure that a homeless person with a priority need secures permanent accommodation if that authority are of the opinion that neither the applicant nor any person who might reasonably be expected to reside with him has a local connection with their area and the applicant or any person who might reasonably be expected to reside with him has a local connection with the area of another housing authority in England, Scotland or Wales. In such a case it becomes the duty of the other housing authority, after being notified by the authority to which the homeless persons originally applied, to secure that accommodation is made available.[2]

(a) Definition of local connection

The legislation defines a local connection as arising in one of four circumstances:

(i)   because the applicant is or was in the past normally resident in the

---

1. Section 61 of the Housing Act 1985; section 27 of the Housing (Scotland) Act 1987.
2. See Chapter 7 below.

authority's area and his residence in it is or was of his own choice; or

(ii) because he is employed in the authority's area; or

(iii) because of family associations; or

(iv) because of any special circumstances.

It is important to note that in *R. v. Eastleigh Borough Council, ex p. Betts*[3] the House of Lords held that local connection is not defined as meaning "normal residence", "employed", "family associations", or "special reasons" but is only:

> "[E]stablished by a period of residence; or a period of employment; or by family associations which endured in the area or by the other special circumstances which spell out a local connection in real terms."

It would seem therefore that whereas in assessing whether has a local connection with their area an authority must have regard to these four factors, the question whether there is a local connection turns on a detailed consideration of each factor and its inter-relationship, if any, with these other factors.

(i) Normal residence

The legislation does not define "normal residence" but paragraph 2.5(i) of the Agreement on Procedures for Referrals of the Homeless[4] suggests that a working definition of "normal residence" shall be that:

> "[T]he household has been residing for at least six months in the area during the previous twelve months, or for not less than three years during the previous five year period."

The rigid application of this working definition of "normal residence" was held by the Court of Appeal to be an unlawful fetter on the authority's discretion in *R. v. Eastleigh Borough Council, ex p. Betts*[5] where it was suggested that the phrase "normally resident" should be interpreted more widely.

The Court of Appeal held that, apart from the failure to exercise discretion by rigidly following the working definition in the *Agreement*, there was sufficient material on which the Council could have formed the opinion that the Betts were, or had been, normally resident in the Eastleigh area according to the natural and ordinary meaning of those words. This finding was based on the move by the family into the Southampton area in 1980 when Mr. Betts took up employment with

---

3. [1983] 2 AC 613.
4. ADC/AMA/LBA, 6 June, 1979.
5. [1983] 1 WLR 774.

Southern Television. In 1980 they moved to Netley Abbey in the borough of Eastleigh not far from Southampton on a six months tenancy. The following month Southern Television lost their I.B.A. franchise and as a result Mr. Betts was made unemployed. He fell into arrears with his rent and in February 1981 a possession order was made against him. When he applied for assistance the Council considered that he had a local connection with the district of Blaby south of Leicester where he had worked between 1978 and 1980.

Lord Justice Stephenson stated that the weight of authority seemed "to show that a person may be normally resident where he intends to settle, not necessarily permanently or indefinitely and may have at different times, more than one normal residence". This view was roundly rejected by the House of Lords.[6] In that case it was accepted that there was nothing improper or illegal in an authority operating a policy or established guidelines such as those contained in the *Agreement*, provided that each case was determined on its individual merits. Further, it was stated that while it would not be wrong for authorities to have regard to the definition of normal residence put forward in the Court of Appeal, the question to be decided was not whether an applicant was normally resident but whether he had established a local connection with their area by reason of normal residence. This question could be answered by taking the guidelines provided by the *Agreement* into account:

> "Has the normal residence of the applicant in the area been of such a duration as to establish for him a local connection with the area? To answer that question speedily it is sensible for local authorities to have agreed guidelines. I see nothing in the least unreasonable with a norm of six months' residence during the previous twelve months."

The "Betts principle" has been applied in subsequent cases. In *Brooks v. Midlothian District Council*,[7] for example, Lord Jauncey upheld the decision of a housing authority that a woman who lived in *temporary* accommodation for over a year in the district of the authority did not have a local connection with their area:

> "[M]ere residence for a period does not of itself necessarily establish that the individual has a local connection with the area, something more may be required. In particular, the character of the residence may be important."

Similarly, in *R. v. Vale of White Horse Council, ex p. Smith and*

---

6. [1983] 2 AC 613.
7. Court of Session (OH) 12 December, 1985; see also *R. v. Islington LBC, ex p. Adigun* (QBD) 20 February, 1986.

Hay [8] and *R. v. Waltham Forest London Borough Council, ex p. Koutsoudis* [9] past residence was held to be too remote to establish normal residence although, in the second case, the family had been resident in the area of the authority for two months short of the 3 year period within 5 years suggested by the *Agreement on Procedures for Referral of the Homeless* and had previously lived in the area for some 14 years.

It is not sufficient that a person is merely "normally resident" in the area of a housing authority to establish residence on which local connection may be founded. The residence must also be the residence must also be the residence of the applicant's *choice*. The legislation states that a residence is *not* a residence of choice if the applicant became resident in it because *the applicant or any person who might reasonably be expected to reside with him* either *was* serving in the regular armed forces of the Crown or *was* detained under the authority of any Act of Parliament (e.g. a prisoner or a person detained under mental health legislation). The Secretary of State is empowered by order to specify other circumstances in which residence is not to be treated as residence of choice.

In *R. v. Vale of White Horse District Council, ex p. Smith and Hay* [10] the applications for judicial review concerned a former member of the regular armed forces and the former wife of a member of the armed forces who had been allowed to remain in possession of married quarters after the termination of service. In both cases Mr. Justice Woolf upheld the decision of the local authority that the applicants had not established a local connection with their authority's area because the applicants' residence there was not residence of their choice. While accepting that if after leaving the armed forces a person established a fresh residence in the area of a local authority this exclusion would not apply and that a fresh residence could be established while, as in this case, the person continued to reside in the same property as he had occupied while serving as a member of the armed forces, Mr. Justice Woolf was of the view that no fresh residence had been established in either of these cases, even though one of the applicants had remained in married quarters for a substantial period of time due to the forbearance of the armed forces in allowing her to remain in married quarters. This provision therefore clearly applies to former members of the armed forces who became resident in the area of a local authority because they *were* serving as members of the regular armed forces and who have not established a fresh residence. Moreover, a fresh residence will not be established merely because the armed forces have delayed in seeking possession to enable former personnel to find alternative accommodation.

---

8. (1984) 17 HLR 160.
9. (QBD) 1 September, 1986.
10. (1984) 17 HLR 160.

The revised Code of Guidance for England and Wales[11] requests authorities not to exclude former servicemen from consideration "simply because they have lived in service quarters ..."

(ii) Employment

The legislation does not define "employment" but a person is considered *not* to be employed in a district of a local authority if he *is* serving in the regular armed forces of the Crown, or in such other circumstances as the Secretary of State may specify by order. The purpose of this provision[12] is to shield authorities with major defence establishments in their area from bearing a heavy responsibility for housing service personnel. The use of the present tense, "is employed", indicates that only *present* employment is relevant but Hoath suggests that a lengthy period of past employment may constitute a local connection because of *special circumstances.*[13] Clearly, however, a brief period of past employment will not be sufficient under either this ground or as a special circumstance.[14]

The Local Authority *Agreement on Procedures for Referrals of the Homeless*[15] suggests that where an applicant claims a local connection as the basis of employment "the local authority should satisfy itself by confirmation from the employer that the person *is in his employment* and that the *employment is not of a casual nature"*. On the basis of *Betts* it is likely that the courts would be willing to permit local authorities to have regard to this restriction on the nature of the employment to be considered.[16] There is no case law which deals directly with this provision but it is clear from the *Digest of Referees Decisions*[17] that problems have arisen in distinguishing between casual and non-casual employment (e.g. probationary employment) and in respect of peripatetic employees, such as commercial travellers and construction workers. Whether it would be lawful to exclude part-time employment or self-employment from consideration is open to questions but Arden suggests that it would be unlawful to do so.[18]

(iii) Family associations

The legislation does not define this phrase and the Code of Guidance

---

11. EC A1.17-1.19.
12. *Hansard,* HC Debates Vol. 934 (8 July, 1977) cols. 169-1700.
13. D. Hoath *Homelessness* (Sweet & Maxwell, London, 1983).
14. *R. v. Vale of White Horse District Council,ex p. Smith and Hay* (1984) 17 HLR 160.
15. Para. 2.5(ii).
16. See *Brooks v. Midlothian District Council* Court of Session (OH) 12 December, 1985, on *temporary accommodation.*
17. London Boroughs Association, December 1986.
18. A. Arden, *Homeless Persons –the Housing Act 1985, Part III* (Legal Action Group, London, 1986) para. 7.17.

offers no advice on its meaning. However, the Local Authority *Agreement on Procedures for Referral of the Homeless* [19] states that "family associations *normally* arise where an applicant, or a member of his household, his parents, adult children or brothers or sisters are currently residing in the area." Only in *exceptional* circumstances, the Agreement continues, should the residence of more distant relatives be taken to establish a local connection. The Agreement also suggests that before such a relationship is to be treated as a "family association" so as to form the basis of a local connection two further conditions should be satisfied: (i) the relative in question must have been *resident in the area for at least 5 years*; and (ii) the applicant must express a wish to be near to them. Again, in the absence of case law, it is difficult to give proper guidance on the meaning of this provision but the *Digest of Referees Decisions* indicates that the following points are noteworthy: (i) if there is a family association it is irrelevant that there are *stronger* family associations elsewhere;[20] (ii) cousins are usually too remote to form the basis of a family association;[21] (iii) that the 5 year residence for relatives has been accepted as a guideline.[22]

(iv) Special circumstances

Again, neither the legislation nor the Code of Guidance explains the meaning of "*special* circumstances" which may be taken into account as forming the basis of a local connection. The *Agreement on Procedures for Referral of the Homeless*,[23] provides that "an authority is free to decide that an applicant has a local connection with its area (but not in another authority's area without its agreement) for *any reason* it may decide." The Agreement, nonetheless, gives two examples of special circumstances on which, it suggests, a local connection might be based: (i) households returning from abroad or discharged from the armed forces who do not have a local connection because of normal residence or employment or family associations; and (ii) an applicant seeking to return to an area where he was brought up or had lived for a considerable length of time.

The question of what constitutes "special circumstances" has been considered in three cases to date. In the first case, *R. v. Vale of White Horse District, ex. p. Smith and Hay* [24] it was submitted on behalf of the second named applicant that membership of a local evangelical church,

---

19. Para. 2.5(iii).
20. See *R. v. McCall, ex p. Eastbourne Borough Council* (1981) 8 HLR 48.
21. *Ibid.*
22. *R. v. Eastleigh Borough Council, ex p. Betts* [1983] 2 AC 613.
23. Para. 2.5(iv).
24. (1984) 17 HLR 160.

around which, it was said, the lives of the applicant and his wife revolved, was a special circumstance on which local connection could be founded. the Council's housing aid officer, however, rejected their association with the church as being a special circumstance. The argument ran that if membership of local institutions or organisations constituted "special circumstances" it would be necessary "to open the gates to active members of churches, political parties, sports clubs, operatic and dramatic societies." In deciding that the couple's association with this church did not amount to a special circumstance in *this* case, Mr. Justice Woolf concluded, the officer had not acted unlawfully. He did, however, comment that that was *not* to say that such an association could not be a special circumstance in an appropriate case.

In the second case, *R. v. Islington London Borough, ex p. Adigun*,[25] Mr. Justice Mann stated that a genuine desire not to return to the area of a local authority, in this case Liverpool, because of fear of possible domestic violence, did not establish a 'special circumstance' for establishing a local connection with the area of the authority to which the applicant had applied for assistance. In other words, that the *special circumstances properly must relate to the area of the authority with which it is argued that there is a local connection*. A mere desire to live in Islington was not, of itself a "special circumstance". Lastly, in *R. v. Waltham Forest London Borough Council, ex p. Koutsoudis*[26] the applicant was returning to the area where he and his family had previously lived for some 14 years, where they had friends, and where their children had attended school. On his behalf it was argued, relying in para. 2.5(iv) of the Local Authority Agreement, which states that "[t]he fact that an applicant seeks to return to an area where he was brought up or had lived for a considerable length of time in the past may be a ground for finding a local connection because of special circumstances", that the authority had acted unlawfully in failing to take account of these matters. Mr. Justice Taylor, however, following *R. v. Hillingdon London Borough Council, ex p. Puhlhofer*,[27] came to the conclusion that, as the authority had considered these guidelines but decided that in the circumstances of this case there were not any special circumstances which could justify the finding of a local connection on this basis, that the decision of the authority should not be overturned for being *ultra vires*.

From the cases and the *Digest of Referees' Decisions* it should be noted that 'special circumstances' is an alternative ground on which a local connection may be established. It is not a means of extending the other grounds to cover the particular circumstances of an applicant which do not, as in *Koutsoudis*, satisfy any of the other criteria.

---

25. (QBD) 20 February, 1986.
26. (QBD) 1 September, 1986.
27. [1986] AC 484.

It should also be said that in the only cases in which a referee has found that there were 'special circumstances' the applications related to deserted wives of former members of the forces. In each case there were very pressing reasons why the applicants wish to remain in the area of the authority to which they applied – support of friends, social services, and the resting place of one of her children in one case, and the fact that in the other the applicant had spent her entire adult life in the area and had friends there – which in the view of the referees constituted special circumstances.

Finally, it should be noted that an applicant who is found not to have a local connection with the district authority may re-apply when he does have a local connection. For example, in *Wyness v. Poole District Council* [28] an unemployed couple who had moved to Poole to find work were found not to have a local connection and the housing authority therefore arranged for responsibility to be transferred to an authority with which they had a local connection. However, they did not wish to return to that area and refused the offer of accommodation made by that authority. The husband later was successful in obtaining employment and re-applied to Poole for assistance. It was held that they could re-apply once there had been a material change of circumstances, in this case obtaining employment which formed the basis of a local connection with Poole. [29]

(b) Administrative arrangements [30]

The Secretary of State for the Environment in exercise of his powers has made two Orders concerning the administrative arrangements for the transfer of the duty to provide accommodation for homeless persons. [31] These Orders are supplemented by the revised local authority *Agreements on Procedure for Referrals of the Homeless Persons*.

Responsibility for securing that accommodation is made available to homeless persons, pending agreement, rests with the notifying authority. [32] This principle was unequivocally stated by the Divisional Court in *R. v. Beverley Borough Council, ex p. McPhee.* [33] Rejecting the Council's

---

28. [1979] JSWL 368.
29. *Delahaye v. Oswestry Borough Council, The Times*, 29 July, 1980.
30. Section 67 of the Housing Act 1985; section 33 of the Housing (Scotland) Act 1987.
31. The Housing (Homeless Persons) (Appropriate Arrangements) Order 1978 (SI No. 69/1978); the Housing (Homeless Persons) (Appropriate Arrangements)(No. 2) Order 1978 (SI No. 661/1978).
32. Section 68 of the Housing Act 1985; section 34 of the Housing (Scotland) Act 1987.
33. *The Times*, 27 October, 1978. See also *Delahaye v. Oswestry Borough Council, The Times*, 29 July, 1980.

argument that they were relieved of their duty to house Mrs. McPhee, Mr. Justice Wien pointed out:

> "Nor were Beverley Council relieved of their duties by praying in aid section 5 [of the Housing (Homeless Persons) Act 1977], as they did in their letter. That section dealt with the responsibility as between housing authorities for a homeless person and provided for one notifying the other that it should take responsibility in certain circumstances. By section 5(6) [of the 1977 Act] however, it was "the duty of the notifying authority to secure that accommodation is available for occupation by the person to whom the notification relates until it is determined" whether the notifying authority or notified authority were to assume ultimate responsibility."

An authority may not seek to transfer responsibility, the Code states, on the ground that a person who has a local connection with that area has a greater connection with the area of another authority. Arrangements may be made between authorities, however, for another authority to take responsibility for the applicant provided that they take account of the full wishes of that applicant. The requirement to take the wishes of the applicant fully into account was one of the matters discussed in *R. v. Wyre Borough Council, ex p. Parr.* [34]

In this case the Wyre Council attempted to discharge their obligations to provide permanent accommodation to a family who had a local connection with their area by providing them with accommodation in Birmingham, an area with which they did not have a local connection. The Court of Appeal, overturning the decision of Mr. Justice Phillips, held that whilst the Council undoubtedly could discharge that duty by securing that an applicant obtained accommodation from a third party, they could only do so if they made it plain in their written reasons. They had to deal with why they considered the accommodation to be reasonable in all the circumstances of the case and establish that the wishes of the applicant were taken into account. Lord Denning added that where an applicant is to be housed by a third party in an area with which he has no local connection, there is an implicit requirement to take into account the wishes of the applicant.

(c) Threat of domestic violence

There can be no transfer of the duty to provide permanent housing if either the applicant or any person who might reasonably be expected to reside with her will run the risk of domestic violence in the area of the authority with which they have a local connection. In considering this

---

34. (1982) 2 HLR 71.

matter it is appropriate to take account of the fears and wishes of those concerned.

The measure of whether a person runs the risk of domestic violence is defined in the legislation as being if the applicant runs the risk of violence from any person with whom, but for the risk of violence, she might reasonably be expected to reside or, from any person with whom she formerly resided, or if she runs the risk of threats of violence from any such person if these are likely to be carried out.[35]

The Scottish Code stresses that because of fear of further violence it may be impossible to obtain evidence in the usual form and in such cases the women's fears may be considered as sufficient evidence. In no circumstances, the Scottish Code adds, should an applicant be required to provide evidence from her husband or any other person who may be the source of the violence. The existence of a court order ordering the partner not to molest the woman or enter the home patently does not necessarily mean it is safe for her in that locality and housing authorities should be aware of this danger.[36]

Two points may be made in relation to this provision. First, it is only risk of *domestic* violence which is relevant. Thus the risk of non-domestic violence, such as that which was present in *H.*,[37] *Preen* [38] and *Wood*,[39] would not prevent the transfer of responsibility to permanently rehouse. Second, there are very real difficulties in assessing the *risk* of domestic violence as is illustrated by *R. v. Islington London Borough Council, ex p. Adigun.*[40] In this case a woman left her husband because of domestic violence. She applied to the housing authority which decided that as she had no local connection with their area but had a local connection with Liverpool City Council, to transfer responsibility for permanently rehousing the applicant to that authority. This decision was challenged as being unlawful as she would be at risk of domestic violence from her husband if she returned to Liverpool. Mr. Justice Mann, however, upheld the authority's decision on the ground that the authority had contacted Liverpool City Council and had been informed that her former matrimonial home had been re-let and it was *believed* that her husband had returned to Nigeria. This information, it was said, was sufficient to enable the authority to conclude that there would be no risk of domestic violence.[41]

---

35. Housing Acts 1985 s. 67 (3); Housing (Scotland) Act s. 33(3).
36. SC para. 2.11 (b).
37. *R. v. Hillingdon London Borough Council, ex p. H* (QBD) 17 May, 1988.
38. *R. v. The Vale of White Horse District Council, ex p. Preen* (QBD) 18 April, 1983.
39. *R. v. Warwick District Council, ex p. Wood* (QBD) 15 August, 1983.
40. (QBD) 20 February, 1986.
41. See also *R. v. Bristol City Council, ex p. Browne* [1979] 3 All ER 344; *R. v. Purbeck District Council, ex p. Cadney* (1985) 17 HLR 534; *R. v. Eastleigh Borough Council, ex p. Evans* (1984) 17 HLR 515.

(d) Local connection outwith Great Britain

The territorial restriction whereby a person is homeless if he has no accommodation in England, Scotland, or Wales also applies to the transfer of the duty to permanently rehouse applicants. Thus if an applicant has no local connection with the housing authority to which he applies *and* no local connection with any other housing authority in those three countries the duty to provide permanent accommodation remains with that authority.[42]

Under articles 48-51 of the Treaty of Rome and EEC Regulation 1612/68, workers who are nationals of Member States of the European Economic Community are entitled to treatment, in relation to housing, equal to persons entitled to stay in Great Britain. Therefore where an applicant from Italy, France or any other Member State applies to a housing authority for assistance, they must be treated in exactly the same way as any other applicant.[43]

The position of immigrants from outwith the EEC is somewhat more complicated. A homeless immigrant from outwith the EEC who has a priority need and did not become homeless intentionally is also entitled to permanent accommodation notwithstanding the fact that he or she has no local connection with the area of any housing authority in Scotland, England or Wales. A case which demonstrates the inter-relationship between immigration law and housing law is *R. v. Hillingdon London Borough Council, ex p. Streeting*.[44]

The applicant in this case, an Ethiopian with a young son, had innocently entered into a bigamous "marriage" with an Englishman. They lived together abroad for four years until 1979 when her "husband" died while working in Libya. At this time the applicant and their child lived in a flat provided for them by her "husband" in Athens. Mrs. Streeting came to England for his funeral and was granted limited permission to stay. However, she was refused permission to enter Greece of her return there and understandably was reluctant to return to the volatile political climate of Ethiopia. She therefore sought and was granted refugee status in Britain. Later when her "husband's" former employer refused to continue to provide hotel accommodation for the applicant and her child she approached Hillingdon for assistance. Hillingdon, although providing them with temporary accommodation refused to provide the applicant with permanent accommodation on the ground that "no duty was owed to an applicant who has or had no local connection with the area of any housing authority in Great Britain."

This argument was rejected by both the Divisional Court and the

---

42. *R. v. Hillingdon London Borough Council, ex p. Streeting* [1980] 3 All ER 413.
43. See *De Falco, Lambert, Browne and H* (above).
44. [1980] 3 All ER 413.

Court of Appeal. Mr Justice Griffith pointed out in the Divisional Court that housing authorities were protected from a flood of immigrants seeking to take advantage of our benign housing laws by three important factors:

(i) Immigration law

"Immigration was strictly controlled,and it was not realistic to suppose that large numbers of persons would be allowed to enter the country, either on a temporary or permanent basis, when they have nowhere to stay while they were here."

(ii) Intentional homelessness [45]

"A person abroad cannot give up accommodation and expect to be housed by a local authority under the Act because by intentionally making himself homeless abroad the person would have disentitled himself to relief (more exactly permanent accommodation) under the Act."

(iii) Transfer of responsibility for permanent rehousing [46]

"Nor was there anything to prevent an authority from discharging its duty by arranging for accommodation to be provided in the country from which the applicant had come."

It may be observed, in relation to this provision, that the *Parr* [47] decision lays down two requirements in terms of the reasonableness of accommodation and taking into account the wishes of the applicant which a housing authority must satisfy if they are to transfer responsibility for the permanent rehousing of an applicant who has no local connection with the area of any housing authority in Great Britain.

The Court of Appeal upholding *Streeting* [48] argued that the Act was not to be construed extra-territorially, i.e. to exclude all persons who were not nationals of Member States of the EEC. Lord Justice Walton correctly pointed out that sections 5(5) and 18(2), of the Housing (Homeless Persons) Act 1977, clearly showed that the Act was not to be construed in such a manner. [49]

As regards the position of illegal immigrants, housing authorities

---

45. See *De Falco* and *Lambert*.
46. See *R. v. Bristol City Council, ex p. Browne* [1979] 2 All ER 344.
47. *R. v. Wyre Borough Council, ex p. Parr*, (1982) 2 HLR 71.
48. [1980] 3 All ER 413.
49. Interestingly, Lord Denning's decision that the Act should be construed extra territorially was based on a misconception of the effect of territorial construction on members of the Armed Forces. As we pointed out earlier, members of the Armed Forces return to their normal residence for the purposes of local connection.

are not under a duty to house illegal immigrants under the Act because they are not persons under the Act. As Lord Denning stated:[50]

" ... If he is an illegal entrant, if he enters unlawfully without leave, or if he overstays his leave and remains here unlawfully, the housing authority are under no duty whatever to him."[51]

Indeed, Lord Denning went on to suggest that in such circumstances the authority may report the applicant to the immigration authorities, a suggestion which appears to have been followed by a number of authorities.[52]

Where an authority accept responsibility for an applicant, it may be possible to discharge this duty by securing that accommodation becomes available for the applicant from a third party. This not only includes other authorities or private landlords within Great Britain but also the possibility of arranging for the applicant to return to his or her country of origin. The cases of *Nimako-Boateng, Mayor and Burgesses of Brent, Streeting, Parr,* and *Browne* however, indicate that housing authorities must not seek to return homeless persons to their country of origin without first carrying out detailed inquiries as to the potential risk of domestic and non-domestic violence to the applicant, the reasonableness of the accommodation, and taking the wishes of the applicant fully into account.

If there is a local connection outwith Great Britain, however, the authority may secure accommodation becomes available in that place provided that there would be no risk to the applicant if she returned and it is not unreasonable to do so.

In *R. v. Bristol City Council, ex p. Browne* [53] the Court of Appeal held that the legislation implicitly gives authorities the opportunity to secure that permanent accommodation becomes available for occupation by an applicant through an agency outwith Great Britain. In this case a battered woman and her seven children fled from Tralee in Ireland to Bristol to escape domestic violence. The authority, however, were able to discharge their duty to provide permanent accommodation by ensuring that the woman was returned to the town from which she had originally fled. The community welfare officer from her home town, Tralee, had assured them that there was housing available for Mrs. Browne and that there would be no risk of domestic violence. This case differs from *De Falco* because there was no question of the applicant here being

---

50. [1980] 3 All ER 413 at 420.
51. See *R. v. Crawley Borough Council, ex p. The Mayor and Burgesses of the London Borough of Brent* (QBD) 24 March, 1983.
52. See *Roof* (1980) 67 and 132.
53. [1979] 3 All ER 344.

homeless intentionally. It also differs from *Streeting* because Greece was unwilling to allow Mrs. Streeting to return to Athens.

(iv) Summary

As the position of homeless immigrants is fairly complex it may be helpful to provide a brief summary of the rules which may be applied in determining their rights under the legislation:

1. As immigration from outwith the EEC is strictly controlled, it is not realistic to suppose that large numbers of homeless immigrants will be allowed to enter this country and therefore it is unnecessary to formulate special principles to deny them the benefits conferred by the 1977 Act.

2. Immigrants from within the EEC must be treated in exactly the same way as persons entitled to stay in this country.

3. Where a homeless immigrant has no local connection with the area of any housing authority in Great Britain the duty to provide assistance under the legislation rests with the housing authority to which the applicant first applies.

4. If, however, a person voluntarily relinquishes accommodation abroad which is reasonable for him to occupy and available for him to occupy, the housing authority may be justified in finding him intentionally homeless.

5. A housing authority may take account of the reasons why an immigrant has left the accommodation abroad.

6. In determining whether it would have been reasonable for a homeless immigrant with permanent accommodation abroad to continue to occupy that accommodation, the housing authority may take into account the housing conditions in their own area.

7. A housing authority may discharge their duty to provide a homeless immigrant with permanent accommodation by securing that accommodation is made available by a third party either in his country of origin or elsewhere.

8. However, if a housing authority seek to discharge their duty to provide accommodation by securing that a homeless immigrant obtains accommodation from a third party, the housing authority must satisfy themselves that the accommodation is reasonable in the

circumstances and that there will be no risk of domestic violence or political prosecution to the applicant if he returns home and must take into account the wishes of the applicant.

2. Transfer of Responsibility to Provide permanent Accommodation Between Housing Authorities

In addition to the general power of a housing authority to secure that a homeless person obtains accommodation from some other person, the legislation[54] provides that a housing authority in certain circumstances may transfer their duty to provide *permanent* [55] accommodation to another housing authority.

(a) When can an authority notify?

There are three conditions which must be satisfied if there is to be transfer of responsibility to provide permanent accommodation:[56]

(i) neither the applicant nor any person who might reasonably be expected to reside with him has a local connection with the area of the authority to which the application has been made;[57] *and*

(ii) neither the applicant nor any such person has a local connection with the area of another housing authority in England, Scotland or Wales;[58] *and*

(iii) neither the applicant nor any such person will run the risk of domestic violence in the area of that housing authority.[59]

There can be no notification until the notifying authority have completed their inquiries since no *transferable* duty arises until that point in time.[60]

---

54. Section 67 of the Housing Act 1985; section 33 of the Housing (Scotland) Act 1987.
55. Any attempt to transfer a duty other than the duty to provide *permanent* accommodation is unlawful: *White v. Exeter City Council* (1981) LAG 281.
56. Section 67 of the Housing Act 1985; section 33 of the Housing (Scotland) Act 1987.
57. In *R. v. Eastleigh Borough Council, ex p. Betts* [1983] 1 WLR 744, Lord Stephenson stated that if there is a local connection the referral procedure does not come into operation.
58. If there is no local connection with a housing authority in one of these three countries there can be no referral: see *R. v. Hillingdon LBC, ex p. Streeting* [1980] 1 WLR 1430; *R. v. Bristol City Council, ex p. Browne* [1979] 3 All ER 344 on the provision of accommodation outwith Great Britain.
59. *R. v. Bristol City Council, ex p. Browne supra,* and *R. v. Islington LBC, ex p. Adigun* (QBD) 20 February, 1986.
60. *R. v. Crawley Borough Council, ex p. The Mayor and Burgesses of Brent LBC* (QBD) 24 March, 1983.

(b) Who may be notified?

If the authority are satisfied that these three conditions are met, to affect a transfer of responsibility for permanent rehousing the housing authority to which the applicant applied (the "notifying authority") must notify the housing authority of the area with which the applicant or a member of the applicant's family unit has a local connection (the "notified authority"). Such notification must indicate an application for accommodation has been made and that, in the opinion of the notifying authority, the three conditions for transfer of responsibility for the provision of permanent accommodation have been satisfied.

Where the applicant or a member of his family unit has multiple local connections, the Code of Guidance states that the notifying authority should take account of their wishes in deciding which authority to notify.[61]

If the notified authority are satisfied that (i) the applicant or a member of the applicant's family unit has a local connection with their area and (ii) neither the applicant nor family member will run the risk of domestic violence in that area,the notified authority are obliged to provide permanent accommodation for the occupation of the applicants and their family.

It remains, however, the duty of the notifying authority to provide accommodation until the question of responsibility is determined,[62] and if the conditions for transfer of responsibility are not satisfied, to provide permanent accommodation. The temporary duty to provide accommodation ends when the question whether the conditions for referral are determined either by agreement between the authorities or, failing agreement, by arbitration.[63]

The legislation provides that the question of whether the conditions for referral are satisfied should be determined in the first instance by agreement between the notifying and notified authorities or, failing agreement, according to the appropriate arrangements.[64]

When there is a dispute about whether or not an applicant has a local connection the authority are required to make up their mind whether or not there is a local connection. If there is material on which a reasonable authority properly directing themselves and properly interpreting the statute could form the opinion that no such connection existed, the court would not substitute their own determination. Where, however, there is plainly a local connection with the authority approached by the applicant there can be no referral on the grounds of "closer local

---

61. See EC 5.3; SC 5.3 and *R. v. McCall, ex p. Eastleigh Borough Council* (1981) 8 HLR 48.
62. *R. v. Beverley Borough Council, ex p. McPhee, The Times,* 27 October, 1978.
63. *Delahaye v. Oswestry Borough Council, The Times,* 29 July, 1980.
64. Housing (Homeless Persons) (Appropriate Arrangements) Order 1978 (SI 1978 No. 69) and

connection". The point was emphasised by Lord Justice Stephenson in *R. v. Eastleigh Borough Council, ex p. Betts*: [65]

> "If there was plainly a local connection, as defined in the statute, correctly understood, section 5 [of the Housing (Homeless Persons) Act 1977] did not come into operation at all. Referral to another authority, whether or not there was also a local connection with them, did not get off the ground. The duty remained with the authority who wanted to notify and could not be transferred to the authority that they wanted to be notified."

Where a notifying authority seek to transfer responsibility for housing an applicant, the determination of the notifying authority that the applicant has a local connection with the notified authority is conclusive[66] subject only to the notified authority either invoking the arbitration arrangements or challenging the determination of the notifying authority by way of judicial review.[67]

(c) Administrative arrangements

The Secretary of State for the Environment in exercise of his powers under the legislation has made two orders concerning the administrative arrangements for the transfer of the duty to provide accommodation for homeless persons.[68] These orders are supplemented by the revised local authority *Agreement on Procedure for Referrals of the Homeless*.[69] This informal agreement is not legally binding, and does not displace the statutory duties imposed by the Act upon housing authorities but authorities are entitled to have regard to the guidance provided by the Agreement *providing* they deal with each application on its merits. This point was settled by the House of Lords in *Betts*.[70]

As has been said, an authority may not seek to transfer responsibility for permanent rehousing, on the ground that a person who has a local connection with that area has a "greater" local connection with the area of another authority.[71] Arrangements may be made between authorities, however, for another authority to take responsibility for the applicant

---

Housing (Homeless Persons) (Appropriate Arrangements) (No. 2) Order 1978 (SI 1978 No. 661).

65. [1983] 1 WLR 744.

66. *R. v. Slough Borough Council, ex p. Ealing Borough Council* [1981] QB 801.

67. *Ibid;* and see also *R. v. Crawley Borough Council, ex p. The Mayor and Burgesses of Brent LBC, supra* and *R. v. Tower Hamlets LBC, ex p. Camden LBC, The Times,* 12 December, 1988.

68. Section 67 of the Housing Act 1985; section 35 of the Housing (Scotland) Act 1987; see also footnote 64.

69. Dated 6 June, 1979.

70. [1983] 2 AC 613.

71. EC 2.22; SC 2.23; see also *R. v. McCall, supra.*

provided that they take full account of the wishes of that applicant.[72]

As with the problem of intentional homelessness, if members of a family unit have local connections with the areas of different authorities, it is not necessary but perhaps is advisable for them to make separate applications to secure that the authority to which they apply notify *each* authority with which they have a local connection.

For example, in *R. v. McCall* [73] a mother had a local connection with Eastbourne whereas her son, with whom she resided, had a local connection with Manchester. It was held that it was unnecessary for her to apply separately and that the referee was entitled to take account of the *wishes* of the family to go to Eastbourne rather than Manchester in determining which of these two notified authorities had responsibility for housing them.

Where a person is recognised by the Home Office to be a "refugee" it would appear that the person must be regarded as being homeless and not being intentionally homeless.[74] "Refugee" is defined by Article 1 of the Convention relating to the status of refugees agreed at Geneva on 28 July, 1951 (as extended by Article 1(2) of the Protocol relating to the status of refugees agreed at New York on 31 January 1967) as any person who:

> "[O]wing to well-founded fear of being persecuted for reason of race, religion, nationality, membership of a particular social group or political opinion, is outside his country of nationality and is unable or, owing to such fear, is unwilling to avail himself of the protection of that country: or who, not having a nationality and being outwith the country of his former habitual residence ... is unable or, owing to such fear, is unwilling to return to it."[75]

---

72. *Ibid.*
73. (1981) 8 HLR 48.
74. See *R. v. Wandsworth LBC, ex p. Nimako - Boateng* (1984) HLR 192 and *R. v. Crawley Borough Council, ex p. The Mayor and Burgesses of Brent LBC, supra.*
75. See L. Grant and I. Morton, *Immigration Law and Practice* (Cobden Trust, London, 1981) Ch. 15 and First Supplement (1985) p. 157 and J.A. Macdonald, *Immigration Law and Practice* (Butterworths, London, 1983) Ch. 10.

Chapter 7
The Duties of Housing Authorities

The legislation imposes a series of duties upon housing authorities. Where a person applies to a housing authority for assistance or accommodation *and* the authority "have reason to believe" that the applicant may be homeless or threatened with homelessness the authority are obliged to carry out inquiries into the applicant's personal circumstances and the circumstances leading up to his application. Depending on the result of their inquiries the authority will be under a duty to provide advice and appropriate assistance or to take reasonable steps to avert homelessness or to provide temporary or permanent accommodation.[1] Additionally, where the decision of the authority is an adverse one, for example, where the authority determine that their obligation is merely to provide temporary rather than permanent accommodation, they are obliged not only to notify the applicant of their decision in writing but also to give their reasons for that decision.[2] Other duties, such as the duty to protect the applicant's property,[3] arise as a consequence of the housing authority's initial determination as to the nature and level of assistance to be provided. As these duties form the core of the legislation it is proposed to examine them in some detail.

1. Notification

The legislation requires housing authorities on completion of their inquiries to notify applicants of their decision in writing.[4] Their decision must notify the applicant whether the housing authority believe him to

---

1. Section 65 of the Housing Act 1985; section 31 of the Housing (Scotland) Act 1987.
2. Section 64 of the Housing Act 1985; section 30 of the Housing (Scotland) Act 1987.
3. Section 70 of the Housing Act 1985; section 36 of the Housing (Scotland) Act 1987.
4. See fn. 2, *supra.*

be homeless or threatened with homelessness and to have a priority need for accommodation. In the case of a priority need applicant the housing authority must at the same time notify him whether they believe him to have become homeless or threatened with homelessness intentionally and whether they have notified or intend to notify another housing authority in order to transfer responsibility for providing permanent accommodation to that authority.

(a) Adverse decision

In addition to notifying applicants of their decision, where a housing authority make an adverse decision in relation to: (i) whether the applicant is homeless or threatened with homelessness; or (ii) whether he has a priority need; or (iii) whether he became homeless or threatened with homelessness intentionally; or (iv) if they have notified or intend to notify another housing authority; or (v) if a housing authority cease to be subject to a duty to protect property or where they have exercised their power to protect property in cases where they are not under a duty to do so and cease to have that power, the legislation places a duty upon the housing authority to notify the applicant of their reasons.[5]

(b) Reasons

The Code does not provide detailed guidance as to the adequacy of reasons for adverse decisions. However, the Code does state that "the authority should inform the applicant of their decision as quickly as possible and give him a sufficient and straightforward indication of the reason for their decision."[6]

The law relating to the adequacy of reasons is difficult to state with any precision because the courts recognise that bodies of varying degrees of formality and expertise with different statutory functions cannot be expected to meet the same standard of exposition.[7] However, the courts do expect decision-makers to give proper and adequate reasons which are both intelligible and deal with the substantive points raised.[8] It is seldom acceptable therefore for decision-makers merely to

---

5. Sections 64 and 70 of the Housing Act 1985; sections 30 and 36 of the Housing (Scotland) Act 1987.
6. EC 2.24; SC 2.26.
7. *Metropolitan Property Holdings v. Laufer* (1974) 29 P & CR 172; *Albyn Properties v. Knox* 1977 SLT 41; *R. v. National Insurance Commissioners, ex p. Viscusi* [1974] 1 WLR 646; R(A) 1/73; R(A) 1/72; R(A) 1/73; and *French Kier Developments v. Secretary of State for the Environment* [1977] 1 All ER 296.
8. *Re Poyser and Mills' Arbitration* [1964] 2 QB 467; *Westminster City Council v. Great Portland Estates PLC* [1985] AC 661.

repeat the statutory authority for their decision rather than dealing with issues of substance and explaining, so far as is possible, the basis of their decision.[9]

In general, the view taken by the courts of the statutory duty imposed on housing authorities to give applicants reasons for adverse decisions is that it is not an onerous one. In *Tickner v. Mole Valley District Council*,[10] Lord Denning stated:

> "Local authorities are entitled to look at the problems quite broadly; and to give their reasons quite simply. Their decision and their reasons are not to be analysed in minute detail. They are not to be gone through as it were with a tooth comb. They are not to be criticised by saying: 'They have not mentioned this or that'."

On this view housing authorities would appear to be required to give very little detail in their reasons for their decisions. However, it should be noted that a number of decisions have been quashed by the courts because the reasons given by the housing authorities failed to demonstrate that they had given proper consideration to the matters which they were obliged to consider.[11] For example, in *R. v. Gloucester City Council, ex p. Miles* where a housing authority purported to find an applicant intentionally homeless, their decision was quashed because they had failed to state, as required by the legislation:

> "(a) that the authority is satisfied that [the] applicant for accommodation became homeless intentionally; (b) when he or she is considered to have become homeless; (c) why he or she is said to have become homeless at that time, i.e. what is the deliberate act or omission in consequence of which it is concluded that at that time he or she ceased to occupy accommodation which was available for his or her occupation, and (d) that it would have been reasonable for him or her to continue to occupy it." [12]

It is equally important that in formulating their reasons for adverse decisions, housing authorities should not seek to rely upon court decisions in preference to the words of the statute. In *R. v. Reigate and Banstead*

---

9. *Albyn Properties v. Knox* (above) and *Guppys (Birdport) v. Sandoe* (1975) 30 P & CR 69 and *Edwin H. Bradley and Sons v. Secretary of State for the Environment* (1982) 264 EG 926.

10. LAG (1980) 187 see also *Lambert v. Ealing LBC* [1982] 1 WLR 550; *De Falco v. Crawley LBC* [1980] QB 460; *R. v. Swansea City Council, ex p. John* (1982) 9 HLR 56; *R. v. Westminster City Council, ex p. Chambers* (1982) 81 LGR 401; *R. v. Wandsworth LBC, ex p. Wells* (QBD) 23 November, 1983; *Mazzaccherini v. Argyll and Bute District Council* 1987 SCLR 475; *R. v. London Borough of Tower Hamlets, ex p. Monaf, The Times*, 18 April, 1988; and *R. v. Wandsworth LBC, ex p. Woodall* (QBD) 12 July, 1988.

11. See, for example, *Re Islam* [1983] 1 AC 688; and *R. v. Tynedale District Council, ex p. Shield* (QBD) 5 November, 1987.

12. (1985) 17 HLR 292.

Borough Council, ex p. Paris,[13] where an authority worded their 'notification letter' on the formula used by the housing authority in *De Falco*, Mr. Justice McCullough observed that if they had addressed themselves to the words of the 1977 Act rather than *De Falco* (which, as it related to the availability of an interlocutory injunction, was inappropriate for their purpose) they might have appreciated the need to consider whether accommodation was available to the applicants in Italy and whether it was reasonable for them to continue to occupy it.

It must be said that there is a tendency for the courts to construe the obligation of authorities to give reasons for adverse decisions "benevolently". For example, although in *R. v. Swansea City Council, ex p. John* [14] a housing authority gave the wrong reason for finding an applicant to have become homeless intentionally, Mr. Justice Woolf refused to quash their decision on the ground that it was properly reached:

"... if a decision is properly reached then the fact that proper reasons have not been given to an applicant does not prevent the council from justifying their decision by reliance upon the proper reason."

While this view is in accordance with the earlier cases on the adequacy of reasons it is submitted that the courts should take the more robust view of the question evidenced in *Miles* and *Paris* and should be less willing to "re-write" the decisions of authorities to meet the requirements of the legislation. For if, as Lord Justice Megaw recognised in *Thornton v. Kirklees Metropolitan Borough Council,*[15] the purpose of this requirement is to enable an applicant to see whether or not to apply for judicial review, it is submitted that the leniency of the courts towards the adequacy of housing authority reasons in cases where the reasons given by authorities are plainly inadequate, encourages applicants to embark on futile actions.

(c) Procedure

The procedure for notification includes the provision that any notification of and, where appropriate, reasons for a decision shall be made available for a reasonable period by the housing authority at their office for collection by the applicant or by another person acting on his behalf.[16] In addition, it is provided that on the cessation of the duty or power to

---

13. (1984) 17 HLR 103.
14. (1982) 9 HLR 56.
15. [1979] QB 626.
16. Section 64 of the Housing Act 1985; section 30 of the Housing (Scotland) Act 1987.

protect property the housing authority must notify the applicant by delivery of the notification to the applicant by leaving it at his last known address or by sending it by post to him at that address.[17]

The legislation obliges authorities to give the applicant written reasons for an adverse decision at the time as notifying the applicant of that decision. Nonetheless, in *Dyson v. Kerrier District Council* [18] Lord Brightman treated this obligation as being a technicality: "merely confirmation of the previous decision which had been communicated to her.

(d) Relationship of "accommodation duty" to "notification duty"

In this context it may be noted that the duties of housing authorities towards homeless persons arise independently of their duty to notify applicants of their decision. Thus in *R. v. Beverley Borough Council, ex p. McPhee* [19] the submission of the Council that their duties to Mrs. McPhee and her four children, under the Housing (Homeless Persons) Act 1977, did not arise until they notified Mrs. McPhee of their decision as required by section 8 of that Act, was rejected by Mr. Justice Wien in the Divisional Court as fundamentally flawed. The duties to provide accommodation, he explained, were the immediate consequences of their decision that the McPhee family was homeless.

2. Nature of Assistance

The nature of assistance which a housing authority must provide to an applicant depends on the result of their inquiries into whether the applicant:

(i)   is homeless or threatened with homelessness;
(ii) has a priority need;
(iii) became homeless intentionally; and
(vi) has a local connection with the area of another authority.

There are basically FOUR forms of assistance available to applicants depending on their circumstances:

---

17. Section 70 of the Housing Act 1985; section 36 of the Housing (Scotland) Act 1987.
18. [1980] 1 WLR 1205.
19. *The Times,* 27 October, 1978. See also *R. v. Ealing Borough Council, ex p. Sidhu,* (1982) 2 HLR 45 on an unsuccessful attempt to "spin out" a response to an application.

(a) advice and appropriate assistance;
(b) reasonable steps to secure that accommodation does not cease to be made available;
(c) temporary accommodation; and
(d) permanent accommodation.

It is important to note at the outset, however, that *to qualify for any kind of assistance the housing authority must be satisfied that the applicant is homeless or threatened with homelessness and to qualify for accommodation the authority must be satisfied that the applicant has a priority need.*

(a) Advice and appropriate assistance

The duty of a housing authority towards a homeless person, who is regarded as having a non-priority need or whom the housing authority are satisfied became threatened with homelessness intentionally, is limited to providing the applicant with advice and appropriate assistance.

"Advice" is not defined by the Act, but the Code of Guidance requests housing authorities to respond "as helpfully and constructively as they are able" and indicates this should be met "by providing advice as fully as for those who have priority need". Examples of the kinds of advice which should be given to avert homelessness include financial aspects of accommodation, housing benefits and mortgages and the possibility of registering on the housing waiting list. Help should be available through housing aid centres supplying lists of accommodation agencies, hostels, lodgings and arrangements with registered housing associations.

"Appropriate assistance" is defined by the legislation as "such assistance as a housing authority consider it appropriate in the circumstances to give [the applicant] in any attempts that he may make to secure that accommodation becomes or does not cease to be available for his occupation."[20]

The Code also urges authorities to be positive in giving advice and assistance and that housing authorities should maintain contact with applicants and be prepared to offer further advice and assistance if the applicant's efforts are not initially successful. Additionally, the Code suggests that housing authorities may be able to give positive assistance to single people by making use of accommodation which may not be

---

20. Section 22 of the Housing Act 1985 and section 20 of the Housing (Scotland) Act 1987 provide that one of the categories of persons who are to be given a reasonable preference in the selection of persons to whom local authorities allocate their tenancies are persons who are homeless or threatened with homelessness, irrespective of whether they have a priority need.

suitable for families, such as tower blocks, and by exercising their discretion to provide some measure of flexibility in applying the laws prohibiting multiple occupation of their own stock.

(b) Reasonable steps to avert homelessness

Where a priority need applicant is threatened with homelessness and the housing authority are not satisfied that he became threatened with homelessness intentionally, the legislation requires the housing authority "to take reasonable steps to secure that accommodation does not cease to be available for his occupation." The legislation does not define the meaning of "reasonable steps". It is clear that what is envisaged in such cases is a more positive approach than the duty to furnish advice and appropriate assistance to applicants who become threatened with homelessness intentionally. Although what will constitute "reasonable steps" to avert homelessness will vary with the circumstances of each case and in particular the nature of the family unit and the reasons why the applicant is threatened with homelessness, examples of preventive action which housing authorities may wish to consider are:

(i) discretionary payments towards rent arrears under section 12 of the Social Work (Scotland) Act 1968 or section 1 of the Child Care Act 1980;

(ii) payment of fuel costs direct to the Electricity or Gas Boards by deduction from Income Support under the Social Security (Claims and Payments) Regulations;

(iii) the payment of housing benefit direct to the landlord under Social Security and Housing Benefit Act 1982 and Regulations thereunder;

(iv) checking that the applicant is taking up all welfare benefits – including housing benefits, income support, child benefit, family credit, unemployment benefit, sickness benefit and disability benefits – to which he or any member of his family may be entitled, and that the amount of welfare benefits received has been correctly calculated;

(v) advice on the legal rights which attach to the occupancy under the common law or statute; and

(vi) where necessary referral to a legal advice centre or solicitor for further legal advice or representation.

(c) Temporary accommodation [21]

The legislation imposes a duty upon housing authorities to provide

21. Sections 63, 65 and 68 of the Housing Act 1985 and sections 29, 31 and 34 of the Housing (Scotland)

temporary accommodation in three specific circumstances. Firstly, pending the completion of their inquiries under the legislation housing authorities are obliged to secure that accommodation is available to an applicant whom they have reason to believe is homeless and has a priority need. This duty prevents housing authorities leaving homeless priority need applicants on the streets and is enforceable in the courts.[22]

Secondly, in addition to furnishing advice and appropriate assistance to an intentionally homeless person with a priority need, the legislation requires housing authorities to secure that accommodation is made available for the applicant's occupation for such period as they consider will give him a reasonable opportunity to secure accommodation for his occupation.

In relation to the provision of temporary accommodation to the intentionally homeless, the Code of Guidance recommends that authorities should:

> "[N]ot arbitrarily nor too quickly withdraw the provision of accommodation [and that] those concerned should be afforded a full opportunity to secure their own accommodation with the benefit of the advice and assistance offered and in the light of their individual circumstances at the time, unless they wilfully decline to take advantage of advice and assistance offered."

What amounts to a reasonable opportunity to secure accommodation for occupation will vary with each case. *Lally v. Kensington and Chelsea Royal Borough Council* [23] indicated that this duty may require housing authorities to make accommodation available for a period of three or four months or even longer in areas of acute housing scarcity.[24]

There is some doubt about the point of time from which the period of temporary accommodation runs. In *De Falco v. Crawley Borough Council* [25] Lord Justice Bridge stated that the period was to be reckoned from the date on which the authority's adverse decision was communicated to the applicant, but Lord Denning took the view that the entire period when temporary accommodation was provided, including the period during which enquiries were being made, could be counted. Other cases[26] would appear to favour Lord Bridge's approach to this question. And lastly, it is the duty of a notifying authority to secure that accommodation is made available until completion of the transfer process.[27]

Act 1987.

22. See "Remedies for the Homeless" below at pp. 208-42; *Galbraith v. Midlothian District Council* 1979 SCOLAG 122 and *Purves v. Midlothian District Council* 1986 SCOLAG 144.

23. *The Times*, 27 March, 1980.

24. See below at p. 202.

25. [1980] QB 460

26. *Dyson v. Kerrier District Council* [1980] 1 WLR 1205 and *Smith v. Bristol City Council* (1981) LAG 287.

27. See Ch. 5, *supra.*

Where a housing authority in Scotland provide temporary accommodation or secure that another person provide temporary accommodation, paragraph 5 of Schedule 2 to the Housing (Scotland) Act 1987 states that "a tenancy shall not be a secure tenancy if the dwellinghouse is being let to the tenant expressly on a temporary basis, in the fulfilment of a duty imposed on a local authority by Part II [of the Housing (Scotland) Act 1987]." Provided it is expressly stated that the letting is a temporary one, this exclusion is wide enough to cover not only temporary accommodation provided under sections 29, 31(3) or 34(2) but also where accommodation is provided on a temporary basis under section 33(2).

However, the position in English Law is significantly different. Under paragraph 4 of Schedule 1 to the Housing Act 1985 it is stated that:

"A tenancy granted in pursuance of sections 63, 65(3) or 68(1) of the Housing Act 1985 is not a secure tenancy before the expiry of a period of twelve months beginning with the date [on which that tenant received the notification required by section 64(1) of that Act or, if he received a notification under section 68(3) of that Act, the date on which he received that notification], unless the tenant is notified by the landlord that the tenancy is to be regarded as a secure tenancy."

This provision is narrower than its Scottish equivalent in the sense that it only applies to temporary accommodation provided under sections 63, 65(3), and 68(1) and it is possible in this case, but not in relation to temporary accommodation granted by Scottish housing authorities, for the tenancy to become a secure tenancy after the expiry of twelve months from the date of notification.

(i) The nature of the occupancy

Before the occupancy of temporary accommodation may be converted into a secure tenancy under the Housing Act 1985 there must be a tenancy or a licence which gives the licensee exclusive possession. For example, in *Eastleigh Borough Council v. Walsh* [28] the House of Lords held that where an applicant was provided with temporary accommodation under section 3(4) of the Housing (Homeless Persons) Act 1977[29] his tenancy became a secure tenancy after the lapse of twelve months from the date of notification.[30] However, in *Family Housing Association v. Miah* [31] the Court of Appeal held that as the housing association granted each homeless family a "non-exclusive licence" they could not become

---

28. [1985] 1 WLR 525.
29. See now section 63 of the Housing Act 1985; section 29 of the Housing (Scotland) Act 1987.
30. See also *London Borough of Newham* Inv. No. 67/Y/83.
31. (1982) 5 HLR 94.

secure tenants after the twelve month period, and section 48 of the Housing Act 1980 (which has the effect of granting secure tenant status to licensees)[32] could not operate. This view was followed in *Restormel Borough Council v Buscombe and Kensington* and *Chelsea Royal London Borough Council v. Hayden* [33] in which the Court of Appeal doubted whether a licence in the sense used by section 48 of the Housing Act 1980 was in fact created by a housing authority when providing temporary accommodation under section 4(3) of the 1977 Act.[34]

(ii) The twelve month period

The twelve month period only begins to run from the date on which the tenant actually received notification. Thus in *Family Housing Association v. Miah* [35] it was held that as notification had not been given to the applicants they could not become tenants and that it was irrelevant that notification ought to have been given if in fact it was not given.

The authority can end the running of the twelve month period after notification has been given if the occupancy is validly terminated before the expiry of that period.[36] It was the failure of the authority validly to terminate the applicant's tenancy in *Eastleigh Borough Council v. Walsh* [37] which led to the applicant obtaining the status of secure tenant. Where an occupancy is validly terminated the occupant becomes a trespasser and therefore incapable of becoming a secure tenant under section 79 of the Housing Act 1985.[38]

In this context it has been suggested that the twelve month suspension period only applies in cases where the applicant is notified that he is entitled to permanent accommodation and continues to occupy the same property which he occupied under section 63. If the applicant is provided with other premises under section 63 by a landlord who is capable of creating a secure tenancy then he becomes a secure tenant immediately.[39]

(d) Permanent accommodation [40]

The duty of a housing authority towards a homeless priority need

---

32. See now section 79(3) of the Housing Act 1985.
33. (1982) 14 HLR 91; (1984) 17 HLR 114; see also *Ogwr Borough Council v. Dykes, The Times,* 10 November, 1988.
34. See now section 65(3) of the Housing Act 1985; section 31(3) of the Housing (Scotland) Act 1987.
35. (1982) 5 HLR 94.
36. *Restormel Borough Council v. Buscombe* (1982) 14 HLR 91.
37. [1985] 1 WLR 525.
38. See *Harrison v. Hammersmith and Fulham LBC* [1981] 1 WLR 650; *Restormel Borough Council v. Buscombe* (1982) 14 HLR 91.
39. A. Arden, *The Housing Act 1985,* (Sweet & Maxwell, London 1980), para. 4 of schedule 1.
40. Section 65 of the Housing Act 1985; section 31 of the Housing (Scotland) Act 1987.

applicant who they are satisfied did not become homeless intentionally, is to secure that accommodation becomes available for his occupation. The housing authority therefore are obliged to take positive action in relation to this category of applicant. In addition to providing accommodation from their own housing stock, the legislation enables a housing authority to perform this and their other housing duties by securing that an applicant obtains accommodation from a third party or by giving an applicant such advice or assistance to enable them to obtain accommodation from some other person. We have noted in the case of *R. v. Bristol City Council, ex p. Browne* [41] that a housing authority may discharge their duty to an applicant by providing her with such advice and assistance as would enable her to obtain accommodation outwith Great Britain.[42] This decision was subsequently approved by both the Divisional Court and the Court of Appeal in *R. v. Hillingdon London Borough Council, ex p. Streeting* [43] in relation to homeless immigrants. In that case Mr. Justice Griffith stated in the Divisional Court that there was nothing in the legislation to prevent the authority from discharging their duty by arranging for accommodation to be provided in the country from which the applicant had come.

The Code of Guidance also sets out a number of suggestions, in addition to the allocation of local authority housing, as to how permanent accommodation may be secured. Briefly these are:

(i)   the advance of a mortgage, where house purchase is possible, either by the local authority themselves or by a building society;
(ii)   advice and assistance in obtaining accommodation in the private rented sector;
(iii)   obtaining accommodation from another local authority (which is of particular relevance in the case of battered women);
(iv)   obtaining accommodation from New Towns (especially relevant where it is desirable to give a homeless family a fresh start);
(v)   obtaining accommodation from housing associations and other voluntary bodies which may be able to offer accommodation particularly to persons with special needs;
(vi)   the provision of mobile homes for single persons; and
(vii)   arranging for the provision of a parking site or mooring place.

3. Nature of Accommodation

The legislation states that "accommodation is only available for a

---

41. [1979] 3 All ER 344.
42. Neither the Housing Act 1985 nor the Housing (Scotland) Act 1987 apply to Northern Ireland. Separate legislation for Northern Ireland is being introduced by order.
43. [1980] 3 All ER 417.

person's occupation if it is available for occupation by [the applicant]" and "any other person who might reasonably be expected to reside with him",[44] and thereby attempts to prohibit the splitting of homeless families[45] and the housing of homeless families in overcrowded accommodation.[46] The legislation fails to provide detailed guidance on the nature, standard or location of accommodation which housing authorities should offer homeless applicants. The Code of Guidance, however, does provide suggestions on this matter.

Although the manner in which housing authorities perform their duties to provide accommodation is largely left to their own discretion the Code points to the importance, whenever possible, of avoiding undue disruption for homeless families of education, employment, family and other ties, particularly in the case of battered women and one-parent families where the support of friends and relatives "can be of great assistance ... to overcome the problems of isolation and loneliness." The Scottish Code makes clear that while "people should not be expected to stay in interim accommodation for lengthy periods of time" the provision of interim accommodation may be necessary where it is not possible to arrange a long-term solution immediately. Examples of this type of accommodation are the use of publicly owned property in housing action areas,[47] or short-life properties,[48] local authority reception areas or hostels, or *as a last resort* bed and breakfast accommodation.[49]

The Code emphasises that because interim accommodation is inherently unsatisfactory for family life it should not be considered as fulfilling the housing authority's duty to provide permanent accommodation or to be used to punish the homeless, adding that:

"Permanent accommodation should be secured as soon as possible and homeless people should not be obliged to spend a certain period in interim accommodation as a matter of policy."

The Code also urges housing authorities to treat homeless persons in the same way as other applicants under their housing allocations systems in relation to areas offered and numbers of offers. Employment, schooling, family and social ties should be taken into account where practicable and reasonable in the allocation process.

---

44. Section 75 of the Housing Act 1985, section 41 of the Housing (Scotland) Act 1987; see also Ch. 4. *supra*, at pp. 69-72.
45. On the practice of splitting homeless families, see above at p.70. A cohabitee is a person who might reasonably be accepted to reside with an applicant (*R. v. Wimborne District Council, ex p. Curtis*, (1985) 18 HLR 79) but an *extended* family may be split up (*R. v. Lambeth LBC, ex p. Ly* (1987) 19 HLR 51).
46. See 'Homeless', Ch. 1, *supra*, at pp. 41-42.
47. Part IV of the Housing (Scotland) Act 1987 and Part VIII of the Housing Act 1985.
48. R. Bailey, *The Homeless and the Empty Houses* (1977).
49. See, however, J. Conway and P. Kemp, *Bed and Breakfast: Slum Housing of the Eighties* (1985).

Housing authorities are now obliged to include homeless persons as a priority need category of application in their housing allocation policies. Initially studies into the ways in which the Act was operated indicated the persistence of the practice by some authorities of dumping homeless persons in hard-to-let accommodation, hostels, guest-houses, mobile homes, short-term accommodation, pre-fabricated buildings and disused army camps.[50]

These practices were frowned upon in a number of early decisions which made it clear that the provision of insanitary housing or housing that is in poor repair may not be sufficient to discharge the housing authority's obligations to provide temporary or permanent accommodation. In *Galbraith v. Midlothian District Council*,[51] for example, Lord Avonside indicated that the let of a vandalised, damp and fire-damaged property would not be sufficient to discharge the District Council's obligations to provide permanent accommodation. Subsequently, Lord Justice-Clerk Wheatley observed in *Brown v. Hamilton District Council*[52] that whereas a pig-sty may well be accommodation available for occupation by the applicant it would not be reasonable accommodation. In addition in *Parr*[53] the Court of Appeal indicated that accommodation had to be appropriate or reasonable.

This view was accepted by the House of Lords in *Brown v. Hamilton District Council,* although Lord Fraser did add a rider which reflects the past policies of some local authorities:

> "[T]he accommodation must be reasonable, but as it is provided only temporarily pending the decision of the housing authority it might, I think, be adequate although falling below the standard of adequacy for permanent accommodation."[54]

Later cases, however, highlight a marked reluctance to follow this view. Indeed, a degree of hostility towards the idea of providing homeless persons with decent accommodation appears to be the hallmark of each of these cases, culminating in *Puhlhofer*.[55] The approach of the House of Lords in *Puhlhofer* was so at odds with the spirit of the original legislation that an amendment was successfully introduced in 1986.[56]

---

50. "Where Homelessness Means Hopelessness", Shelter (1978). See also *Delahaye v. Oswestry Borough Council, The Times,* 29 July, 1980.
51. (1979) SCOLAG 122; *Glasgow Herald,* 20 December, 1978; *Scottish Daily Express,* 21 December, 1978.
52. (1983) SLT 397 at p. 403.
53. *R. v. Wyre Borough Council, ex p. Parr* (1982) 2 HLR 71.
54. *Brown v. Hamilton District Council* 1983 SLT 397 at 417.
55. [1986] AC 484.
56. See now section 58 (2A) of the Housing Act 1985; section 24(3)(d) of the Housing (Scotland) Act 1987.

The specific issues which have been raised cover:

(a) type of permanent accommodation;
(b) location of permanent accommodation;
(c) standard of temporary and permanent accommodation;
(d) length of tenure of permanent accommodation;
(e) "staged" performance of the duty to provide permanent accommodation;
(f) allocation; and
(g) refusal of offer.

(a) Type of permanent accommodation

The cases which have discussed the suitability of permanent accommodation provided by housing authorities have related to:

(i)   mobile homes;
(ii) squats; and
(iii) accommodation which has not been adapted for the disabled.

(i) Mobile homes

In the first of these cases, *Wood v. Doncaster Metropolitan Borough Council*,[57] the guidance given by the Code can be usefully contrasted with the view of the courts. Paragraph A2.8 of the English Code states that:

> "[A]lthough a mobile home may sometimes provide suitable accommodation for single people or childless couples, authorities will wish to bear in mind the findings of the Mobile Homes Review that *mobile homes are not satisfactory for families with children or as a form of interim accommodation for homeless persons."* [58]

Notwithstanding this clear expression of the unsuitability of mobile homes as accommodation for families with children, the housing authority in this case sought to fulfil their duty to provide permanent accommodation to an applicant and her family by offering her a caravan. When the case was heard in the county court Judge Pickles accepted that it was open to an authority to penalise unintentionally homeless families who had been "bad rent-payers" by allocating caravan accommodation:

> "In the case of good tenants one would doubtless apply paragraph A2.8, but

---

57. Court of Appeal, 29 November, 1983.
58. Our emphasis.

the applicant and her husband are not in that category. They cannot expect to be treated in the same way as those who have in the past carried out their obligations as tenants. The [housing authority] have acted reasonably in putting them at the bottom of their list and providing them with less attractive accommodation."

The Court of Appeal did not comment adversely on this statement and implicitly accepted it.

(ii) Squats

The issue in *R. v. Westminster City Council, ex p. Wahab* [59] was whether the offer of premises occupied by squatters discharged an authority's duty to provide permanent housing to an applicant. In this case, the applicant, an Asian waiter with three children, was offered accommodation by the housing authority but when he got there he found that it was occupied by squatters who had changed the locks. What transpired at this stage was disputed by the applicant but it was accepted by Mr Justice Taylor that the housing officers explained to the applicant that it was possible for the squatters to be evicted within a week under section 7 of the Criminal Law Act 1977 and that the accommodation would be available to him within a week. In these circumstances the offer of this accommodation was accepted by the court as discharging the authority's duty on the grounds that it could be made available within a few days and that the applicant's real reason for refusing it was that he did not wish to live in this part of London.

(iii) Accommodation not adapted for the disabled

In *R. v. Hillingdon London Borough Council, ex p. Oatley* [60] a disabled applicant argued that the accommodation provided by an authority did not discharge their duty to provide permanent accommodation because it did not have a shower unit. This contention was rejected by Mr. Justice Taylor on the ground that the authority were entitled to accept the assessment of their Senior Clinical Medical Officer that as a bath was provided a shower unit was not justified in his case.

(b) Location of permanent accommodation

Another aspect of the *Wood* case was whether the accommodation

---

59. (QBD) 28 June, 1983.
60. (QBD) 2 October, 1984.

provided could be regarded as "appropriate" accommodation given that the location of the caravan site was over 20 miles from Doncaster where the couple's families resided, the poor public transport facilities, and the expense of travelling between the site and Doncaster. While Judge Pickles referred to *Parr* as authority that a housing authority providing accommodation under the legislation, is under a duty to ensure that it is suitable as regards geographical location, he found that the accommodation was suitable for the applicants and that this discharged the authority's obligation to provide permanent accommodation:

> "The plaintiff and her husband came from Doncaster, but that did not deter them from accepting the offer of a caravan in Miserton. They can travel into Doncaster by bus on a Saturday for £1 return [two buses during the week -- single fare £1.30] and they use this facility. I appreciate that it would be more convenient for the [applicant] and her husband to have accommodation nearer to Doncaster, but I do not consider that this factor in itself makes the caravan inadequate."

When this case was heard before the Court of Appeal, Lord Justice Cumming-Bruce stated that while he:

> "[B]egan at one stage to feel that perhaps Miserton was rather a long way from the metropolitan centre of Doncaster for the purposes of employment, the concern was due to a failure on my part to recognise that the pleaded geographical unsuitability was simply a regret of [the applicant] that she could not keep in closer contact with her extended family."[61]

In *Keyte v. South Holland District Council*[62] the applicant objected to both the location and the standard of housing offered by the authority. Her principle objection was to the location of the accommodation which she described as being "a problem area, an area in which delinquents abound and therefore an area which was unsuitable for her and her two young daughters." However, she also objected to the condition of the housing which she stated was unsuitable: "there is no inside water-closet; the toilet is outside in the garden and ... that is unsatisfactory if it has to be used at night ... the garden is very neglected, with an overgrowth several feet high." Lord Justice Stephenson said that he could "well understand her objection to the accommodation she had been offered" and that it may well be said that "it was reasonable for her to refuse the offer of this alternative permanent accommodation; and it may even be said that it was unreasonable of the Council to offer it." However, the question was not whether her refusal of the Council's offer

61. Court of Appeal, 29 November, 1983 and *The Daily Telegraph,* 11 November, 1988, which reported Dorset were considering housing the homeless in Oldham.
62. (1985) 84 LGR 347.

was unreasonable but rather "was the Council's view that this was appropriate accommodation so unreasonable that no reasonable authority ... could have reached it?"

The answer which the Court of Appeal gave to this question was a negative one. However, the Court of Appeal reminded housing authorities that according to their earlier decision:

> "[A] council's housing duty is not discharged by the offer of 'any old' accommodation; they must offer appropriate accommodation. What is appropriate is of course a question, and often a very difficult question, of fact which must needs be a troublesome exercise on the part of the authority, housing no doubt being short and homeless persons being numerous and it not being by any means always possible to provide anything like ideal accommodation for unintentionally homeless persons."[63]

The sweeping nature of Lord Brightman's remarks in *Puhlhofer* would seem to suggest that objections on the grounds of location are irrelevant. This clearly was the view taken by Lord Mayfield in *Mackenzie*[64] where he stressed that his hands were tied as far as interfering on the grounds of the unsuitability was concerned, except in rare circumstances where:

> "[I]t remains open to an applicant to object to the location of permanent accommodation on the grounds that no reasonable authority would make such an offer."

Bearing in mind the acceptance by the judiciary that the problem of homelessness is a standard one of an under-supply of decent affordable houses the chances of success are limited.

Where an applicant is dissatisfied with the location of permanent accommodation offered to him, he may obtain a more satisfactory solution by complaining to the Local Ombudsman, rather than seeking redress through the courts, as the following complaint by a battered woman demonstrates. The problem of allocating housing in a suitable area to a battered woman is one which the Scottish Code[65] states requires a sensitive approach by housing authorities which reflects both the need of battered women for family support and to ensure that a reasonable distance is placed between a battered woman and her violent partner. The failure of a housing authority to respond to the needs of battered women in such a manner can lead to a repetition of violence or increase the isolation of estranged spouses.

For example, in one complaint a woman separated from a violent spouse was aggrieved that she had been offered accommodation near to

---

63. *R. v. Wyre Borough Council, ex p. Parr* (1982) 2 HLR 71.
64. *Mackenzie v. Strathkelvin District Council*, 8 May, 1985 (authors' notes).
65. SC 4.3.

where she was living. Her complaint revealed serious deficiencies in the policy of the housing authority for dealing with housing applications from separated couples under the 1977 Act[66] and as a consequence the authority not only offered her a house in another area but decided to carry out an urgent review of their policy to ensure that homeless women who had been subjected to matrimonial violence would not be put in such a position again. As this was a satisfactory response the Local Ombudsman discontinued his investigation.

(c) Standard of accommodation

In *Brown v. Hamilton District Council* [67] Lord Fraser indicated that different standards apply to temporary and permanent accommodation provided by housing authorities under the legislation:

> "*[T]he accommodation must be reasonable*, but as it is provided only temporarily pending the decision of the housing authority it might, I think, be adequate although falling below the standard of adequacy for permanent accommodation." (Our emphasis)

(i) Temporary accommodation

This dictum was clarified by Mr. Justice Nolan in *R. v. Ryedale District Council, ex p. Smith.*[68] In this case the applicant was a 67 year old man who had acute bronchitis, chronic fibrosis of the lungs and emphysema and showed evidence of clubbing of fingers and breathlessness. At the time of his application he was living in a caravan at a site in Yorkshire where the standard of hygiene was exceptionally low . According to his doctor's sworn affidavit:

> "[T]he site was full of faeces and there had been many cases of clamydial infection of the gut and one or two of salmonella ... At this time the conditions on the caravan site, so far as Sydney Smith was concerned, were most unsatisfactory, and in my opinion his health was seriously at risk."

Pending the completion of their inquiries, the housing authority offered the applicant temporary accommodation in a caravan on another site which he refused. The question before the court therefore was whether in these circumstances the offer of this temporary accommodation to the applicant discharged their duty towards him. Mr. Justice Nolan held that it did not:

---

66. See City of Glasgow District Council (Inv. No. 150/82).
67. 1983 SLT 397.
68. (1983) 16 HLR 66.

"It is common ground that the word 'accommodation' in this context must be read as a reference to suitable or appropriate accommodation for the applicant. Plainly, the quality of the accommodation cannot always be high, but the section appears to me to contemplate that the suitability of the accommodation, in the particular applicant's case, is to be judged by reference to the results of the appropriate inquiries. These must cover *inter alia* the matters referred to in s.2(1)(c) of the Act [see now s.59(1)(c) of the Housing Act 1985 and s.25(1)(c) of the Housing (Scotland) Act 1987], which covers the cases in which an applicant, or any person who resides with him is vulnerable as a result of old age, mental illness or hardship, physical disability or other special reasons ... I am not prepared to accept that the accommodation was shown to have been suitable as temporary accommodation [for a man of sixty-seven years, suffering from emphysema] ..."

This decision is important for two reasons. First, while adhering to the view that temporary accommodation provided under the Act need not be of as high a standard as permanent accommodation, it must be appropriate to the needs of the applicant and his family. Secondly, it casts doubt on the use of mobile homes as temporary accommodation to house homeless applicants, particularly where the applicant is vulnerable as a result of old age or physical disability.

Against this decision, however, it is possible to cite the case of *R. v. Southampton City Council, ex p. Ward*.[69] In this case, the alternative accommodation offered to a gypsy family was a rat-infested caravan site which frequently flooded and on which there were no heating or lighting facilities. A social services worker stated in her *affidavit* that the land had been used for the dumping of rubbish and that she had seen it flooded and with rats living on it, adding that "the condition of the site was jeopardising the health and welfare of the children." Notwithstanding the atrocious conditions of the site, Mr. Justice McCullough held that in providing it the housing authority had discharged their duty to provide temporary accommodation.

The standard of temporary accommodation was also discussed in *R. v. Exeter City Council, ex p. Gliddon*.[70] In this case the temporary accommodation provided by the authority was in a deplorable condition; the standard of repair and maintenance was very unsatisfactory, there was extensive damage to wall and ceiling plaster, and the standard of decoration was poor. However, it was held that as the property was not unfit for human habitation it could not be said that it was of such a standard that it amounted to a failure of the authority to discharge their duty.

In arriving at this conclusion Mr. Justice Woolf, echoing Lord

69. (1984) 14 HLR 114.
70. [1985] 1 All ER 493.

Fraser in *Brown*, stated that the standard of temporary accommodation does not require to be of the same standard as permanent accommodation but it has to be accommodation. What is accommodation for this purpose, he added, is to be assessed in terms of the fact that the authority have many calls upon their stock of accommodation and the courts should not be too ready to come to the conclusion that the duty to provide temporary accommodation has not been fulfilled even though the accommodation provided is in many respects unsatisfactory.

(ii) Permanent accommodation

It is now specifically provided that the accommodation offered by a local authority must satisfy a minimum standard. For Scotland it is provided that "accommodation" does not include accommodation that is overcrowded[71] *or* which may endanger the health of the occupant.[72] In England the "accommodation" provided must be "suitable accommodation", having regard to slum clearance, overcrowding and houses in multiple occupancy.[73] Both of these amendments were designed to overcome the restrictive view of the meaning of accommodation put forward by Lord Brightman in *Puhlhofer*[74] and therefore can be regarded as in part restoring the long line of authority disturbed by the decision of the House of Lords in that case.[75] The standard adopted by the Housing Act 1985 is obviously more flexible than that adopted by the Housing (Scotland) Act 1987. It may be thought that the former standard is to be preferred to the latter.[76] However, in *R. v. Blackpool Borough Council, ex p. Smith*[77] Mr. Justice Schiemann indicated that the question of whether a property is reasonable or suitable was a question of fact for the authority in question and it is therefore unlikely that a successful challenge could be mounted unless it was shown that the property was so unsuitable that no reasonable authority could regard it as being suitable. The "Scottish standard" has then at least the merit of being an objective one.

---

71. Section 135 of the Housing (Scotland) Act 1987.
72. Section 32(5) of the Housing (Scotland) Act 1987; section 24(3)(d) which refers to accommodation which is overcrowded *and* a danger to health.
73. Section 69(1) of the Housing Act 1985, as amended by section 14 of the Housing and Planning Act 1986.
74. [1986] AC 484.
75. See, for example, *Brown v. Hamilton District Council* 1983 SLT 397; *R. v. Wyre Borough Council, ex p. Parr* (1982) 2 HLR 71; *R. v. South Herefordshire District Council, ex p. Miles* (1983) 17 HLR 82 and *R. v. Dinefwr Borough Council, ex p. Marshall* (1984) 17 HLR 310.
76. T. Mullen, "The New Law on Homelessness" (1987) SCOLAG 7.
77. (QBD) 29 July, 1987; see also *R. v. Westminster City Council, ex p. Tansey,* (QBD) 6 March, 1987.

(d) Length of tenure of permanent accommodation

The duty to secure that accommodation becomes available for occupation by an applicant is a duty to make accommodation available on an indefinite or permanent basis.[78] In *R. v. Camden London Borough Council, ex p. Wait* [79] an attempt to discharge the duty to provide accommodation by providing accommodation for the unexpired period of a 3 months licence was held to be unlawful as the duty of the authority was to provide accommodation on an indefinite basis. Nevertheless, it would appear to be lawful to provide insecure accommodation, such as hostel or hotel accommodation, in discharge of this duty provided it is on an indefinite basis.[80]

(e) "Staged" performance on the duty to provide permanent accommodation

The Code of Guidance provides that permanent accommodation is to be provided as soon as possible and that homeless persons should not as a matter of policy be forced to spend a specific period in interim accommodation. In *R. v. East Hertfordshire District Council, ex p. Hunt* [81] it was accepted that it was open to an authority to perform this duty in stages; for example, they could provide bed and breakfast accommodation before allocating permanent accommodation.

(f) Allocation

Section 22 of the Housing Act 1985 and section 20 of the Housing (Scotland) Act 1987 provide that homeless persons are to be given a reasonable preference by housing authorities in the selection of their tenants under their allocation policies. In this context the Code of Guidance[82] talks of homeless persons as "persons who are homeless whether or not they have priority need or became homeless intentionally." What amounts to a "reasonable preference" is unclear but the adoption of allocation policies designed to discriminate unfairly against homeless persons may give grounds for application for judicial review[83] or complaint to the Local Ombudsman.

---

78. *Din v. Wandsworth LBC* [1981] 1 AC 657.
79. (1986) 18 HLR 434.
80. *R. v. Westminster City Council, ex p. Tansey* (QBD) 6 March, 1987.
81. (1985) 18 HLR 51.
82. SC 6.3; EC 6.3.
83. *R. v. Canterbury City Council, ex p. Gillespie* (1987) 19 HLR 7; *R. v. Port Talbot Borough Council, ex p. Jones, The Independent,* 5 January, 1988.

(g) Refusal of an offer of accommodation

In *R. v. Westminster City Council, ex p. Chambers*,[84] Mr. Justice McCullough held that if a homeless person unreasonably refused an offer of appropriate accommodation and there are not separate circumstances which give rise to a separate incidence of homelessness, then there is no obligation on a housing authority to keep making offers of accommodation.[85] This decision has been misconstrued as meaning that one offer of accommodation is sufficient to discharge the obligation of housing authorities to unintentionally homeless applicants. However, it is clear that this will only be the case where the original offer was an offer of appropriate accommodation and there has not been a material change in the applicant's circumstances between the date of the offer and his later request for assistance. If there is a change of circumstances the authority's duty towards him is revived.

This point was reaffirmed by the Court of Appeal in *R. v. Ealing London Borough Council, ex p. McBain*.[86] In this case a pregnant woman approached the housing authority for assistance. They found that she had a priority need for accommodation and that she was unintentionally homeless and therefore offered her the tenancy of a premises in Southall. The applicant refused the offer on the ground that it was unsuitable for her and the child she was expecting. A year later when she was expecting the birth of a second child she again approached the authority for assistance under the Housing (Homeless Persons) Act 1977. Relying on *Chambers* the authority informed her that as there had been no material change in her circumstances they had discharged their duty and had no further duty to offer her accommodation. Following *Chambers*, the Court of Appeal held that there was no duty on a housing authority to keep making offers of accommodation unless there was a material change in the applicant's circumstances. The question therefore was whether the second pregnancy provided such a change.

On this question Lord Justice Ackner was in no doubt that there had been a material change in the applicant's circumstances:

"To my mind it would seem most odd if, because Miss McBain rejects the Council's offer, thereby taking it upon herself to provide accommodation for herself and her child, she therefore forfeits the rights to assistance under the Act if her circumstances so change that the accommodation originally offered would, in the event, have been quite unsuitable ... of course, where a Housing Authority, pursuant to its statutory obligations under the Act, makes a proper offer of accommodation which is unreasonably declined, the

---

84. (1982) LGR 401.
85. See also *R. v. Hammersmith and Fulham LBC, ex p. O'Brian* [1985] 17 HLR 471 and *R. v. East Hertfordshire District Council, ex p. Hunt* [1985] 18 HLR 51.
86. [1986] 1 All ER 13.

Housing Authority has at that stage performed that statutory obligation. On my judgement, however, it can be properly inferred from the provisions of the Act, that *the obligation is revived by a material change in the circumstances of the applicant. To establish a material change, the applicant must show that there has been a change in his or her circumstances to make the accommodation offered clearly unsuitable.* Because conditions vary from area to area, in judging the alleged unsuitability regard must be had to the general conditions prevailing in relation to housing in the area of the Housing Authority ... If the applicant can establish such a situation, as indeed Miss McBain has done, then he or she has established an occasion which requires the duty to be performed yet again." [87] (Our emphasis)

Where an offer is made an applicant must be given a *reasonable opportunity* to accept or reject the offer. For example, in *R. v. Wandsworth London Borough Council, ex p. Lindsay* [88] it was stated that an applicant must be given a "proper opportunity of considering an offer, both by being told sufficient details about the premises and being given time to take a decision." However, in that case a period of less than one week was held to be sufficient to enable the applicant to decide to accept or reject an offer.

4. Charging for Accommodation

In addition to the power of a housing authority to charge rent where they provide accommodation to homeless persons from their own housing stock,[89] the legislation empowers them to require homeless persons to pay such reasonable amount as the housing authority may determine in respect of sums payable by the housing authority for accommodation made available to homeless persons by other persons.[90] Neither the legislation nor the Code provides guidance as to how a housing authority should exercise this discretion. However, from general principles of administrative law one can infer that where a housing authority fail to exercise their discretionary powers to determine what is a reasonable charge by adopting a blanket policy, such as charging all homeless persons the full cost or a fixed charge for accommodation,[91] or by refusing to consider to consider the individual charge in each case,[92] their

---

87. Ibid. at 17 (our emphasis).
88. (1986) 18 HLR 502; see also *R. v. Wyre Borough Council, ex p. Parr* (1982) 2 HLR 71 and in Scotland *Mackenzie v. Strathkelvin District Council* (above) where 48 hours was an inadequate time to decide.
89. Section 24 of the Housing Act 1985; section 210 of the Housing (Scotland) Act 1987.
90. Section 69 of the Housing Act 1985; section 35 of the Housing (Scotland) Act 1987.
91. See 'Split Families – the dividing rule', *Roof*, March/April 1981, p.3.
92. On fettering discretionary powers see *R. v. Eastleigh Borough Council, ex p. Betts* [1983] 2 AC 613; *R. v. South Hertfordshire District Council, ex p. Miles* (1983) 17 HLR 182; and *R. v. Canterbury City Council, ex p. Gillespie* (1987) 19 HLR 7.

failure to do so may be unlawful.

What amounts to a reasonable charge for accommodation has been the subject for litigation and has figured in an investigation by the Local Ombudsman. A case involving Argyll and Bute District Council[93] arose from adoption by that Council of a policy of charging homeless persons the full cost of temporary accommodation. The Sheriff in a summary court action decided that the Council were only entitled to recover a reasonable amount and not the full cost of providing the accommodation. He also stated that it was incumbent on the authority to make a detailed assessment of the financial circumstances of the applicant in order to determine what is a reasonable amount for *him* to pay. As the full cost of the accommodation in this case was more than double what the applicant received in social security it could not be a reasonable charge.

In a complaint against Nairn District Council[94] the complainant's grievance was that he was required to contribute towards the cost of bed and breakfast accommodation. The Local Ombudsman held that, while it would have been better if the housing authority had informed the complainant in writing that he would be expected to contribute towards the cost of accommodation, as he should have been aware that he would have to pay something, there was not maladministration on the part of the authority due to their failure to inform him of this fact. The Local Ombudsman considered whether the charge of £70 per week made by the authority for the period of stay was reasonable. This sum represented about half of the actual cost of the accommodation and half the amount of supplementary benefit paid to the couple. In these circumstances the Local Ombudsmen found that the charge was not unreasonable.

5. Protection of Property [95]

Where a housing authority are obliged by the Act to provide either temporary or permanent accommodation or to take reasonable steps to avert homelessness and have reason to believe that there is a danger of loss of, or damage to the personal or moveable property of an applicant falling within these categories by reason of his inability to protect or deal with the property and that no other suitable arrangements have been made or are being made, the housing authority are obliged to take reasonable steps to prevent the loss of the property or prevent or mitigate damage to it. In other circumstances, where there is a danger of loss or damage and suitable arrangements have not been made, a housing authority are empowered but not obliged to take any steps they consider

93. (1986) SCOLAG 100.
94. Inv. No. 830016.
95. Section 70 of the Housing Act 1985; section 36 of the Housing (Scotland) Act 1987

to be reasonable to protect the property of an applicant.

A housing authority are empowered, in the discharge of their duty or in exercise of their power to protect property at all reasonable times, to enter the residence or former residence of an applicant and to deal with the property in any way which is reasonably necessary. The Code of Guidance suggests that a housing authority may, in the discharge of their duty or exercise of their power, store the property or arrange for its storage or, with the agreement of the applicant, leave the property in the applicant's former residence if it can be adequately protected there or arrange for its transportation.

Housing authorities are also empowered to decline to discharge their duty or to exercise their power to protect property except upon appropriate conditions. "Appropriate conditions" are defined as such conditions as a housing authority consider appropriate in a particular case and may include:

(i) reasonable charges for the protection of property; or
(ii) disposal of property in specified circumstances, such as abandonment.

The duty or power to protect the personal or moveable property of an applicant ceases when in the opinion of the housing authority there is no longer any reason to believe that there is a danger of loss of or damage to the property by reason of the applicant's inability to protect or deal with it. However, property placed in storage may be kept in store after the expiry of the duty or power.

The value of this provision to homeless persons depends on the manner in which housing authorities interpret "reason to believe" in relation to their duty or power to protect property and the conditions, particularly in relation to reasonable charges, which the housing authorities may impose if they are not to decline to discharge their duty or to exercise their power.

The failure of a housing authority to exercise reasonable care in relation to property under their control can result in them being found liable for damages for negligence. In *Mitchell v. Ealing London Borough Council*[96] where an authority voluntarily agreed to store the property of a couple evicted from a squat it was held that they were liable in negligence when most of the goods were found to be missing and that the couple were entitled to damages.

When a housing authority failed to fulfil their duty to protect moveable property, the Local Ombudsman has found that their failure amounted to maladministration. In one case a regional social work department and a housing authority failed to take adequate steps to

---

96. [1979] QB 1.

safeguard the belongings of a disabled pensioner who had been made homeless following the flooding of her house. The Local Ombudsman found that the failure to do so constituted maladministration from which she suffered injustice. As a consequence of this report a substantial sum was offered by way of compensation and the housing authority and social work department reviewed their joint procedures for dealing with emergency homelessness cases to provide that the housing authority would be responsible for removals and the protection of property after notification by the social work department.[97]

---

97. See Strathclyde Regional Council and City of Glasgow District Council Inv. Nos. 199/80 and 200/80.

Chapter 8

Remedies For The Homeless

The National Assistance Act 1948 imposed a duty upon local authorities to provide temporary accommodation "for any persons who are in urgent need thereof, being need arising in circumstances which could not reasonably have been foreseen." Where a local authority failed to implement this somewhat limited duty the Minister of Health was empowered by section 36(1) of that Act to compel the authority to do so. This duty was replaced by sections 3 and 4 of the Housing (Homeless Persons) Act 1977 which required housing authorities to provide, secure or help to secure accommodation for homeless persons and those threatened with homelessness.

However, unlike its predecessor, the Housing (Homeless Persons) Act 1977 did not provide either the Secretary of State for the Environment or the Secretary of State for Scotland with a default power, or any other extra-judicial mode of redress; neither does the Housing Act 1985 nor the Housing (Scotland) Act 1987. Hence a homeless person seeking to challenge the decision of a housing authority under the legislation must, in the main, do so before the courts. Many difficulties face homeless persons in attempting to obtain redress in the courts and therefore in this section we attempt to provide a short guide to the remedies which are available to homeless persons. As this problem continues to exercise those advising homeless persons on both sides of the Border, we have attempted to state the law on the matter, drawing comparisons where it is thought appropriate to do so, with the position of homeless persons seeking redress under Scots law and English law.

For some time it was far from clear what remedies were available to homeless persons seeking redress in the Scottish courts. The Court of Session had approved the use of section 91 petition procedure under the Court of Session Act 1868 to compel the performance of a statutory obligation under the Act.[1] However, differing opinions were expressed as to the competence of the sheriff court as a forum to determine a number of actions arising from attempts to challenge decisions of housing authorities.[2] This matter was finally dealt with in the House of Lords in *Brown v. Hamilton District Council*.[3] In an unanimous decision their Lordships decided that only the Court of Session had jurisdiction to supervise Scottish local authority decision-making and there was no role for the sheriff court in this process.[4] Apart from this challenge by way of judicial review an aggrieved applicant could enforce a statutory duty under the legislation by way of a decree *ad factum praestandum* or bring an action for damages for breach of statutory duty in that court. In addition to these remedies a homeless person may seek an interdict or interim interdict against a housing authority, for example, to prevent the premature withdrawal of temporary accommodation.

The major legislative change in respect of remedies has been the introduction of a new simplified procedure for judicial review in Scotland. The new procedure was introduced by Act of Sederunt[5] and came into effect on 30 April, 1985. Form 39A provides a model form of petition to be used under this procedure. The new procedure broadly follows the proposals of the Dunpark Working Party which was set up in 1983 to devise a simplified form of procedure for judicial review in the Court of Session.[6] In essence the new procedure vests considerable discretion in the Court of Session in relation to both procedure and remedies. Rule 260B (4) provides that the court:

"[I]n exercising supervisory jurisdiction in respect of an application for judicial review, may;
(a) grant or refuse the application or any part of it, with or without conditions;
(b) make such order in relation to the decision in question as it thinks fit, whether or not such an order was sought in the application, being an order that could be made if sought in any action or petition, including an

---

1. *Galbraith v. Midlothian District Council* (1979) SCOLAG 122; *Mackenzie v. West Lothian District Council* (1979) SCOLAG 123, 1979 SC 433.
2. *Williamson v. Moray District Council* 1980 SLT (Sh Ct) 32; *Roughead v. Falkirk District Council* (1979) SCOLAG 188; *Brown v. Hamilton District Council* 1980 SLT (Sh Ct) 81.
3. 1983 SLT 397.
4. *Argyll and Bute District Council* (1986) SCOLAG 100 in which the reasonableness of a charge for temporary accommodation was successfully challenged in the sheriff court and *Purves v. Midlothian District Council* (1986) SCOLAG 144.
5. Rule of Court 260(B); 1985 SLT 137 Introduced by Act of Sederunt (Rules of Court Amendment No. 2) Judicial Review 1985.
6. A.C. Page 'Just and Reasonable: Report of the Working Party on the Procedure for Judicial Review of Administrative Action' 1984 SLT 290; J.L. Murdoch, 'Reviewing Administrative Action' (1984) SCOLAG 160; T. Mullen, *A Guide to Judicial Review in Scotland* (Shelter (Scotland), Edinburgh, 1987); J. St Clair and N. Davidson, *Judicial Review in Scotland* (W. Green and Son, Edinburgh, 1986).

order for reduction, declarator, suspension, interdict, implement, restitution, payment (whether of damages or otherwise), and any interim order; and
(c) subject to the provisions of this rule, make such order in relation to procedure as it thinks appropriate in the circumstances."

The importance of the new judicial procedure cannot be over-estimated. Under the new procedure it is possible to expedite the determination of public law actions[7] and the Court of Session may grant whatever remedy it thinks most appropriate to obtain leave to seek judicial review.

The question of availability of remedies in English law has been discussed in three Court of Appeal cases and in the House of Lords. In the first Court of Appeal case, *Thornton v. Kirklee Metropolitan Borough Council*,[8] Lords Megaw and Roskill rejected the view that homeless persons seeking redress against housing authorities under the legislation were confined to a claim for judicial review under RSC Order 53. The Court accepted that as the statute was passed for the benefit of a specified category of persons, a homeless person could bring a civil action for damages in the county court. The decision was later followed in *De Falco v. Crawley District Council*.[9] Lord Denning added in that case that a homeless person may seek redress by action of declaration, injunction, a civil action for damages, judicial review or interim relief in either the High Court or the county court. Subsequently, however, in *Lambert v. Ealing London Borough Council* [10] both Lord Denning and Lord Justice May indicated that it is desirable that homeless persons should challenge the decisions of housing authorities by way of judicial review in the High Court rather than by seeking remedies, such as damages for breach of statutory duty, in the county court.

This line was taken up with some enthusiasm by the House of Lords in *Cocks v. Thanet District Council* [11] where the sole remedy sought was the quashing of a decision of an authority. This remedy, it was said, should be by means of judicial review rather than by a private law action for damages, as to do otherwise would amount to an abuse of the process of the court.

Although there are roughly equivalent remedies in Scots law and English law, there are important differences in the forms, procedure and scope of judicial remedies for the control of administrative acts and omissions. Moreover, both the House of Lords and the Court of Session have expressed some doubt as to the appropriateness of the judicial review being used by homeless persons as a means of testing the legality

7. P. Robson, 'Judicial Review and Homelessness' 1985 SLT 305.
8. [1979] QB 626.
9. [1980] QB 460.
10. [1982] 2 All ER 394.
11. [1983] AC 286. See also a case decided at the same time on the relationship between public law remedies and private law remedies, *O'Reilly v. Mackman* [1982] 3 WLR 604.

of decision-making by housing authorities.[12] Until a locally accessible mechanism for challenge becomes available there is no obvious alternative for dissatisfied applicants.

1. Judicial Review

The Housing (Homeless Persons) Act 1977 did not provide for appeal to the courts on points of law and neither do the consolidated Acts. Housing authorities nevertheless are subject to the supervisory jurisdiction of the Court of Session in Scotland and the High Court in England and Wales. Thus, homeless persons are able to test the legality of housing authority decision-making. The powers of these Courts on application for judicial review, however, are strictly limited.[13] The function of judicial review is merely to ensure that administrative bodies keep within their statutory powers[14] and do not act in breach of the principles of natural justice or fairness.[15] Therefore the grounds upon which the Courts will intervene are extremely narrow.[16]

It is important to bear in mind that, in reviewing the legality of the decisions of housing authorities under the Acts, neither the High Court nor the Court of Session carry out an appellate function. Mr. Justice Glidewell explained the supervisory role of the judge in *R. v. Hertsmere Borough Council, ex p. Sedaghat:* [17]

> "I am not sitting as a Court of Appeal. It is not for me to say what I would have found if I were the [housing authority], or if I had the task of saying whether I thought the [housing authority's] decision was right or wrong ... The question is: Can I say, faced with the evidence which was properly before them, advised as they were properly as to the matters they had to take into account, that no sensible [authority] could properly come to the decision to which they had come?"

The objective of the supervisory function of the courts in reviewing

---

12. *R. v. Hillingdon London Borough Council, ex p. Puhlhofer* [1986] AC 484; *Mazzaccherini v. Argyll & Bute District Council* [1987] SCLR 475; and *R. v. Blackpool Borough Council, ex p. Smith* (QBD) 29 July, 1987.

13. *Don Brothers, Buist & Co. v. Scottish Insurance Commissioners* 1913 SC 607; *Associated Provincial Picture Houses v. Wednesbury Corporation.* [1948] 1 KB 223.

14. *Forbes v. Underwood* (1886) 13 R 465; *Anisminic Ltd. v. Foreign Compensation Commission* [1969] 2 AC 147.

15. *Moss Empires v. Assessor for Glasgow* 1917 SC (HL) 1; *Ridge v. Baldwin* [1964] AC 40.

16. These are discussed by Lord Greene in the leading case on the judicial review of administrative action: *Associated Provincial Picture Houses v. Wednesbury Corporation* [1948] 1 KB 223 at 228.

17. (QBD) 7 March, 1984; see also *CCSU v. Minister for the Civil Service* [1985] AC 374; R. v. *Hillingdon London Borough Council, ex p. Puhlhofer* [1986] 1 AC 484; *R. v. Secretary of State for the Environment, ex p. Nottingham County Council* [1986] AC 240; *R. v. Wycombe District Council, ex p. Mahsood* (QBD) 30 August, 1988.

the legality of housing authority decision-making is broadly to ensure that they keep within their statutory powers and do not act in breach of the principles of natural justice or fairness.[18] From these basic tenets, six specific grounds upon which the courts may intervene by way of judicial review can be identified from the case law on homeless persons:

(a) the exercise of discretion by the housing authority   must be a real exercise, in the sense that the administrative body must consider the merits of each application rather than slavishly follow predetermined policy;

(b) the housing authority must have regard to matters which the statute directs them to consider and conversely must disregard all irrelevant or collateral matters;

(c) the housing authority must not act dishonestly or in bad faith;

(d) the decision of the housing authority must not be so unreasonable that no reasonable authority could have come to it;

(e) the housing authority in exercising their   administrative   functions must act fairly; and

(f) the housing authority must give adequate reasons for their decision.

These principles of administrative law are sometimes known as the "Wednesbury principles".[19] To elucidate these principles in action the following example may be useful:

(a) A real exercise of discretion

The question whether there has been a real exercise of discretion by a housing authority has arisen in two specific contexts; the fettering of discretion by the adoption of a blanket policy, and the delegation of decision-making to a body not authorised to exercise discretion.

(i) Blanket policies

While it is open to an administrative body to fashion guidelines to enable them to obtain consistency in decision-making, they must not adopt policies which in effect disable them from exercising their discretion[20] or slavishly follow policy and thereby fail to consider the individual

---

18. See, for example, *R. v. Basingstoke and Dean District Council, ex p. Webb* (QBD) 6 November, 1987; *R. v. Tynedale District Council, ex p. Shield* (QBD) 5 November, 1987, and *R. v. Mole Valley District Council, ex p. Burton, The Independent,* 14 April, 1988.

19. *Associated Provincial Picture Houses v. Wednesbury Corporation* [1948] 1 KB 223.

20. *Williams v. Cynon Valley District Council* (1980) LAG 16, and *Barry v. Newham Borough Council* (1980) LAG 142.

merits of a case.[21]

These principles were central to both *R. v. Eastleigh Borough Council, ex p. Betts* [22] and *R. v. Preseli District Council, ex p. Fisher*.[23] In *Fisher* the decision of the housing authority was based on their fear that by housing an applicant they would "be opening the doors of Preseli to any nomad who wants to come into the area." By choosing to follow a policy which discriminated against persons with a nomadic lifestyle rather than considering the individual merits of the application, Mr. Justice McCullough held that the authority had acted unlawfully. In *Betts* the question before the House of Lords was whether in applying the definition of "normal residence", in paragraph 2.5 of the *Agreement on Procedures for Referrals of the Homeless*,[24] a housing authority had fettered their discretion. When this case was before the Court of Appeal[25] Lord Justice Stephenson held that they had unlawfully fettered their discretion by a rigid application of the definition contained in the Agreement. However, the House of Lords held that they had not fettered their discretion but had operated the policy established in the guidelines, adding that, provided the question of "normal residence" was considered on its merits in each case, there was nothing improper or illegal in an authority applying the definition provided in the Agreement.[26]

Although this decision can be criticised on the ground that it conflates the questions of the legality of the policy and whether there was a real exercise of discretion based on a lawful policy,[27] it is authority for the view that the Agreement provides lawful guidelines which may be applied by housing authorities in determining whether an applicant has a local connection with their area.

(ii) Delegation of decision-making

Where a body fails to exercise discretion vested in them by statute and in effect delegates their decision-making powers to a body not authorised to make that decision, the courts will hold the decision to be invalid.[28] Therefore, where a housing authority merely "rubber stamped" the decision of another authority that an applicant had become homeless

---

21. *British Oxygen Co. Ltd. v. Board of Trade* [1971] AC 610 and *Attorney-General ex rel. Tilley v. Wandsworth LBC* [1981] 1 All ER 1162. *R. v. Canterbury District Council, ex p. Gillespie* (1986) 19 HLR 7.
22. [1984] 2 AC 613.
23. (1984) 17 HLR 147; see also *R. v. Canterbury District Council, ex p. Gillespie* (1986) 19 HLR 7.
24. Revised 6 June, 1979.
25. [1983] 1 WLR 774.
26. See *British Oxygen Co. Ltd v. Board of Trade* (above).
27. [1984] JSWL 365.
28. *Lavender (H) and Son Ltd. v. Minister of Housing and Local Government* [1970] 1 WLR 1231; see also *R. v. Port Talbot Borough Council, ex p. Jones, The Independent*, 5 January, 1988.

intentionally without making their own inquiries, as they were obliged to do under section 3 of the Housing (Homeless Persons) Act 1977, the High Court stated that they had acted unlawfully because in so doing they had failed to perform their statutory duty.[29] However, it should be noted that where authorities do carry out appropriate enquiries they are entitled to rely on the advice of other housing authorities.[30]

(b) Relevant matters

It is fundamental to administrative decision-making that an authority have regard to the matter to which statute directs them to have regard and disregard any collateral or irrelevant matters.

(i) The statute

It should not be necessary to state that housing authorities must have regard to the provisions of the statute— now the Housing Act 1985 or Housing (Scotland) Act 1987— in determining applications made under it but a surprisingly large number of authorities seem to ignore them.

Where a housing authority fail to address the question they are required by the Act to address, and refuse assistance on other extraneous grounds, their decisions will be held to be invalid. Thus in *R. v. Preseli District Council, ex p. Fisher*[31] Mr. Justice McCullough overturned the decision of a housing authority that an applicant had become intentionally homeless because of her nomadic lifestyle and based their decision on the irrelevant consideration that they would be opening their doors to other nomads who wanted to come into their area on the ground that the authority had failed to address themselves to the questions laid down by statute on which a decision of intentional homelessness must be founded.[32]

(ii) The Code of Guidance

The relevance of the Code of Guidance is somewhat more complex. *De*

---

29. *R. v. South Herefordshire District Council, ex p. Miles* (1983) 17 HLR 82; see also *R. v. Basingstoke and Dean District Council, ex p. Webb* (QBD) 6 November, 1987.
30. *R. v. Bristol City Council, ex p. Browne* [1979] 1 WLR 1437; and *R. v. Warwick District Council, ex p. Wood* (QBD) 15 August, 1983; *R. v. Islington LBC, ex p. Adigun* (1980) 20 February, 1986.
31. (1984) 17 HLR 147.
32. See also *R. v. Wandsworth LBC, ex p. Rose* (1984) 11 HLR 105; *R. v. Eastleigh Borough Council, ex p. Beattie* (1983) 10 HLR 134; *R. v. Wimborne District Council, ex p. Curtis,* (1985) 18 HLR 79; *R. v. Exeter City Council, ex p. Gliddon* [1985] 1 All ER 493; *R. v. Mole Valley District Council, ex p. Minnett* (1983) 12 HLR 44; *R. v. Hillingdon LBC, ex p. Wilson* (QBD) 6 July, 1983; *R. v. Portsmouth City Council, ex p. Knight* (1983) 82 LGR 184; *R. v. Reigate and Banstead Borough Council, ex p. Paris* (1984) 17 HLR 103; *R. v. Basingstoke and Dean Borough Council, ex p. Bassett* (1983) 10 HLR 125.

Falco [33] establishes that the Code of Guidance is directory only and not mandatory in the sense that housing authorities must follow the guidance it provides. However, the failure of a housing authority to have regard to the Code resulted in their determination being held to be unlawful in *Kelly and Mallon v. Monklands District Council.* [34] In that case Lord Ross quashed the finding of a housing authority that two 16 year old girls did not have a priority need due to vulnerability because the housing authority failed to have regard to the need to co-operate with the social work department in determining the question, [35] as recommended by the Code. [36] Subsequently, however, Lord Jauncey, in *Mazzaccherini v. Argyll and Bute District Council* [37] endorsed the limited role for the Code envisaged by Lord Denning in *De Falco:*

> "[I]f a housing authority considered that in a particular case the circumstances do not merit the rigid application of a part of the Code I do not consider that they could be faulted in law or said to have acted unreasonably."

(c) Irrelevant considerations

If an authority make a decision on the basis of irrelevant considerations, that decision will be held to be unlawful. In *Fisher* it was held that the fear of a nomadic invasion was not a relevant consideration in assessing whether an applicant had become intentionally homeless. Similarly, in *R. v. Mole Valley District Council, ex p. Minnett,* [38] it was held that the fact that a family had "squatted" in council property *after* leaving rented accommodation was not relevant to the question whether an applicant had become homeless intentionally when she relinquished her former dwelling. Equally, when an applicant formed the intention to become homeless is not relevant to the questions why and how she became homeless. [39]

(d) Unreasonable decisions

Where the decision reached by an authority is unreasonable, in the narrow sense that it is so unreasonable that no reasonable authority could

33. [1980] QB 460.
34. 1986 SLT 165.
35. See also *R v. Wyre Borough Council, ex p. Joyce* (1983) 11 WLR 72 on "wanton or persistent failure to pay rent or mortgage instalments".
36. SC 7.5-7.7; EC 7.5 and A4.1-A4.3.
37. 1987 SCLR 475.
38. (1984) 12 HLR 49.
39. See *R. v. Gloucester City Council, ex p. Miles* (1985) 83 LGR 607.

have come to it,[40] the courts will quash it. For example, in *R. v. Penwith District Council, ex p. Trevena* [41] the authority held that an applicant had become homeless intentionally because he had acquiesced in his wife's decision to give up her tenancy of council accommodation. The evidence, however, indicated that he was hostile to it and therefore the court held that the decision was unlawful on the ground that no reasonable council could on the material before them have come to it.[42]

(e) The duty to act fairly

Although in carrying out inquiries under the Act housing authorities are carrying out an administrative function, and therefore are not subject to the principles or rules of natural justice, they are required to act fairly.[43] This amorphous duty requires authorities in discharging the obligation to make inquiries, to make sufficiently detailed enquiries to enable them to determine the nature and level of assistance to be provided to an applicant and may also oblige them to afford the applicant an opportunity to comment upon the evidence on which they propose to base their decision.

(i) Nature and scope of inquiries

Where an authority receive an application for assistance under the Act it is necessary for them to carry out sufficient inquiries to provide them with adequate evidence upon which to base their decision. The failure of authorities to conduct such inquiries or to obtain adequate evidence led them to make unlawful decisions in *R. v. Eastleigh Borough Council, ex p. Beattie;*[44] *R. v. Westminster City Council, ex p. Ali;*[45] *R. v. Wandsworth London Borough Council, ex p. Rose; R. v. West Dorset District Council, ex p. Phillips;* [47] *R. v. Bath City Council, ex p. Sangermano;* [48] *R. v.*

---

40. *Wednesbury* (above) and *CCSU v. Minister for the Civil Service* [1985] AC 374: "absurd, illogical, perverse".
41. (1984) 17 HLR 526.
42. See also *R. v. Woodspring District Council, ex p. Walters* (1984) 17 HLR 73; *R. v. Bath City Council, ex p. Sangermano* (1984) 16 HLR 94; *R. v. South Herefordshire District Council, ex p. Miles,* (1983) 17 HLR 82; *R. v. Eastleigh Borough Council, ex p. Beattie* (No. 2) (1984) 17 HLR 168; *R. v. Westminster City Council, ex p. Ali* (1984) 11 HLR 83; *R. v. Surrey Heath Borough Council, ex p. Li* (1984) 16 HLR 79.
43. *Stubbs v. Slough Borough Council* (1980) LAG 16; *Afan Borough Council v. Marchant* [1979] JSWL 367; (1980) LAG 15.
44. (1983) 10 HLR 134.
45. (1984) 11 HLR 83.
46. (1984) 11 HLR 105.
47. (1984) 17 HLR 336.
48. (1984) 17 HLR 95.

Eastleigh Borough Council, ex p. Beattie No. 2;[49] *R. v. Rydedale District Council, ex p. Smith;*[50] *R. v. Reigate and Banstead Borough Council, ex p. Paris;*[51] *R. v. Preseli District Council, ex p. Fisher,*[52] *and R. v. East Northamptonshire District Council, ex p. Spruce.* [53]

In *Paris,* to take one example, the failure of an authority to ascertain if the accommodation a couple left in Italy was available to them was held to invalidate their decision of intentional homelessness.

(ii) Fair hearing

Although an authority are not obliged to afford an applicant an opportunity to be heard in relation to all matters which arise from their inquiries[54] the failure of an authority to give an applicant an opportunity to comment may invalidate the housing authority's decision.[55]

For example, in *R. v. South Herefordshire District Council, ex p. Miles* [56] an authority based their decision that an applicant had become homeless intentionally on information provided by another authority without checking its accuracy with the applicant or affording him an opportunity to comment on it. The High Court held their decision to be unlawful.

(f) The duty to state reasons

Although the requirement placed on housing authorities to state reasons for adverse decisions made under the Act is far from onerous,[57] the Court of Appeal held in *R. v. Gloucester City Council, ex p. Miles* [58] that it is necessary for them to spell out in their reasons that they considered all the questions which the legislation requires them to consider before making that decision.

---

49. (1984) 17 HLR 168.
50. (1983) 16 HLR 66.
51. (1984) 17 HLR 103.
52. (1984) 17 HLR 147.
53. (QBD) 17 February, 1988.
54. See *R. v. Reigate and Banstead Borough Council, ex p. Henry* (QBD) 16 December, 1982 (Smythe HC 17); *R. v. Southampton City Council, ex p. Ward* (1984); *R. v. Vale of White Horse District Council, ex p. Lyle* (QBD) 6 July, 1983.
55. See *R. v. Wyre Borough Council, ex p. Joyce* (1984) 11 HLR 73; *R. v. South Herefordshire District Council, ex p. Miles* (1983) 17 HLR 82.
56. *Ibid.*
57. See 'The Duties of Housing Authorities' *supra* pp. 182-86 and *R. v. London Borough of Tower Hamlets, ex p. Monaf* (CA) 27 April, 1988.
58. (1985) 83 LGR 607; *Mazzaccherini v. Argyll and Bute District Council* 1987 SCLR 475.

2. Interim Interdict and Interlocutory Injunctions

Although the legal tests for granting interim interdicts and interlocutory injunctions differ,[59] the effect of the remedies is broadly the same. In each case an interim interdict or interlocutory injunction may be obtained to preserve the *status quo* pending the outcome of a court case. These remedies are particularly useful in preventing a housing authority from withdrawing temporary accommodation until the court determines whether the housing authority are entitled to find an applicant to be intentionally homeless.[60]

In England and Wales homeless persons should be able to obtain interlocutory injunctions to prevent the withdrawal of temporary accommodation with greater ease than their Scottish counterparts. However, the advantage, which the more liberal test laid down by the House of Lords in *American Cyanamid Co. v. Ethicon Ltd* [61] should provide, has been substantially eroded by the Court of Appeal. In *De Falco* Lord Denning explained why, in his view, the general test of whether there is a serious issue to be tried should be rejected in the case of homeless persons in favour of a more onerous test of a strong *prima facie* case.[62]

> "This is not the same sort of case as *American Cyanamid Co. v. Ethicon Ltd.* because the plaintiffs here cannot give any worth-while undertaking in damages. No injunction should be granted unless the plaintiffs make out a strong *prima facie* case that the council's finding of 'intentional homelessness' was invalid. I would go further. It should not be granted unless it is a case in which, on an application for judicial review, *certiorari* would be granted to quash their decision and *mandamus* issued to command them to consider the case afresh."

The effect of this ruling arguably may be demonstrated by comparing the outcome of applications for interlocutory injunctions prior to and following *De Falco*. In *Fanning v. London Borough of Wandsworth* [63] and *Bailey and Bendix v. Cardiff City Council*,[64] applicants successfully obtained interlocutory injunctions on the ground that as their claims

---

59. In Scots law the test is whether there is a *prima facie* case to be tried. A matter which is settled on a balance of convenience: see *Scottish Milk Marketing Board v. Paris* 1935 SC 287 per Lord Fleming at 302 *NWL Ltd. v. Woods* [1979] 1 WLR 1294 at 1310 per Lord Fraser at *Love v. Montgomerie*, 1982 SLT (Sh Ct) 60. In English law the test is the much less onerous test of whether there is a serious issue to be tried. A matter which is satisfied provided the plaintiff's claim is neither frivolous nor vexatious. See *American Cyanamid Co. v. Ethicon Ltd.* [1975] AC 396 and *De Falco v. Crawley Borough Council* [1980] QB 460.
60. See *Roughead v. Falkirk District Council* (1979) SCOLAG 188.
61. [1975] AC 396.
62. *De Falco v. Crawley Borough Council* [1980] QB 460.
63. (1980) LAG 16.
64. *Ibid.*

were neither frivolous nor vexatious the balance of convenience favoured them. However, following *De Falco* the Court of Appeal set aside an interlocutory injunction granted by Mr. Justice Browne in the High Court on the ground that he had applied the wrong test.[65] And in *Miller v. Wandsworth London Borough Council* [66] Mr. Justice Walton applying the *prima facie* test laid down by the Court of Appeal in *De Falco* refused a motion for a mandatory interlocutory injunction to force the housing authority to secure temporary accommodation for a homeless person under section 4(3) of the 1977 Act on the ground that they had not satisfied that test.

Subsequently, in *R. v. Kensington and Chelsea Royal Borough Council, ex p. Hammell* [67] the Court of Appeal granted a mandatory injunction ordering the housing authority to accommodate a homeless person pending the hearing of her application for judicial review. In this case the applicant was a divorced woman with three young children. She had fled from her home in Alloa because of violence and intimidation by her ex-husband. After staying with her sister in a one-bedroomed flat for a period of time she applied to the housing authority for assistance as a homeless person. The authority were not satisfied that the applicant was homeless or threatened with homelessness because she remained a tenant of the council house in Alloa and was entitled to occupy it. Holding that the inquiries made by the housing authority as regards the accommodation in Alloa had been insufficient to deprive the applicant of her private law right to temporary accommodation, Lord Justice Parker stated that in his view the applicant had shown a "very strong *prima facie* case" that the housing authority had not fulfilled their duty and that their decision had been unlawful.

3. Declarator and Declaration

The purpose of declarator in Scots law and declaratory proceedings in English law is to provide litigants with an authoritative ruling on their respective legal rights and duties. As these common law remedies merely provide the parties with a declaration by the court of their legal position, action for declarator or declaration are frequently combined with other remedies.

Declarator is available in the Court of Session and declaratory proceedings may be instituted in the High Court or the county court, provided that in the latter court it forms part of a damages action, but

---

65. *Tickner v. Mole Valley District Council* (1980) LAG 187.
66. *The Times,* 19 March, 1980.
67. *The Times,* 23 August, 1988; see also *R. v. Broxbourne Borough Council, ex p. Willmoth* (QBD) 29 July, 1988.

declaration of homelessness cannot be obtained in advance.[68] The availability of these remedies to declare the rights of homeless persons and the concomitant obligations of housing authorities was explicitly recognised by the House of Lords in *Brown v. Hamilton District Council*[69] and the Court of Appeal in *De Falco v. Crawley Borough Council*.[70]

While the competence of declaratory proceedings in relation to the legislation has been accepted in England and Wales in *Lambert v. Ealing London Borough Council*[71] Lord Denning and Lord Justice May questioned the appropriateness of initiating actions for declaration and damages in the county court. In *Cocks v. Thanet District Council*[72] the House of Lords emphasised that whilst declaration was competent in the county court, *certiorari* in the High Court "remained the primary and most appropriate remedy". In Scotland the competence of raising an action of declarator in the sheriff court was fiercely debated.

In the first case in which the issue was raised, *Williamson v. Moray District Council*,[73] Sheriff Principal Gimson held that the sheriff court neither had jurisdiction nor competence to determine matters arising under the 1977 Act by way of declarator. That decision, however, was overruled by the majority decision of the Court of Session in *Brown v. Hamilton District Council*.[74] Lord Justice Wheatley, delivering the leading majority judgment in this case, rejected the argument put forward on behalf of the housing authority that if the jurisdiction of the sheriff court was extended to include review by way of action for declarator, this had to be expressly by statute and not by implication. If a remedy is *ex facie* available in the sheriff court, as declarator was by way of section 5 of the Sheriff Court (Scotland) Act 1907, Lord Wheatley argued "there is no need for any specific mention of a mode of appeal or review in the statute."[75]

The argument that the action for declarator was in fact a covert action of reduction, which is not competent in the sheriff court,[76] was also rejected by Lord Wheatley who indicated that the practical solution to this argument was that the decision of the housing authority would not be effective and as a responsible public body, they would accept the legal consequences of declarator if it went against them and would take the

---

68. *R. v. Hillingdon London Borough Council, ex p. Tinn, The Independent*, 14 January, 1988.
69. 1983 SLT 397.
70. [1980] QB 460.
71. [1982] 2 All ER 394.
72. [1983] AC 286.
73. 1980 SLT (Sh Ct) 32.
74. 1983 SLT 397 and (1982) SCOLAG 5. This decision confirmed the earlier decision of Sheriff Lockhart in the case: see 1980 SLT (Sh Ct) 81 at p. 82.
75. See *Brown* above.
76. See *Reduction and Certiorari*, below.

appropriate steps to make a proper legal decision. In any event, Lord Wheatley concluded, if the housing authority refused to follow the guidance given by the court in this decree of declarator it was possible to raise an action *ad factum praestandum* or to petition the Court of Session for enforcement of that decree. On appeal to the House of Lords this reasoning was rejected as it would involve:

> "[T]reating a decree of declarator by the Sheriff either as being in substance a decree of reduction, in which case it would be granted without jurisdiction, or as a mere *brutum fulmen*, having no compulsive force, in which case it would be futile not to be pronounced."[77]

4. Reduction and *Certiorari*

In Scots law an action of reduction and in English law an order of *certiorari* are available to set aside the unlawful decisions of public bodies. For example, where an administrative body acts beyond their powers, i.e. *ultra vires*, or acts unfairly or in breach of the rules of natural justice, it is possible to raise an action of reduction in the Court of Session or to seek an order of *certiorari* in the High Court to have the unlawful decision of the public body set aside. This remedy was extensively discussed by Lords Wheatley and Dunpark in *Brown v. Hamilton District Council*[78] and while the House of Lords overturned the attempt of the Court of session effectively to extend reduction to the sheriff court, their Lordships did not comment on these remarks and they therefore remain authoritative. Two points of importance emerge from their judgments. Firstly, the Court of Session is the only Scottish court competent to reduce, i.e. set aside, an unlawful act or decision. Secondly, actions of reduction may be sought against acts as well as writings.[79] The English courts have also accepted that *certiorari* is a competent remedy to set aside housing authority decisions.[80] However, in *Din v. London Borough of Wandsworth*[81] Lord Lowry expressed doubts whether in relation to some of the areas of broad discretion which the legislation vests in housing authorities *certiorari* could ever be available. The emphasis on the primacy of *certiorari* in *Cocks v. Thanet District Council*[82] seems to suggest these doubts may be displaced, albeit that the

---

77. 1983 SLT 397.
78. *Ibid*. For an example of a successful action for reduction see *Wincenzen v. Monklands District Council* 1988 SLT 239, upheld by the Inner House, unreported, 7 July, 1988.
79. See *Brown* above.
80. *De Falco v. Crawley London Borough Council* [1980] QB 460; *R. v. Hillingdon Borough Council, ex p. Streeting* [1980] 3 All ER 417.
81. [1983] 1 AC 657 at 679.
82. [1983] AC 286.

doubts expressed by the House of Lords in *Puhlhofer* and by the Court of Session in *Mazzaccherini* about the appropriateness of judicial review must be born in mind.[83]

5. *Mandamus*, Section 91 Petitions and Actions *Ad Factum Praestandum*

This group of remedies, although different in form, serves the same broad purpose, which is to enforce statutory duties.

(a) *Mandamus*

The competence in the English courts of an order of *mandamus* to enforce housing authority duties under the Act has been accepted and there has been little discussion of the merits and demerits of this remedy.[84] This may, in part, be attributable to the availability in the law courts of the mandatory injunction which is an interim enforcement order and in many ways lessens the anxiety of English lawyers in relation to positive remedies.[85]

(b) Section 91 of the Court of Session Act 1868

The principal remedy for compelling the non-performance of statutory duties in Scots law is contained in Section 91 of the Court of Sessions Act 1868.

Under this section the Court of Session has general power to compel the performance of a statutory duty. This remedy is open to an aggrieved person who may apply by way of summary petition to the Court of Session to obtain an order or interim order requiring the implementation of a statutory duty.[86] In granting such an order it is competent for the Court of Session to attach whatever conditions and

---

83. See fn. 12, *supra*.
84. *Thornton v. Kirklees Metropolitan Borough Council* [1979] QB 626; *R. v. Slough Borough Council, ex p. Ealing LBC* [1981] 1 All ER 601; *R. v. Wyre Borough Council, ex p. Parr*, (1982) 2 HLR 945; *R. v. Beverley Borough Council, ex p. McPhee, The Times*, 27 October, 1978, in which Wien J. doubted that a court would ever grant an order of *mandamus* because of the nature of the legislation.
85. *R. v. Kensington and Chelsea Royal Borough Council, ex p. Hammell, The Times*, 25 August, 1988.
86. Although Lord Fraser observed in *Brown v. Hamilton District Council* 1983 SLT 397 that summary petition would not be a convenient procedure for deciding the particular question raised in the Brown case where the nub of the complaint was the exercise of discretion by the housing authority. Where a clear breach of duty was involved then summary petition would be more appropriate, as in *Galbraith* below.

penalties for non-performance the court deems proper.

Resort has been had to that remedy by homeless persons in two reported cases thus far. In the first case, *Galbraith v. Midlothian District Council*,[87] Mrs. Margaret Galbraith voluntarily terminated the lease of her Scottish Special Housing Association (SSHA) in Dalkeith because of the failure of the SSHA to carry out essential repairs which failure in her view, had rendered the house unfit for habitation. Mrs. Galbraith, together with her three children, approached Midlothian for assistance as a homeless person. As she was homeless and in priority need, it was the duty of Midlothian to provide accommodation for her and her children pending the completion of their inquiries. However, Midlothian refused to provide temporary accommodation and suggested that she should return to her SSHA house. Mrs. Galbraith applied to the Court of Session for an interim order under section 91 requiring Midlothian to fulfil their duty to secure that temporary accommodation be made available to her for such a period as would provide her with a reasonable opportunity to obtain accommodation for herself, together with an order requiring them to secure that permanent accommodation be made available. Midlothian had clearly acted in breach of their duty by refusing Mrs. Galbraith and her family temporary accommodation, and the Court of Session issued an interim order compelling Midlothian to provide temporary accommodation. At a subsequent hearing on 20 December 1979, Midlothian gave the court an undertaking that they would provide Mrs. Galbraith with permanent accommodation in a different estate and therefore it was unnecessary for the court to deal with the second part of her petition which related to the temporary accommodation provided for her in her original SSHA house.

In the second case, *Mackenzie v. West Lothian District Council*,[88] Mr. Mackenzie who was evicted from his council house by West Lothian District Council was placed in temporary accommodation in a block due for demolition. A petition was presented under section 91 requesting the court to compel the authority to secure that accommodation be made available on a permanent basis and, pending the housing authority supplying him with such accommodation, for an order prohibiting the authority from evicting him and his family. In this instance the petition was refused on the grounds that the court was not satisfied that Mackenzie had discharged the onus of proof. He had to demonstrate that the decision of the Council on intentionality was unlawful. it was not enough for him simply to give his version of what took place.

The importance of this remedy has diminished substantially since the introduction of the Rule 260(B) procedure.

---

87. (1979) SCOLAG 122.
88. 1979 SC 433.

(c) *Ad factum praestandum*

While the procedures laid down by section 91 of the Court of Session Act 1868 and Rule 260(B) provide litigants with a remedy whereby both interim and permanent relief against the non-implementation of statutory duties can be obtained, they do suffer from a number of disadvantages. The most obvious is that these remedies are exclusive to the Court of Session, a factor which may result in additional delay, expense and inconvenience for the applicant. Other less obvious considerations relate to the section 91 petition as a remedy. As Lord Dundas has remarked, it is a "peculiar and drastic" remedy and it is for those who seek to invoke it to state clearly in what way a statutory duty has not been performed and in precise terms the order which they wish the court to grant.[89] This factor led to Mackenzie's failure in his action against West Lothian District Council.

6. Damages

The right of a homeless person to bring an action of damages for breach of statutory duty by a housing authority has been explicitly recognised by both the Court of Appeal in England and the Court of Session in Scotland. In *Thornton v. Kirklees Metropolitan District Council* [90] and *De Falco v. Crawley Borough Council*[91] the Court of Appeal stated that a homeless person was entitled to seek damages in the county court of High Court. The House of Lords in *Cocks v. Thanet District Council*[92] accepted that action for damages was appropriate in the High Court and the county court once the existence of a duty to provide accommodation had been established. In Scotland an aggrieved person can raise an action for damages in the Court of Session.[93]

While these decisions are important insofar as they give recognition to a right of action in damages, the Court of Appeal recognised in *Thornton* that there are a number of difficulties facing homeless persons seeking to recover damages from a housing authority for breach of statutory duty:

"... All the necessary elements ... fall to be proved. Amongst other things,

---

89. *Carlton Hotel Co. v. Lord Advocate* 1921 SC 237 p.248.
90. [1979] QB 626.
91. [1980] QB 460.
92. (1983) AC 286.
93. *Brown v. Hamilton District Council* 1983 SLT 397 and (1982) SCOLAG 5; *Mallon v. Monklands District Council* 1986 SLT 347; *Purves v. Midlothian District Council* 1986 SCOLAG 144, where damages were awarded in the sheriff court apparently because the district council did not dispute the failure to carry out the objections.

it would be necessary for a plaintiff to prove that he had indeed suffered damage which is regarded by the law as being the consequence of breach of duty; and he would have to prove all the various other matters which may often be matters which it would be extremely difficult to prove, particularly where Parliament has expressly left a discretion to the housing authority in such phrases as 'if the housing authority is satisfied...'"[94]

In that case Lord Justice Roskill also made the point that:

"[I]t would be quite wrong to allow emotive considerations of sympathy, which must inevitably arise in these cases, to have any influence on the determination of difficult problems which obviously may arise under the statute ..."[95]

In this area it would appear that the judiciary have experienced few difficulties in banishing emotional considerations, judging from the amount of damages awarded to the homeless. In *Williams v. Cynon Valley District Council*,[96] for example, a mother of three forced to spend four months in a women's refuge as a result of the unlawful application of a blanket policy was awarded £75 damages by the county court. In *Stubbs v. Slough Borough Council*[97] where the housing authority acted in breach of the rules of natural justice by refusing to allow a couple an opportunity to comment on the grounds for their eviction from private rented accommodation, £100 was awarded. Similar sums have been awarded by the courts in other cases but the smallest sum awarded in damages known to us is £30.[98]

It is not inconceivable that if the courts do not award exemplary damages some housing authorities may be tempted to make a cynical calculation of the cost of providing accommodation to homeless families and any damages which may be awarded against them.[99]

7. Other Judicial Remedies?

A number of test cases have been brought up in an attempt to establish a remedy whereby statutory duties might be enforced in the sheriff

---

94. [1979] QB 626 per Lord Justice Megaw at p. 640.
95. *Ibid.* at p. 644.
96. (1979) *Roof* 195; (1980) LAG 16.
97. (1980) LAG 16.
98. *Lally v. Kensington and Charles Royal Borough, The Times,* 27 March, 1980.
99. See *R. v. Camden LBC, ex. p. Gillan, The Independent,* 13 October, 1988; see also *Scotland on Sunday,* 30 October, 1988 for examples of the financial pressures put on housing authorities and their reactions to such.

court.[100] In *Brown v. Hamilton District Council*. Sheriff Lockhart held that performance of a statutory duty under the 1977 Act could be enforced either by way of a section 91 petition in the Court of Session or by way of a decree *ad factum praestandum* in the sheriff court. This decision was upheld on appeal by the majority of the Second Division of the Court of Session.[101] In the leading majority judgment Lord Justice-Clerk Wheatley stated that whereas the Court of Session alone was entitled to review the decisions of bodies exercising "judicial" or "quasi-judicial" functions, the Court of Session and the sheriff court could review the decisions of bodies exercising "administrative" functions. Lord Wheatley added that if the function of a public body is an administrative function then "an aggrieved person can go to any court which had jurisdictional power to grant him the remedy he seeks." Lord Wheatley concluded:

> "I find comfort in finding that the Sheriff court has jurisdiction for judicial review of controversies of this nature under the Act. Having regard to the administrative nature of the decision which falls to be reviewed judicially by the court in its supervisory capacity and the convenience of all concerned throughout the length and breadth of Scotland, the sheriff court is appropriately suited for the purpose. To require the Court of Session to find time to determine the kind of issue likely to be involved is somewhat akin to taking a sledge hammer to crack a nut."[102]

This decision was overturned in the House of Lords where the "subtle distinctions" between administrative and judicial decisions were finally laid to rest. They were deemed no longer relevant for England in *O'Reilly v Mackman* [103] and Lord Fraser suggested "it would be strange if they were to linger on it in Scotland."[104]

It was also suggested in *Brown v. Hamilton District Council*[105] that it was worthwhile considering reviving the ancient remedies of advocation and suspension. Lord Fraser stated that an advantage similar to that provided by English prerogative orders might be derived from a resuscitation of these remedies. In *Remedies in Administrative Law*, Professor Bradley indicates that suspension was most appropriate for preventing the infringement of a right[106] since it involved retaining matters in their

---

100. *Williamson v. Moray District Council* 1980 SLT (Sh Ct) 32; *Brown v. Hamilton District Council* 1980 SLT (Sh Ct) 81; *Edwards v. Lothian Regional Council* 1980 SLT (Sh Ct) 107 and 1981 SLT (Sh Ct) 41.
101. 1983 SLT 397.
102. *Ibid.* at 402.
103. [1983] 2 AC 237.
104. *Brown v. Hamilton District Council* 1983 SLT 397 at 415.
105. *Ibid.* at p. 418.
106. Scottish Law Commission Memorandum No. 14, 1972; A.W. Bradley, 'Administrative Law', *Stair Memorial Encyclopaedia of the Laws of Scotland*, Vol.1.

current position until the right of parties could be determined by a final judgement. The role it might play in challenging the determinations of authorities is less clear. As far as advocation in civil matters is concerned, this was the method by which cases from an inferior court were brought before a superior court for review. Typically this was used in supervising the operation of the poor law in Scotland. Lord Fraser suggested that the procedure was competent, citing as authority a case of 1843, *Pryde v. Heritors and Kirk Session of Ceres*,[107] which confirmed the right of the Court of Session to make a determination that the allowance paid to a destitute and pregnant widow was insufficient and remit the matter back to the parish authorities for a reasonable addition. With the introduction of the appeal procedure in the Court of Session Act 1868 this ancient form of remedy was expressly substituted by section 65. Lord Fraser also noted that advocation was still available in Scots criminal law.

8. The Local Ombudsman

Members of the public who feel that they have suffered injustice because of local government maladministration may complain to the Local Ombudsman. The Commissioners for Local Administration in England, Wales and Scotland (the Local Ombudsman) were introduced after local government re-organisation in the mid-seventies and provide one possible means of redress to homeless persons who feel dissatisfied with the way their applications have been treated by a local authority.

The Local Ombudsman has emerged as an important avenue of redress for homeless persons aggrieved by the decisions of housing authorities. The jurisdiction and powers of the Local Ombudsman are described in detail elsewhere[108] and we do not propose to rehearse them here. However, it is necessary to explain why this avenue of redress is important. Firstly, although the Local Ombudsmen have no power of enforcement, the number of authorities who decline to accept their recommendations is very small. In the years 1975-85 the Local Ombudsman for Scotland found it necessary to issue only 11 further reports against local authorities which failed to take appropriate action following the issue of a report finding that injustice had been caused as a result of maladministration.[109] This represents a "failure" rate of about 5%. When measured against the number of cases in which maladministration with injustice was found this is a tiny proportion. However, it must be said that even this small proportion of failures may be regarded as an over-estimate because of the number of complaints where local authorities

---

107. (1843) 5 D. 552.
108. J.G. Logie and P.Q. Watchman, *The Local Ombudsman* (T. & T. Clark, Edinburgh, 1989).
109. *Ibid.*, Ch. 5.

have remedied injustices or improved procedures, policies or practices despite there being no evidence of maladministration or injustice.

Secondly, as the average time taken for the Local Ombudsmen to complete their investigation varies between six months and a year, it may be thought that it is futile for homeless persons to complain to the Local Ombudsman. However, pessimism about delay is unjustified and indicates a failure to understand the way in which the Local Ombudsman operates. The rolling investigation procedure of the Local Ombudsman is specifically designed to maximise the opportunities for local authorities to informally remedy grievances. In particular, where a satisfactory settlement has been reached at the pre-investigation stage it will be unnecessary for the Local Ombudsman to conduct an investigation. The settlement of grievances at this stage may be attained in one of three ways:

(a) where a local councillor is approached by the complainant with a request to refer a complaint to the Local Ombudsman the councillor may be able to negotiate a settlement of the dispute with the authority on behalf of the complainant;

(b) where the authority is notified of the complaint and satisfactorily remedies the grievances before the Local Ombudsman has decided to initiate an investigation, the Local Ombudsman may either reject the complaint because as a result no injustice is evident or exercise his discretion not to investigate; or

(c) lastly, the Local Ombudsman's revised operating procedures now provide a further formal pre-investigation stage whereby the local authority are given an additional opportunity to take remedial action.

Even if the complaint goes beyond the pre-investigation stage it is still possible that it will be settled before the investigation has proceeded very far. In such cases, it is open to the Local Ombudsman to discontinue his investigation. In Scotland over 10% of all investigations are discontinued and the majority of discontinued complaints are discontinued[110] because of the offer of a council house.

(a) General guidelines

There are four points to note in relation to this particular extra-judicial remedy:

(i)   Complaints.
(ii) Maladministration.

---

110. *Ibid.*, Ch. 6.

(iii) Alternative modes of redress.

(iv) Delay in the Ombudsman process.

(i) Complaints

Complaints to the Local Ombudsman must be made *in writing* either through an elected member of the relevant authority or direct to the Local Ombudsman[111] within twelve months of the action complained of.[112]

(ii) Maladministration

Complaints are limited to the issue of *maladministration* rather than the merits of the decision of the authority. There is no statutory definition of what constitutes "maladministration". However, the "Crossman Catalogue"[113] is used by the Ombudsman as a guide. Under this catalogue maladministration arises from the following:

> "[B]ias, neglect, inattention, delay, incompetence, ineptitude, perversity, turpitude, arbitrariness and so on."

(iii) Alternative modes of redress

Where there is an alternative mode of redress through, for example, the courts, there can normally be no investigation.[114] One additional preliminary matter which is worthy of mention is that none of the Local Ombudsmen regard the availability of judicial review as a bar to investigation, and that complaints from homeless persons about maladministration will be investigated because they do not consider that it is reasonable for homeless persons to have to resort to such proceedings.[115]

(iv) Delay in the Ombudsman process

The time involved in the investigation by the staff of the Ombudsman means that the gap between the receipt of the complaint and the issuing of a report can be lengthy. The Ombudsman currently averages between

---

111. Local Government Act 1988; Local Government (Scotland) Act 1988.

112. Local Government (Scotland) Act 1975 Part II; Local Government Act 1974 Part II.

113. In the House of Commons 18 October, 1966, Richard Crossman attempted a definition of maladministration in what has become known subsequently as "The Crossman Catalogue". This was referred to with approval in *R. v. Local Commissioner for Administration for the North and East Area of England, ex p. Bradford Metropolitan City Council* [1979] QB 287. See also J.G. Logie and P.Q. Watchman, *The Local Ombudsman*, op. cit., Ch. 4.

114. Local Government Act 1974, Sch.5; Local Government (Scotland) Act 1975, Sch.5.

115. See *Report of the Commissioner for Local Administration in Wales*, dated 29 April, 1982.

9 and 10 months for this process[116] but many complaints are resolved at a fairly early stage.

(b) Principles of decisions

The Reports of the various Local Commissioners in Scotland, Wales and England are not classified in terms of the forms of maladministration which may arise. However, it is possible to identify some general principles from the decisions which have been made on complaints relating to the operation of the homeless legislation:

(i)   Delay.
(ii)   Inadequate Inquiries.
(iii)   Unfair Treatment.
(iv)   Misinterpretation.
(v)   Unhelpful attitude and inaccurate advice.

(i) Delay

One of the goals of the legislation is that the homeless should not have to wait interminably while the wheels of bureaucracy grind slowly on. This was explicitly recognised by the Local Ombudsman when investigating a complaint concerning a local connection dispute between Bury, Rochdale and Manchester:

> "I recognise the administrative complexities; but Parliament's purpose in placing this Act upon the statute book will have been to house the homeless ... without unreasonable delay."[117]

This principle was followed in a complaint concerning a woman with four children who was provided with temporary accommodation for seven months. Her wait for permanent accommodation had been extended due to the Council's policy regarding a court order for custody of the children. The difficulties of coping with children in temporary accommodation resulted in the family being split up for five months thus causing "considerable injustice" to the complainant. The Local Ombudsman in making this finding stressed the importance of speed in

---

116. See *Report of the Commissioner for Local Administration in Scotland for the Year ended 31 March, 1988*, and *The Local Ombudsman: Report for the Year ended 31st March, 1988 of the Commission for Local Administration in England*.

117. Complaint No. 109/C/78 against the Bury Metropolitan Borough Council, the Rochdale Metropolitan Borough Council and the Manchester Metropolitan City Council, dated 30 December, 1978, at p. 13 (six month period living in parents' home while the councils argued about which were responsible for the homeless family).

resolving the housing difficulties of families:

> "[T]he heavy social and economic costs involved required the Council vigorously to pursue all the available options with the aim of reuniting the family - which they clearly failed to do."[118]

Complaints concerning delay largely stem from inadequate administrative procedures, for example, delay in being informed of the need to provide supportive medical evidence in order to be classified as "vulnerable".[119]

An important report on a complaint about homelessness from the Commissioner for Local Administration in Scotland involved a wife who was turned out of the marital home by her husband in May 1978. She applied to Bearsden and Milngavie District Council under the 1977 Act and stayed temporarily with her mother in a room-and-kitchen flat in Glasgow. The complainant was informed that she was on the homeless list in June 1978 but no offer of accommodation was made. It was December 1978 before a housing official visited the accommodation which she and her daughter were sharing with her mother. In February 1979 the complainant was informed that it was not possible to accelerate her application as other applicants were also occupying unsatisfactory conditions. There was some publicity for her situation in a local newspaper in July 1979 but no action was taken until March 1980 when her mother asked her to leave the room-and-kitchen flat. After consultation the Council wrote guaranteeing to offer "suitable permanent accommodation before the end of June 1980." The Report of the Local Ombudsman in March 1980 did not find maladministration in respect to the delay of over two years to house the complainant. However, it did harshly criticise the Council's actions:

> "I am concerned that the Council did not make more detailed enquiries [apart from asking her to complete an application form] to establish the exact circumstances of the complainant's eviction until some six months after they had received her application and that they did not explain to the complainant at an early date that, although her application was included within the 'Homeless Category' of their Housing Waiting List, this category described applicants who were subtenants and/or living with relatives, and did not in fact relate to applicants who were without any accommodation whatsoever and who were considered to be 'homeless' in terms of the Act."[120]

---

118. Complaint No. 22/S/78 against the London Borough of Lambeth, dated 15 January, 1979 at p.15.
119. Complaint No. 715/H/78 against Sedgemoor District Council, dated 28 March, 1980.
120. Report of Investigation of a Complaint against Bearsden and Milngavie District Council, dated 21 March, 1980.

(ii) Inadequate inquiries

Failure to carry out adequate inquiries may amount to maladministration because authorities must have sufficient facts on which to base their decisions.[121] The Local Ombudsman, for example, upheld an allegation of maladministration against Leominster District Council[122] where the failure to investigate was crucial. The complainant who registered on the housing waiting list in 1978 was turned out of his rented furnished flat in Leominster in June 1979. Although 66 years old he received no help from the District Council. After a period seeking accommodation elsewhere he returned to Leominster in August 1979 and applied for housing assistance. In late September he received a letter from the Council indicating that they did not regard him as their responsibility as he had no local connection with Leominster. As a result of further discussions with the complainant in November, it was decided to assist him and two months later he was re-housed.

Although the Council first interviewed the complainant in August 1979 the Local Ombudsman concluded that they had failed to make appropriate inquiries and to follow up the initial interview. Their overall failure to react to the complainant's condition amounted to maladministration which caused injustice to the complainant.[123]

(iii) Unfair treatment

The way in which an authority treats an applicant has also been interpreted as amounting to "maladministration" by the Local Ombudsman. In 1978 Slough Borough Council[124] rejected an application from a man and wife who had been living with the wife's parents. Relations had become strained due to a combination of circumstances. The father had suffered a heart attack and had become irritable and the couple had had a baby. The accommodation that they occupied was far from satisfactory, consisting of a bedroom shared with the wife's 10 year old sister. However, in the deliberations of the special sub-committee of three councillors which dealt with their applications, hearsay information was submitted by another councillor who made representations to the sub-committee. Whilst it was not proved that this information (which subsequently turned out to be without foundation) had any effect on the sub-committee's decision to reject the complainant's application, the Local Ombudsman was uneasy about the whole procedure which had been adopted in Slough and upheld the complaint of maladministration:

---

121. See also "Processing Applications" *above* at pp. 74-76.
122. Complaint No. 304/H/79, dated 31 March, 1980.
123. See also Complaint No. 207/H/80 against Huntingdon District Council, dated 12 January, 1981.
124. Complaint No. 387/H/77 against Slough Borough Council dated 22 February, 1978. See also (c) "Dissatisfaction with action taken by an authority" below at pp. 237-38.

"Councillor T took no steps himself to check whether the allegations he passed on to the Sub-Committee were genuine [for instance by obtaining signed statements or further details] nor did he pass on the information to ... The Chairman of the Sub-Committee, or to the housing officers before the meeting for them to check its accuracy and relevance ... [this amounted to] maladministration by the Council causing injustice to the complainant in that he will never know whether his application was treated fairly. Nor will he know whether any future dealings he has with the Council will be prejudiced unless the record is put straight."[125]

A discrepancy between stated policy and practice may also form the basis of a successful complaint of maladministration.[126]

(iv) Misinterpretation

As we have indicated, investigation by the Local Ombudsman is supposed to take place only if other avenues of redress, such as court action, are inappropriate. In practice, the line between what amounts to maladministration and misapplication of the law is a fine one. A number of councils have had complaints of maladministration against them upheld because of their failure to assess complainants' circumstances correctly as well as for taking the wrong facts into account in operating the legislation.

There have, for example, been difficulties in deciding what amounts to "vulnerability". In a complaint against Sedgemoor District Council[127] it was revealed that a couple who were homeless both had fairly minor medical problems. The Chief Housing Officer took the view that "vulnerable" meant a "serious disadvantage when seeking alternative accommodation as compared to someone in normal health and under retirement age".[128] Whilst the Local Ombudsman did not criticise this test he did indicate that it was not enough to look simply at the medical evidence and stated that "social factors may also help in the assessment of vulnerability".[129]

An allegation of maladministration stemming from a failure to identify a homeless situation correctly was raised in a complaint against Glanford Borough Council.[130] The complainant's house was badly

---

125. *Ibid.* at pp. 23-24.
126. Complaint No. INV/171/S/81 against the London Borough of Southwark, dated 7 January, 1982.
127. Complaint No. 715/H/78 against Sedgemoor District Council, dated 28 March, 1980.
128. *Ibid.* at p. 10.
129. *Ibid.* at p. 26; see also Complaint No. 10/H/78 against Castle Point District Council, dated 2 October, 1978, on allegations that medical circumstances were not taken into account by the authority. *R. v. Lambeth LBC, ex p. Carroll, The Independent,* 8 October, 1987.
130. Complaint No. 158/C/81 against Glanford Borough Council, dated 12 November, 1981; *R. v. Camden London Borough Council, ex p. Wait, The Times,* 12 July, 1986.

damaged by fire in September 1980 and was rendered uninhabitable. Apart from providing for the complainant to stay one night in a hotel the Council provided no housing assistance. They contended that since they had served a Notice to Quit for rent arrears of £27 some months before, the tenancy had ended. The arrears had been reduced and no possession order had been sought. The Council did not accept that the complainant was in priority need even though his homelessness seemed to stem directly from the fire. They took the view that he was homeless "directly through his failure to pay rent, and that failure was intentional". As noted above, the category of priority need includes those who become homeless as a result of "any emergency such as flood, fire or any other disaster."

The complaint of maladministration was upheld on the basis that the Council had muddled up the questions of priority need and intentional homelessness. Those homeless as a result of an emergency such as a fire are defined by the Act as being in priority need. The second question was whether a person was homeless intentionally. Presumably an individual who was homeless due to a fire would only be intentionally homeless if he deliberately set fire to his own home.

This confusion of questions was deemed to amount to maladministration causing injustice to the complainant and the Council were urged "to sort out their procedures so that when dealing with future cases of homelessness, they [would] do so in a more ordered way and in full compliance with the Act."[131]

The relevance of custody orders for children in determining whether a complainant has a priority need was at issue in a complaint against the London Borough of Lambeth.[132] One of the grounds of complaint was the refusal of the Council to offer a homeless woman permanent accommodation until she had obtained a custody order for her children. She had care and control of the children until they were taken into local authority care due to her homelessness in August 1977. "Short life" housing unsuitable for young children was then offered to the complainant. Her attempts to get an offer of accommodation which would allow her to be re-united with her children were unsuccessful due to the "custody" requirement. she was repeatedly told that she could not be rehoused permanently until she had obtained custody of the children. The Council could have discovered the likelihood of whether or not she would get custody by asking her solicitors to advise on the probability without waiting until just before the custody hearing.

The lack of urgency in asking the right questions meant that the children were unnecessarily in the Council's care for over five months

---

131. *Ibid.* at p. 4.
132. Complaint No. 22/S/78 against the London Borough of Lambeth, dated 15 January, 1979; *R. v. Ealing LBC, ex p. Sidhu* (1982) 2 HLR 45; see also "Delay" *above* at pp. 230-231.

and was part of a finding of maladministration causing "considerable injustice" to the complainant and her children.

In a later complaint against Bournemouth Borough Council the Council were held to have "acted with maladministration" where they refused to accept that the complainant was threatened with homelessness until he was actually the subject of a possession order.[133] The Council's planning department took enforcement action against the owner to prevent multiple occupation in July 1981. The complainant approached the housing department who refused to treat him as threatened with homelessness until there was a possession order. In "taking the line that he could not be regarded as potentially homeless until he was actually the subject of Possession Order", the Council were deemed to have "acted with maladministration".[134] It seems to be the case that failure to follow the advice of the Code of Guidance may also amount to maladministration. In one case[135] temporary accommodation in a caravan was provided for a homeless couple who were vulnerable but they received no early offers of permanent housing. The Local Ombudsman discussed Council policy in his report:

"The Council said that they offered tenancies of purpose-built Council accommodation to homeless persons only after they had spent six months in short-stay accommodation. That was contrary to the Code."[136]

The actions of the Council were deemed to amount to maladministration but "because at the time there was no suitable alternative accommodation available for which [the complainants] were qualified they did not suffer any injustice."

There have been successful complaints and findings of maladministration on a variety of other issues, such as failure of housing authorities to treat disabled applicants as having a priority need;[137] failure to consider the possibility that applicants were homeless;[138] discriminatory treatment of the homeless in the allocation of council properties;[139] the allocation of housing to battered women in the areas where their violent spouses lived;[140] and the policy of a council to refuse to rehouse homeless persons without rights of occupation until they were physically evicted from squats.[141]

---

133. Complaint No. 304/H/81 against Bournemouth Borough Council, dated 26 January, 1982.
134. *Ibid.* at p.9.
135. Complaint No. 715/H/78 against Sedgmoor District Council, dated 28 March, 1980.
136. *Ibid.* at p.27.
137. See *Report of the Commissioner for Local Administration in Wales*, dated 29 April, 1982.
138. See North Warwickshire Borough Council [No. 30/J/82] and Portsmouth City Council [No. 365/J/83].
139. See Breckland District Council [No. 365/J/82].
140. See City of Glasgow District Council [No. 150/82].
141. See London Borough of Waltham [No. 383/Y/83].

(v) Unhelpful attitude and inaccurate advice

Although, as has been mentioned, the Local Ombudsman tends to make findings of maladministration on quite specific grounds it seems that s significant factor in some complaints has been the helpfulness or otherwise of the approach to the homeless taken by housing authorities. In one of the cases mentioned above involving Lambeth District Council[142] the way in which they advised the complainant was part of the maladministration finding. Discussing the "custody first" policy of the authority the Local Ombudsman stated:

> "Not only was Mrs. A given misleading information but Council officers themselves were confused about what was the Council's policy or practice in these situations. I consider that the Council failed to give Mrs. A accurate or consistent advice in what must have been for her the most trying of circumstances."[143]

Minor lapses by an authority have been held not to amount to maladministration such as where an authority failed to issue a written notification.[144] Huntingdon District Council, for example, did not notify the complainant of their decisions and the reasons for them as required. However, since the complainant was informed that he could not expect an early offer of accommodation, this technical failure did not cause the complainant injustice.

The question of maladministration in cases such as these also seems to turn on the level and nature of communications between the complainant and council officials. In a complaint against Bournemouth Borough Council the manner in which the complainant was treated was the major issue.[145] As the applicant was a single man in his fifties without any medical or other considerations which might amount to vulnerability, the Council's obligations were relatively limited. Nevertheless, by failing to be helpful to the complainant, in not supplying information of property which had planning permission for multiple occupancy, the Council incurred the displeasure of the local Ombudsman:

> "I am not at all satisfied with the way the council have treated Mr. A. It is astonishing that they should show themselves so unhelpful to someone who was facing homelessness through the Council's own action [i.e. enforcement action against multiple occupation without planning permission], however necessary that action may have been. I consider that in not being more

---

142. See fn. 144.
143. *Ibid.* at p.16.
144. Complaint No. 207/H/80 against Huntingdon District Council, dated 12 January, 1981; see also "The Duties of Housing Authorities" above at pp. 182-83.
145. Complaint No. 304/H/81 against Bournemouth Borough Council, dated 26 January, 1982.

helpful to Mr. A ... the Council acted with maladministration."[146]

The Commissioner recommended that the Council tender the complainant a "generous apology".

(c) Dissatisfaction with action taken by an authority

When the Commissioner is of the opinion that there has been maladministration causing injustice his report must be sent by the relevant authority to the complainant and, if appropriate, the referring councillor.[147] The report must also be drawn to the public's attention through newspaper advertisements and be available for inspection in three weeks.[148] The authority must consider the report and notify the Commissioner of the action they are taking in the light of the report. If the Commissioner does not receive such notification within a reasonable time or if he is not satisfied with the action taken by the authority in response to his report then he must make a further report setting out the facts.

In the complaint mentioned above against Slough Borough Council a further report was issued because the Council decided not to accept the Local Ombudsman's Report.[149] This report had concluded that there had been maladministration by the Council causing injustice to the complainant. Hearsay evidence had been placed before the appropriate sub-committee. The basis of Slough's decision not to accept the Commissioner's conclusions was that the sub-committee had born in mind that hearsay evidence could be unreliable. The Commissioner did not agree:

"As my investigation showed, the impression was given to officers and one of the three members of the Sub-Committee that the allegations were believed to be true. I cannot accept, therefore, that the Council took the view that the allegations could be unreliable, particularly as the Council later wrote to the complainant 'It is permissible and indeed common for local authority committees of this nature to receive and act upon uncorroborated statements which appear to them to come from a reliable source.' I doubt whether the practice is as widespread as the council suggest, but, whether it

---

146. *Ibid.* at p. 8.
147. Local Government (Scotland) Act 1975 section 29(2) and Local Government Act 1974 section 31(2).
148. Subject to the direction by the Local Commissioner that, taking into account the public interest as well as the interests of the complainants and of persons other than the complainant, there shall be no publicity — section 30(7) of the 1975 Act and section 28(7) of the 1975 Act. This occurred in the first Report concerning homelessness which was dealt with by the Commission for Local Administration in Wales.
149. Further Report by the Local Commissioner into Complaint No. 387/H/77 dated 14 November, 1978, at p.2.

is or not, I consider that to reach an important decision affecting the lives of individuals on prejudicial 'uncorroborated statements' is maladministration."

In the event of a local Ombudsman not being satisfied with the action that an authority take following his further Report he may draw attention to the authority's failure in his Annual Report.[150] Although this does not seem to be a major problem the Local Ombudsman for England noted in his Annual Report for 1979 that Slough's response in Complaint No. 387/H/77 was negative.

A further report was also issued against Bournemouth Borough Council[151] because they refused to apologise to a complainant who was threatened with homelessness for their failure to provide him with adequate advice and assistance.

(d) Discontinuation of investigation

The Local Commissioner has discretion as to whether or not to start an investigation and whether or not to abandon an investigation.[152] The criteria which have been advanced for dropping an investigation are important for anyone concerned with the housing problems of the homeless:

> "A decision to discontinue ... is likely to be influenced in the main by two factors: firstly, the stage reached in the investigation and secondly the nature of the matter being investigated. If the investigation is at an early stage and there is no evidence of maladministration up to that stage then I would be inclined to discontinue the investigation on the grounds that the complainant was satisfied, further inquiries might be regarded as unreasonable, and continuation of the investigation would inevitably involve expenditure of time and money which might be put to better use ..."[153]

To see how these principles have been applied in practice we can look at the investigation of a complaint against Hamilton District Council. The complainant had alleged maladministration in the Council's failure to assist him when he returned to Hamilton following redundancy in England. In February 1978 while staying temporarily with his wife's parents the complainant applied in February 1978 for rehousing as a "sub-tenant". As there were outstanding rent arrears from his English

---

150. Local Government Act 1974 and Part II of the Local Government (Scotland) Act 1975.
151. Complaint No. 304/M/81.
152. See Part III of the Local Government Act 1974 and Part II of the Local Government (Scotland) Act 1975.
153. Report of the Commissioner for Local Administration in Scotland for the year ended 31 March, 1982, at p.2.

tenancy, Hamilton would not consider this application. In October 1978 he presented himself as a homeless person. The Council stated that they could not consider such an application. In January 1979 after his arrears were paid off, his application as a subtenant was accepted and he was offered a house by the District Council. He refused this as unsuitable. At the time of complaint to the Local Ombudsman no further offers had been made and the complainant claimed that he had suffered injustice because the Council had not given him notification under the Act as well as complaining about the area he had been offered. A court action had also been raised by the complainant. Prior to the case being heard the Council offered the complainant a flat in an area which he wanted. In the light of this the Commissioner indicated that:

> "Since the allocation of the house at B ... effectively remedied the main complaint to me, I felt that the expense of further action by me would not be justifiable and consequently decided ... to discontinue my investigation."[154]

9. Section 211 of the Local Government (Scotland) Act 1973 [155]

This section provides the Secretary of State for Scotland with a general power to enforce the statutory obligations of Scottish local authorities irrespective of any other form of redress which might be available to a complainant. The enforcement procedure is quite cumbersome and the effectiveness of the remedy largely depends on the view of the Secretary of State as to the gravity of the local authority's failure to act.[156] However it has been resorted to in recent years to enforce the right of public sector tenants to buy their homes under the Tenant's Rights Etc. (Scotland) Act 1980[157] and it may be of limited utility in enforcing housing authority

---

154. Report of Discontinuation of the Investigation of a complaint against Hamilton District Council, Ref. 35/79, dated 27 March, 1980, at p.2.
155. There is no equivalent English remedy. It should be noted, however, that some statutes provide specific enforcement mechanisms and section 211 of the 1973 Act is in addition to, and not in substitution for, other modes of redress on default powers see J.G. Logie 'Enforcing Statutory Duties: The Courts and Default Powers' [1988] JSWL 185.
156. Enforcement must be preceded by a public inquiry and both are dependent on the Secretary of State exercising broad discretionary powers.
157. Following "section 211 inquiries" both Stirling and Dundee District Councils agreed to implement the sale of council houses in their respective areas, section 164 of the equivalent English statute, the Housing Act 1985, empowers the Secretary of State for the Environment to take over the sale of council houses where it appears to the Minister that tenants "have or may have difficulty in exercising the right to buy effectively and expeditiously." See *Norwich City Council v. Secretary of State for the Environment* [1982] 1 All ER 737.

obligations under the Part II of the Housing (Scotland) Act 1987.[158]

10. Commission for Racial Equality

The Commission for Racial Equality (CRE) was established by section 43 of the Race Relations Act 1976 to replace the Race Relations Board and the Community Relations Commission. However, unlike its predecessor, the role of the CRE, like that of the Equal Opportunities Commission, is not merely reactive but is positive and strategic. The broad nature of the CRE's role is reflected by section 43(1) which imposes on the CRE duties to work for the elimination of racial discrimination and the promotion of equality of opportunity.

The power to conduct formal investigations does not appear to have been used particularly effectively. There were some 45 investigations under way by the end of 1981.[159] However, the Commission's record has been criticised by the Select Committee on Home Affairs. Although the number of investigations compare very favourably with those of similar bodies, such as the Equal Opportunities Commission,[160] no major investigations were completed in the first four years of operation and the 10 completed investigations were all into small organisations. The Select Committee commented acidly that:

> "Even one single completed investigation into the practices of a major employer or provider of services would have had a greater effect than the nailing of these small fry."[161]

This tactical error allied to the "snail's pace of the Commission's investigations"[162] was described by the Select Committee as being a "grave indictment of the effectiveness and this aspect of the Commission's operation deserves the most careful scrutiny."[163] To meet these and other criticisms[164] the Home Office and the CRE have commenced a joint review of the Commission's practices in the conduct of investigations

---

158. *See Williamson v. Moray District Council* 1980 SLT (Sh Ct) 32 at pp. 33-35; *Lord Advocate v. Stirling District Council* 1986 SLT 179. It will be interesting to see if the Secretary of State uses this power to force Stirling District to implement their duties to the homeless: *Scotland on Sunday*, 30 October, 1988.
159. *First Report from the Home Affairs Committee*, Parliamentary Papers, Session 1981-82, HC 46-I, para. 43.
160. Equal Opportunities Commission, *Sixth Annual Report*, 1981, at p.5; *Fifth Annual Report*, 1980, at p.7; *Fourth Annual Report*, 1979, at p.10.
161. Home Affairs Committee, Session 1981/82, HC 46-I, para. 43, *supra*.
162. *Ibid.* at para. 55.
163. *Ibid.* at para. 45.
164. L. Lustgarten, *The Legal Control of Racial Discrimination* (1980) pp. 240-252; K. Miller, "Natural Justice in Formal Investigations under Anti-Discrimination Legislation" (1980) SCOLAG 177; G. Applebey and E. Ellis, "Formal Investigations; The CRE and EOC as Law Enforcement Agencies"

with a view to the elimination of prolonged delays.[165]

Nevertheless, the CRE did attempt to investigate the housing policy of Hillingdon London Borough Council, which have been prominent in the campaign for the amendment of the homeless legislations.[166] Although the attempt was unsuccessful, the facts which prompted the Commission to embark on a formal investigation may be stated briefly as the case, in our view, is of some significance. In *R. v. CRE, ex p. Hillingdon London Borough Council* [167] the CRE decided to investigate Hillingdon's handling of applications from homeless immigrants on the basis of two cases. In the first case, the Janmohamed family, an East African family with four children between 12 and 21, arrived at Heathrow Airport from Kenya on November 5, 1978. After spending an evening in the airport lounge Hillingdon provided them with temporary accommodation. On the completion of their inquiries Hillingdon determined that although they were homeless and had a priority need for accommodation their duty to the Janmohamed family was merely to provide accommodation for a further period in order to afford them a reasonable opportunity to secure accommodation for themselves. However, instead of fulfilling this obligation, the Chairman of the Council's housing committee, Mr. Terry Dicks, decided to use the Janmohameds to highlight their grievances concerning the legislation. In what was described by Lord Justice Griffith as "a gesture in the worst possible taste and with an inhuman disregard for the feelings of the unfortunate family", Councillor Dicks had them taken by taxi to the Foreign Office and dumped on the pavement.

In the second case Mr. Turvey, an Englishman, returned to England from Rhodesia with his children aged between eighteen months and thirteen years. It appears that Mr. Turvey, who had been employed as a schoolteacher, voluntarily relinquished his accommodation in that country when his school closed. In this case, however, Hillingdon found that not only was Mr. Turvey homeless and in priority need but that he had not become homeless intentionally. Their duty towards the Turveys in these circumstances therefore was to secure that accommodation became available for their occupation.

The CRE regarded Hillingdon's treatment of these two families as constituting a *prima facie* case of unlawful racial discrimination[168] and wrote to Hillingdon to inform them that they were considering conducting a formal investigation under section 48(1) of the Race Relations Act

---

[1984] PL 236. D. Forbes, *Action on Racial Harassment. Legal Remedies and Local Authorities* (LAG/LHU, London, 1988) Ch. 6.

165. The Government Reply to the First Report from the Home Affairs Committee, Session 1981-82, HC 46-I (HMSO, Cmnd 8547, 1982) p.8.

166. *Roof*, May/June 1980, p. 85.

167. [1981] 3 WLR 520 (CA); [1982] AC 779 (HL).

168. See sections 1, 2, 20 and 21 of the Race Relations Act 1976.

1976. After the procedural requirements which must precede a formal investigation were carried out,[169] the Commission informed the Council that they believed the Council had directly discriminated against homeless applicants on unlawful racial grounds in the provision of housing.

Hillingdon, however, successfully challenged the decision of the CRE to conduct a formal investigation on two counts. Firstly, the CRE did not have reasonable grounds for believing that the Council had unlawfully discriminated against the Janmohamed family on the racial grounds. Lord Denning, in the Court of Appeal, pronounced that it would be unfair to subject Hillingdon to an inquisitorial investigation on such an insubstantial foundation as the disparity of treatment between the Janmohamed and Turvey families. This disparity he believed could "be explained perfectly well by the honest decision of the Council's housing officer" that the former were intentionally homeless and the latter unintentionally homeless. Secondly, the Court of Appeal upheld the Council's contention that the CRE's frame of reference was not specific enough and this resulted, in Lord Justice Griffith's view, in the CRE exceeding its powers.

On appeal to the House of Lords the decision of the Court of Appeal was confirmed. Lord Diplock made it clear that the CRE could not embark on a formal investigation without being specific about the types of unlawful acts they genuinely believed Hillingdon had committed. The Commission could not "throw the book" at Hillingdon nor could they tell the Borough that they believed it "might have done or be doing some acts capable of amounting to unlawful determination". For any investigation to be within the CRE's powers, Lord Diplock considered that there had to be some "particularisation of the kinds of acts of which the Borough was suspected". Their failure to be specific rendered the investigation unlawful.

While the result of this case may be discouraging, it should be noted that the findings of the Court of Appeal and House of Lords were based on procedural irregularities and not the principle of formal investigation and that this decision has been criticised as artificially circumscribing the powers of the CRE.[170]

---

169. These are that the Commission draw up terms of reference for the inquiry, section 49(2); notify the person or body to be investigated, sections 49(3) and 49(4); and afford such a person or body an opportunity to make representations orally or in writing to the Commission, section 49(4).

170. See, for example: (1981) SCOLAG 321; K. Miller, "Formal Investigations by the CRE" (1982) JLSS 449; *R. v. Commission for Racial Equality, ex p. Cottrell & Rothon* [1980] 3 All ER 265; and *Home Office v. Commission for Racial Equality* [1982] QB 385; *In re Prestige Groups PLC* [1984] ICR 473; C. McCrudden, 'The Commission for Racial Equality: Formal Investigations in the Shadow of Judicial Review' in R. Baldwin and C. McCrudden (ed.) *Regulation and Public Law* (Weidenfeld and Nicolson, London, 1987) p.227. Recent housing investigations and reports by the CRE include: *Race and Council Housing in Hackney: Report of a formal investigation* (1984); *Race and Housing in Liverpool: A research report* (1986); *Homelessness and Discrimination: Report of a formal investigation into the London Borough of Tower Hamlets* (1988).

List of Abbreviations

1. Reports of cases

AC	Appeal Cases
All ER	All England Law Reports
CLY	Current Law Yearbook
KB	King's Bench
QB	Queen's Bench
JSWL	Journal of Social Welfare Law
LAG	Legal Action Group Bulletin
SCOLAG	Scottish Legal Group Bulletin
SC	Session Cases
SLT	Scots Law Times
SLT (Sh Ct)	Scots Law Times Sheriff Courts Reports
R	Rettie (Scottish Law Reports 1873-1898)
D	Dunlop (Scottish Law Reports 1838-1862)
Ch	Chancery
ICR	Industrial Case Reports
WLR	Weekly Law Reports
LGR	Local Government Reports
Smythe	SHAC Digest of Cases by John Smythe
Carnwath	Case printed in "A Guide to the Housing (Homeless Persons) Act" (1978)
SCCR	Scottish Criminal Case Reports
SCLR	Scottish Civil Law Reports

2. Journals

LGC	Local Government Chronicle
New LJ	New Law Journal
JLSS	Journal of the Law Society of Scotland
JPL	Journal of Planning and Environmental Law
SJ	Solicitors' Journal
JSWL	Journal of Social Welfare Law
JPN	Justice of the Peace — weekly notes of cases
LG Rev	Local Government Review
EC	English Code of Guidance
SC	Scottish Code of Guidance

Bibliography

1. Parliamentary debates and Circulars.
2. General books and guides.
3. Background to the problems of homelessness before 1977.
4. General comment on the Act and its operation.
5. Specific Issues and Cases
    (a) The nature of the homeless
    (b) The nature of accommodation secured for the homeless
    (c) Intentional homelessness
    (d) Remedies for the homeless
    (e) Comments on specific cases under the Act
    (f) Women and homelessness
    (g) Single homeless
    (h) The politics of the Act.

1. Parliamentary debates and Circulars

For Parliamentary discussion of the Housing (Homeless Persons) Bill, readers are referred to *Weekly Hansard,* No. 1064, 18-24 February, 1977, Col. 896-995; also No. 1076, 20-27 May, 1977, Col. 955-972; also No. 1081, 8-14 July ,1977, Col. 1590-1733.

Ministry of Health, Circular 87/48.
DoE Circular 18/74 on Homelessness.
DoE Circular 166/77 on Housing (Homeless Persons) Act 1977.
SDD 41/1977, SWSG SW/14/1977 *The Housing (Homeless Persons) Act 1977.*
SDD 13/1978, SWSG SW/1/1978 *The Housing (Homeless Persons) Act 1977.*
SDD 27/1980 *The Code of Guidance on the Housing (Homeless Persons) Act 1977.*
SDD 21/1982 *Matrimonial Homes (Family Protection)(Scotland) Act 1981.*

2. General books and guides

Arden, A; *Homeless Persons: the Housing Act Part III*, LAG Publications, 1988.
Carnwarth, R; *A Guide to the Housing (Homeless Persons Act)*, Knight, 1978.

Greve, J. et al; *Homelessness in London,* GLC, London, 1986.

Hoath, D.C; *Homelessness,* Sweet & Maxwell, 1983.

International Federation of Housing and Planning; *Homelessness. An Act of Men,* NFHA, 1987.

Joint Charities Group; *A Guide to the Housing (Homeless Persons) Act, 1977.*

Partington, M; *The Housing (Homeless Persons) Act 1977 and Code,* Sweet and Maxwell, 1978.

Scottish Homeless Group, *Housing (Homeless Persons) Act 1977: A Short Guide,* 1979.

Smythe, J; *Homelessness: A Digest of Court Decisions,* SHAC, 1982.

3. Background to the problem of homelessness before 1977

Bailey, R. and Ruddock J; *The Grief Report,* Shelter, 1972.

Bailey, R; *The Squatters,* Penguin Sp, 1973.

Bailey, R; *Bed and Breakfast,* Shelter, 1974.

Bailey, R; *The Homeless and the Empty Houses,* Penguin Sp, 1977.

Digby, P.W; *Hostel and Lodgings for Single People,* HMSO, 1976.

Glastonbury, B; *Homeless Near a Thousand Homes,* Allen & Unwin, 1971.

Greve, J; *London's Homeless,* Bell, 1964.

Greve, J., Page, D., and Greve, S; *Homelessness in London,* Scottish Academic Press, 1971.

Turner, M; *Forgotten Men,* National Council for Social Service, 1960.

Wates, N. and Wolmar C. (eds); *Squatting,* Bay Leaf, 1980.

4. General comment on the legislation and its operation.

Birkinshaw, P; 'Homelessness and the Law: the Effects and Response to Legislation', *Urban Law and Policy,* (1982), Vol. 5, No. 3, 255.

Brown, A.J. and Harvey, A; 'Housing (Homeless Persons) Act: Two Views', *New L J,* (1978), 128, 971.

Coombes, J.M; 'The Duty to House the Homeless', D. Lasok et al (eds.)*Fundamental Duties* , (1980), 53.

De Friend, R; 'The Housing (Homeless Persons) Act 1977', *Modern Law Review,* 41, (1978), 173.

Evans, A. and Duncan, S; *Responding to Homelessness: Local Authority Policy and Practice,* HMSO, 1988.

Finnis, N; 'The Heartless and the Homeless', *Roof,* (1978), 138.

Gibson, P; 'How Scotland Got the Housing (Homeless Persons) Act', *The Scottish Government Yearbook 1979,* N. Drucker and H.M. Drucker (eds), (1978), 36.

Goss, J; *Working the Act: The Homeless Persons Act in Practice,* CHAR, 1985.

Hoath D.C; 'Homeless Families and Local Authorities: The 1977 Act', *Family Law,* 1978, 99.

Hoath, D.C; 'Housing (Homeless Persons) Act: an Act of gross complacency that is impossible to interpret', *LGC,* (1982), 1308.

Hoath, D.C; 'Homelessness after the Housing and Planning Act 1986: the "Puhlhofer" amendments', *JSWL,* (1988), 39.

Housing Corporation Seminar Reports; 'Action for Housing the Homeless', *Housing Review,* May-June, 1987.

Institute of Housing; *Who Will House the Homeless?,* Institute of Housing, 1988.

Lewis, N. and Birkinshaw, P.J; 'Housing (Homeless Persons) Act', *JPL,* (1978), 524.

McGurk, P; 'Housing the Homeless', *LGC,* (1977), 748.

McIntosh, N; 'Homelessness: Four Big Gaps in the New Act', *New Society,* (1978), 516.

Mullen, T; 'New Law on Homelessness', SCOLAG, 7, 1987, 124.

Robson, P. and Watchman, P; 'The Homeless Persons Obstacle Race', *JSWL,* (1981), 1-15, 67-82.

Scottish Homeless Group, *Housing (Homeless Persons) Act 1977 — a review of the first six months,* Scottish Homelessness Group, 1978.

Scottish Homelessness Group; *No Recourse for the Homeless (on implementation of the Act in Scotland),* Scottish Homelessness Group, 1979.

SHAC; *Working the Act: The Homeless Persons Act in Practice in 6 London Boroughs,* SHAC, 1983.

Shelter, *Ordinary People: Homeless in Housing Crisis,* Shelter, 1982.

Shelter, *Where Homelessness Means Hopelessness,* Shelter, 1982.

Smith, P.F; 'The Housing (Homeless Persons) Act 1977: Four Years On', *JPL,* (1982), 143.

Thompson, L; *An Act of Compromise: an appraisal of the effects of the Housing (Homeless Persons) Act 1977 — ten years on,* Shelter, 1988.

Ware, P; The Problems that Still Persist in the Housing of Homeless Families, *Housing,* November 1979, pp. 18-19.

Wilkinson, M.W; 'Review of the Homeless Persons Act',132 *New LJ,* (1982), 708.

Woodward, P; 'The Housing (Homeless Persons) Act 1977 — A Paper Tiger', *JPL,* (1978), 445.

Woodward, P and Davidge E.M; 'Homelessness Four Years On', *JPL,* (1982), 158.

5. Specific Issues and Cases

(a) The nature of the homeless

Brahams, D. and Weller, M; 'Crime and Homelessness Among the Mentally Ill',135 *New LJ,* (1985), 626 and 761.

Bramley, G. et al; *Homelessness and the London Housing Market,* SAUS,

Bristol, Occasional Paper 32, 1988.

Briscoe, J; 'Jobless and Homeless: Law Relating to the Tied Worker', 135 *New LJ*, (1985), 139 and 159.

Halstead, P; 'Vulnerability', 133 *New LJ*, (1983), 384.

Hoath, D; '"Split Families" and Part III of the Housing Act 1985', *JSWL*, (1987), 15

Randall, G., Francis, D. and Brougham, C; *A Place for the Family: A Report on Homeless Families in London*, SHAC, 1982.

The Boston Foundation, *Homelessness: Critical Issues for Policy and Practice*, 1987

Thornton, R; 'Homelessness Through Relationship Breakdown: The Local Authorities' Response', *JSWL*, (1989), 87.

(b) The nature of accommodation secured for the homeless

Ash, J; 'Hotels for the Homeless: Prodigality and Misery', *Housing Review*, (1985), Vol. 34.

Battersby, S. et al; 'Rooms for Improvement', *Housing Review*, Vol. 37 No. 3, May-June, 1988.

Cairns, M; 'Heartbreak Hotel', *Roof*, (1983), May-June 13.

Conway, J. and Kemp, P; *Bed and Breakfast: Slum Housing of the Eighties*, SHAC Policy Paper No. 7, Shelter (London) 1985.

Franey, R; 'Apart from the Law', *Roof*, (1980), November/December, 172.

Franey, R; 'Split Families - the Dividing Rule', *Roof*, (1981), March/April, 3.

Glasgow SHAC; *No Place Like Home*, Shelter (Scotland), 1984.

Greater London Council; Temporary Accommodation - Long Term Problem, Greater London Council Housing Department, 1984.

Gregory, R; 'When is a Duty Not a Duty?' 1979, *LGC*, 263.

Grosskurth, H; 'When Home is a Bed and Breakfast Hotel', *Roof*, (1984), Jan/Feb, 11.

Hoyler, K; 'Homelessness in London: the environmental health response', *Environmental Health*, Vol. 95 (5), May, 1987.

London Research Centre/Shelter: *Survey of Bed and Breakfast and Homelessness in London*, 1987.

Murie, A. and Jeffers, S ; *Living in bed and breakfasts: the experience of homelessness in London*, SAUS Bristol Working Paper 71, 1987.

Watchman, P; 'Heartbreak Hotel', *JSWL*, (1988), 147.

(c) Intentional homelessness

Harvey, A; 'Homeless by Choice?', 131 *New LJ* (1981) 131.

Holgate, G; '"Intentional homelessness" and the overseas connection', 152 *LGR*, (1988), 827.

Rattenbury T.P.B; 'Din and the Voluntarily Homeless', *JPL* (1983), 4.

(d) Remedies for the homeless

Arden, A; *Enforcing the Homeless Persons Act,* 1979, LAG 283, 1980, LAG 14.

Arden, A; *More on Enforcing the Homeless Persons Act,* 1980, LAG 64.

Gordon, R; 'Judicial Review and homelessness', 130 *SJ,* (1986), 211.

Ogston, V. and Seager P; 'Judicial Review in the Sheriff Court', *JLSS,* (1980), 442.

Robson, P. and Watchman, P; 'Remedies for the Homeless', *JLSS,* (1981), 104.

Robson, P; 'Judicial Review and Homelessness', 1985, *SLT,* 305.

(e) Comments on specific cases under the Act

Arden, A; 'Bashing the Homeless? (how judges have interpreted the Act)', *Roof,* (1982), March/April, 13.

Edwards, R; *No Recourse for the Homeless,* 1979 SCOLAG, 122-123.

MacAllister, A; 'Homelessness Since Puhlhofer', *Legal Action,* (1987), 11.

Robson, P. and Watchman, P; 'Homelessness in the Courts', 1980, 49 SCOLAG, 151.

Samuels, A; 'Legal problems over homelessness', 1980, 144 *LG Rev,* 3.

Samuels, A; 'The Housing (Homeless Persons) Act 1977', 1981, 145 *LG Rev,* 85.

Watchman, P; No recourse for the homeless in Scotland?', 1983, *SLT,* 33.

(f) Women and homelessness

Austerberry, H. and Watson, S; *Women on the Margins: a Study of Single Women's Housing Problems,* Housing Research Group, City University, 1983.

Binney, V., Harkell, G. and Nixon, J; *Leaving Violent Men,* July 1981.

Bryan, D., 'Domestic Violence: A Question of Housing',*JSWL,* (1984) , 195.

Scottish Institute of Housing/ Scottish Homeless Group; *Housing and Marital Breakdown,* Scottish Institute of Housing, 1985.

Watson, S. and Austerberry, H; *Housing and Homelessness: A Feminist Perspective,* RKP, London, 1986.

(g) Single homeless

Brandon, D., Wells, K., Frances, C., and Ramsay, E; *The Survivors,* RKP, 1980.

Campaign for Single Homeless People, *Homeless Single Persons and the Housing (Homeless Persons) Act 1977,* , 1979.

CHAR; *Putting and End to the Workhouse,* CHAR, 1980.

CHAR; *Single and Homeless: The Facts,* CHAR, Occasional Paper No.3, 1983.

CHAR; *Singled Out: Local Authority Housing Policies for Single People,* CHAR, 1985.

Community Action Proects,*Beyond the Hostel: Housing for Homeless Young People,*, 1983.

DoE, *Settling Down: A Study of the Users of DHSS Resettlement Limits*, HMSO, London, 1985.

DoE, *Single and Homeless*, HMSO, 1981.

Franey, R; *Poor Law: The Mass Arrest of Homeless Claimants in Oxford*, CHAR, 1982.

Glasgow Council for the Single Homeless; *Re-housing hostel Residents: The Experience of Glasgow*, Scottish Council for the Single Homeless, 1985.

Grosskurth, A; 'From Care to Nowhere', *Roof*, (1984), 11.

Henry, D. and MacCallum, M; 'Single Homeless in Nottingham', *Housing and Planning Review*, (1984) Dec .10.

Kingham, M; *Squatters in London*, 1968.

Laidlaw, S.I; *Glasgow Common Lodging Houses and the People who live in Them*, 1956.

Middleton, R; 'The end of the line: boarders and single homeless people', S. Ward (ed.), DHSS In Crisis, CPAG, London, 1985.

National Assistance Board; *Homeless Single Persons*, 1966.

Sargaison, M; *Growing Old in Common Lodgings*, 1954.

Scottish Council for the Single Homeless; *Alternatives to Night Shelters*, Scottish Council for the Single Homeless, 1984.

Scottish Council for the Single Homeless; *Coming Out*, Scottish Council for the Single Homeless, 1985.

Scottish Development Department; *Single and Homeless in Scotland — Some Facts*, 1974.

Shelter (Scotland); *Homeless Young People in Scotland*, Shelter (Scotland), 1984.

Young Homeless Group; *Moving On, Moving In: Working Towards Proper Housing for Young People*, NACRO, 1985.

(h) The politics of the Act

Finnis, N; 'The Heartless and the Homeless', *Roof*, 1978, September , 138.

Richards, J; *The Housing (Homeless Persons) Act 1977: a study in policy making*, SAUS, Bristol ,Working Paper 22, 1981.

Roof; 'The Lobby Against the Homeless Persons Act' (on the opposition of a number of London boroughs to the Act), *Roof*, (1980) May/June , 85.

SHAC; *Homelessness: Prospects for the 1980s*, SHAC, 1981.

Index of Cases

Edwards v. Lothian Regional Council, 1980 SLT (Sh Ct) 107; 1981 SLT (Sh Ct) 41 ... 226

Edwin H. Bradley and Sons v. Secretary of State for the Environment, (1982) 264 EG 926 ... 184

Fezoui v. Torbay Borough Council, (CA) 27 July, 1983 ... 115, 117, 130

Family Housing Association v. Miah, (1982) 5 HLR 94 ... 190, 191

Fanning v. London Borough of Wandsworth, (1980) LAG 16 ... 218

Forbes v. Underwood, (1886) 13 R 465 ... 211

French Kier Developments v. Secretary of State for the Environment, [1977] 1 All, ER 296 ... 184

Galbraith v. Midlothian District Council, (1979) SCOLAG 122 ... 38-40, 189, 194, 209, 223

Glasgow District Council v. Douglas (unreported) ... 12

Goddard v. Torridge District Council, (1982) LAG 9 ... 159, 160

Guppys (Birdport) v. Sandoe, (1975) 30 P&CR 69 ... 184

Hadjilucas v. Crean, [1987] 3 All ER 1008 ... 130

Harrison v. Hammersmith & Fulham London Borough Council, [1981] 1 WLR 650 ... 191

Home Office v. Commission for Racial Equality, [1982] QB 385 ... 242

Hynds v. Midlothian District Council, 1986 SLT 54 ... 58, 60, 70, 114, 137, 150, 157

In re Prestige Groups plc, [1984] ICR 473 ... 242

Jennings v. Northavon District Council, (1982) LAG 9 ... 159, 160

Jones v. Bristol City Council, (1981) LAG 163; Smythe 30 April, 1981 ... 123, 135, 145

Kelly v. Monklands District Council, 1986 SLT 169 ... 51, 79, 96, 98, 99

Kelly and Mallon v. Monklands District Council, 1986 SLT 165 ... 95, 215

Kensington & Chelsea Royal London Borough Council v. Hayden, (1984) 17 HLR 114 ... 191

Keyte v. South Holland District Council, Court of Appeal 19 November, 1983; (1985) 84 LGR 347 ... 197

Krishnan v. London Borough of Hillingdon, (1981) LAG 137; SCOLAG 307 ... 53, 66, 74, 110, 155, 156

Lally v. Kensington and Chelsea Royal London Borough Council, *The Times,* 27 March, 1980 ... 66, 103, 189, 225

Lambert v. Ealing London Borough Council, [1982] 2 All ER 394; [1982] 1 WLR 550 ... 41, 84, 127, 130, 152, 155, 157, 174, 175, 184, 210, 220

Lavender (H) and Son Ltd. v. Minister of Housing and Local Govt., [1970] 1 WLR 1231... 213

Lewis v. North Devon District Council, [1981] 1 All ER 27 ... 59, 60, 70, 137, 138, 141, 142

Lord Advocate v. Stirling District Council, 1986 SLT 179 ... 240

Love v. Montgomerie, 1982 SLT (Sh Ct) 60 ... 218

Since completion of the text the following cases have arisen. The * attached to certain cases denotes those of particular significance.

R. v. Islington LBC, ex p. Higgins (QBD) 22 February, 1989 (intentional homelessness - redundant - rent arrears - move from Dublin to Islington - staying with relative - unsuccessful application).

R. v. Nottingham City Council, ex p. Costello, The Times, 14 February, 1989 (intentional homelessness - leaving council accommodation - poltergeist claimed - inadequate inquiries into poltergeist alleged - unsuccesful application).

R. v. Westminster City Council, ex p. Crowe (QBD) 27 January, 1989 (intentional homelessness - giving up a job with accommodation or dismissal - unsuccessful application).

R. v. Tower Hamlets LBC, ex p. Rouf (QBD) 26 January, 1989 (intentional homelessness - accommodation available or not available in Bangladesh - inadequate inquiries - successful application).

R. v. Croydon LBC, ex p. Marchant (QBD) 12 January, 1989 (intentional homelessness - pregnant woman accepted as in priority need and homeless - provided with interim accommodation - not living with parents as claimed but in private rented accommodation - unsuccessful application).

R. v. Thanet DC, ex p. Groves (QBD) 19 December, 1988 (intentional homelessness - eviction from private rented accommodation for arrears of rent - non-acquiescence in rent arrears and reduction in arrears after husband left - successful application). **

R. v. Tower Hamlets LBC, ex p. Camden LBC, The Times, 12 December, 1988 (refusal of validity of referral - applicant homeless, in priority need and not intentionally homeless - local connection referral - previously deemed intentionally homeless by receiving authority - referral lawfully refused). ***

R. v. Wycombe DC, ex p. Homes (QBD) 1 December, 1988 (intentional homelessness - voluntarily leaving council accommodation unsuitable as on a steep hill - applicant hospitalized - waited 3 years for transfer - inadequate inquiries into medical issues - application successful). *

R. v. Wandsworth LBC, ex p. Onyemah (QBD) 15 November, 1988 (intentionally homeless - applicants owners and occupiers of house in London - claim that property owned by cousins in Nigeria - required to sell up and transfer cash back to cousin - unsuccessful application).

R. v. Sevenoaks DC, ex p. Reynolds (QBD) 14 November, 1988 (intentional homelessness - eviction from private rented property for property damage - applicant claimed property repairs ignored - inadequate inquiries - unsuccessful application).

R. v. Merton LBC, ex p. Ruffle (QBD) 11 November, 1988 (intentional homelessness - previous finding of intentionality for coming back to Britain without arranging accommodation - various temporary addresses between unsuccessful first application and current one - accommodation to break chain of causation - unsuccessful application).*

R. v. St Albans City Council, ex p. Tuta Ullah (QBD) 11 November, 1988 (intentional homelessness - parents left H.A. accommodation and went to live with son - son's restaurant business failed - question of son's house as settled residence - unsuccessful application).*

R. v. Maidstone BC, ex p. Reader (QBD) 4 November, 1988 (intentional homelessness - couple evicted by landlady for failing to control their children's behaviour - disputes as to nature of children's behaviour - unsuccessful application).

R. v. Westminster City Council, ex p. Iqbal (QBD) 21 October, 1988 (intentional homelessness - political refugee from Pakistan who fled attacks in Paris - language difficulties and adequacy of inquiries - successful application).*

R. v. Westminster City Council, ex p. Esmail (QBD) 18 October, 1988 (local connection - doctor from Jordan formerly living in Dublin - authority referred to Dublin - successful application).

Index of Statutes

Note: The Housing (Homeless Persons) Act, 1977 is the subject matter of this book and therefore has been omitted from this index.

ss.27-31 54
Housing (Sc) Act 12, 51-54
    s.33 53
    ss.36-38 54
Local Government Act 229
Local Government (Sc) Act 229

Index of Ombudsman Decisions

Subject Index

271

272

intentional 80, 82, 135-138, 149
priority need 92, 188
possession order
 maladministration 235
 twenty-eight day notice 92
Tied accommodation 12
 eviction 160
 intentional homelessness 124, 136, 158-161
Travelling people 89
Treaty of Rome 155, 174 **see also** European
 Community—immigrants
Twenty-eight day notice
 threatened homelessness 92

Ultra vires 221
Unemployment
 intentional homelessness 111, 124, 160, 166
 tied accommodation 158-161

Vagrants 9, 16-18, 26, 27
Vandalism 134
 cause of homelessness 152
Violence
 domestic 22, 51, 52, 76, 83, 85, 88, 89, 94,
 112,130, 137, 176, 178, 179
 local connection 172, 173, 176, 178
 non-domestic 114-123, 130, 131
 young people 98, 134
 see also Battered women
Voluntary organisations 46, 49
 financial assistance from local authority 55

Vulnerability
 assessment of 99-101
 battered women 94, 97
 categories 94-99
 disabled people 96, 97, 99, 200
 elderly people 17, 105
 maladministration 233, 235, 236
 medical evidence 100, 101
 priority need 92-102
 young people 97-99

Waller, Lord Justice 95
Walton, Lord Justice 175, 219
Webster, Lord Justice 59, 76, 108, 141
Wein, Lord Justice 172, 186
Welfare benefits 188
Wheatley, Lord 90, 194, 220, 221, 226
White, Judge 151
Wilberforce, Lord 74, 146
Wilkinson Report 54
Women
 access to housing 21
 violence 112, 115-117
 see also Battered women
Woolf, Mr. Justice   70, 77, 111, 112, 113,
 114,116, 118, 120, 122, 124, 128, 137, 139,
 141, 142, 143, 147, 167, 170, 185, 200

Young people
 intentional homelessness 147-149
 violence 98, 134
 vulnerability 97-99

Other titles available from summer 1989:

Alarm Systems and Elderly People, Malcolm J. Fisk (ed.), £13 approx.

Public Sector Housing Law in Scotland, (3rd edition), Chris Himsworth, £12 approx.

Available from 'Publications', The Planning Exchange, 186 Bath Street, Glasgow G2 4HG

Tel. (041-332-8541).